STAFF RELATIONS IN THE CIVIL SERVICE

FIFTY YEARS OF WHITLEYISM

STAFF RELATIONS IN THE CIVIL SERVICE

FIFTY YEARS OF WHITLEYISM

HENRY PARRIS

Director of Studies in Public Administration, Civil Service College

for the

ROYAL INSTITUTE OF PUBLIC ADMINISTRATION

LONDON

GEORGE ALLEN & UNWIN LTD

Ruskin House   Museum Street

Printed in Great Britain
in 10 point Plantin type
by Alden & Mowbray Ltd
at the Alden Press, Oxford

AUTHOR'S FOREWORD

I was pleased, and flattered, when asked to write a book to mark the fiftieth anniversary of the National Whitley Council. At the same time, I was diffident of my ability to produce a book worthy of the occasion. The difficulty I foresaw was expressed by W. J. Brown, one of the most remarkable men ever to sit on the Council. In his autobiography, he wrote: 'I cannot but be aware that these recollections of far-off controversies and "battles long ago" can possess but little interest for many readers who are not civil servants nor feel any special concern for civil service matters.'[1] Yet fifty years of Whitleyism, like Brown's career, consists very largely of 'far-off controversies and battles long ago'. How could the historian bring out the contemporary importance of the subject, and avoid burying it under a mass of detail about claims for more pay, shorter hours, longer leave, higher travelling allowances, and the like? I have striven hard to overcome this difficulty, and to produce a book which will be not only a memorial to those who have built up the Whitley system in the past, but also a useful guide to those who now and in the future will carry on the work. It is also my hope that enquirers from other countries will find this study of use in deciding whether anything in Whitleyism can usefully be transferred to other environments.

Although the book was commissioned to mark an anniversary, it was made clear to me that it was not intended to be purely an historical narrative. It should emphasize the characteristics of contemporary Whitleyism, and should find space for some discussion of likely future trends. This guidance was welcome to me. There are already two valuable books on Whitleyism in the civil service.[2] This study does not aim to take their place. The reader who wishes to make a fuller study of the subject, or who is especially interested in the early period, is recommended to read them. The emphasis of this account is on the period since the outbreak of the Second World War, and it uses mainly material that was not available to White and Gladden.

At the same time, the treatment by topics should not conceal from the reader the fact that the method of the book is historical. The present becomes the past before the ink is dry upon the page. When, therefore, the present tense is used it does not refer to some timeless dimension in which the eternal essence of Whitleyism is laid up. It refers to the month of July 1969 – the anniversary to mark which the book was commissioned. That is to say, the Civil Service Department had taken over the Treasury's responsibility for the National Whitley Council. But the

[1] W. J. Brown, *So Far*, 1943, p. 98.
[2] L. D. White, *Whitley Councils in the British Civil Service*, Chicago, 1933: E. N. Gladden, *Civil Service Staff Relationships*, 1943.

7

Post Office staff had not yet departed from it. That event was to follow later in the year. And so on.

One convention has been deliberately set aside in this text. No attempt has been made, in referring to individuals, to indicate titles by which they were subsequently known, except where there was some specific object in doing so. The reader will not encounter many such characters as, 'Mr A. B. (later Sir Aloysius) Smith'. To do otherwise would unnecessarily congeal the argument. Take, for example, that distinguished public man, the late Lord Bridges. He would have to appear as 'Edward Bridges (later Sir Edward, and ultimately, Lord Bridges)' in some parts of the text: as 'Sir Edward Bridges (later Lord Bridges)' in others: and as Lord Bridges in yet others, where excerpts from the taped interview he gave for this book are quoted. The intelligent reader should have no difficulty in recognizing Mr Thomas Padmore when he re-appears as Sir Thomas: or in grasping the point that when Sir Albert Day's recollections are quoted, they may refer to a period before he received the honour of knighthood.

In collecting material for this study, two phrases cropped up time and time again: so frequently, in fact, as to acquire the status of proverbs. On the one hand, old Whitley hands told interviewers that 'Whitley superseded nothing'. The idea had already been formulated as early as 1920[1] and Sir Richard Hayward has given a full statement of what it means. 'Recognized associations are older than Whitley Councils. When the Whitley Councils were established, following the 1914–18 war, it was recognized that this novel form of joint consultative machinery merely built upon the existing fabric of staff associations and trade unions: this fact was acknowledged in the dictum "Whitley superseded nothing". At that time a pledge was given by the government that recognized associations would continue to have the right of direct consultation, outside the Councils, on matters affecting their members alone. The pledge has been honoured and today a substantial proportion of the negotiations on conditions of service is conducted by direct discussion between the associations and the Treasury or department, and not through Whitley machinery.'[2]

The other Whitley proverb states that 'Whitley is an umbrella'. That is to say, although it has not superseded anything, it has given the staff associations, in relation to many ends, a choice of means. Business could be raised, either bilaterally, or on Whitley. The choice of means would depend, for example, on the strength of the association. A very powerful group might well see no advantage in pursuing a claim through the Whitley machine, believing it could do at least as well by way of a

[1] See below, p. 106.
[2] R. Hayward, *Whitley Councils in the United Kingdom Civil Service*, 1963, p. 3.

direct approach. A small organization, on the other hand, might feel diffident about the success of a bilateral demand, and might seek to increase its chances of success by raising it on the Staff Side, in the hope of getting the support of other sections of employees. The umbrella metaphor refers to the fruitful uncertainty that has always existed as to the proper limits of Whitley business. A staff leader, confronted with a situation in which doubt exists as to whether a given item should rightly find a place on a Whitley agenda, is not necessarily deterred from doing so. He may feel it will serve the interest of his constituents to try to bring the dubious item under the umbrella. To paraphrase Harold Laski, there is a permanent penumbra of contingent uncertainty about Whitley business. It has contributed very greatly to the growth of the system. No attempt to remove it is made in these pages by defining with any rigour what exactly the scope of Whitley is. Many things are dealt with under its aegis today which were never thought of by its founders. No doubt, its sphere will continue to grow in the future.

My best thanks are due to all those in the Civil Service Department and other departments, in the National Whitley Council Staff Side, in a number of staff associations, and in the Royal Institute of Public Administration, who have helped in the writing of this book. It has been a real pleasure to work with the advisory group set up by the R.I.P.A., and successive drafts have benefited greatly by their criticism. I was fortunate to have one of my former students, Freida Stack, as full-time research assistant for one year. She worked mainly on the documentary material and prepared a number of papers for discussion by the advisory group: I have used them extensively in writing the book. My wife, who undertook most of the interviews, also made a most valuable contribution. Her genius for persuading people to talk shines through large sections of the text. Gratitude of a special kind is due to all those who submitted to interview for the purposes of this study, namely: Dame Elsie Abbot; Sir William Armstrong; Jack Bishop; the late Lord Bridges; the late A. J. Broom; Lord Crook; Sir Albert Day; J. R. M. Dryden; Sir Bruce Fraser; Lord Geddes of Epsom; Sir Richard Hayward; Edward Hewlett; the late Pat Hoey; Douglas Houghton; the late T. R. Jones; W. L. Kendall; Sir John Lang; the late C. L. Leese; W. McCall; Stanley Mayne; the late F. A. A. Menzler; N. G. Morrison; John Newton; Paul Osmond; Sir Thomas Padmore; Sir Harold Parker; Sir Louis Petch; Cyril Plant; Muriel Ritson; Baroness Sharp; J. J. S. Shaw; Sir John Simpson; Leslie Williams; Sir Horace Wilson; and Sir John Winnifrith.

Finally, it is my very agreeable duty to thank the University of Waterloo, Canada, for its hospitality during the year when most of the book was written.   Henry Parris
CIVIL SERVICE COLLEGE

PREFACE

On the approach of the fiftieth anniversary of its establishment in 1919, the Civil Service National Whitley Council invited the Royal Institute of Public Administration to prepare a commemorative volume describing the salient features of the Council's work during its first fifty years. The Institute was particularly pleased to receive this invitation since it was itself created by the staff associations in central and local government, acting together, only a year or two after Whitleyism was introduced into the civil service.

The Institute invited one of its members, Dr Henry Parris, then in the University of Durham and now Director of Studies in the Civil Service College, to undertake this task. Dr Parris already had a notable reputation as an administrative historian, and the Institute is extremely grateful to him for having agreed to add this to his other pressing obligations. Mrs Freida Stack, one of Dr Parris's former students, assembled the documentary material by intensive study of Official and Staff Side records. Her research work was a major contribution to this survey of the Whitley system. The Institute also gratefully acknowledges the skilful help of Dr Parris's wife who undertook much of the interviewing of the leading participants during the period.

Throughout the enterprise Dr Parris was greatly assisted by both the Official and Staff Sides of the Civil Service National Whitley Council. An advisory group, with whom Dr Parris could confer, was established and consisted of the following members:

Sir John Winnifrith, K.C.B., formerly Permanent Secretary, Ministry of Agriculture, Fisheries and Food, and previously Third Secretary, H.M. Treasury

Dame Elsie Abbot, D.B.E., formerly Third Secretary, H.M. Treasury

J. P. Bishop, formerly National Industrial Officer, General and Municipal Workers' Union

Sir Richard Hayward, C.B.E., formerly Secretary-General, Civil Service National Whitley Council (Staff Side)

Sir George Honeyman, C.B.E., formerly Chairman, Civil Service Arbitration Tribunal

*T. R. Jones, O.B.E., formerly Secretary, Civil Service National Whitley Council (Staff Side)

N. G. Morrison, C.B., Deputy Secretary, Civil Service Department

J. M. Newton, C.B., Director, Management Development Department, The Post Office

C. Plant, O.B.E., General Secretary, Inland Revenue Staff Federation

J. J. S. Shaw, C.B., Deputy Secretary, Civil Service Department

* Mr. T. R. Jones died on 15 May 1971.

J. L. Williams, C.B.E., Secretary-General, Civil Service National Whitley Council (Staff Side)

Members of the advisory group gave of their time most generously and both Dr Parris and the Institute are extremely grateful to them. The resulting book must, however, be regarded essentially as the work of Dr Parris.

There has long been a need for an up-to-date account of the system of staff relations that has been developed in the British Civil Service. Originally a pioneer, it still has features that probably make it unique. However that may be, there can be no doubt of the importance of Whitleyism over many years in developing sound staff relationships in one of the world's largest state services. Although approached as a history, Dr Parris indicates throughout the book how past events have a contemporary and continuing importance.

The warmest thanks are due to the Civil Service National Whitley Council for making possible this valuable contribution to the literature of public administration.

CONTENTS

CHAPTER I

THE SETTING UP OF THE NATIONAL WHITLEY COUNCIL

The Civil Service National Whitley Council met for the first time on 23 July 1919. It consisted of twenty-seven representatives of the government as employer, and a like number to speak for civil servants as employees. These groups were referred to in the Council's constitution as 'sides' – the Official Side and the Staff Side. Everyone on the Official Side was a civil servant. Most members of the Staff Side were civil servants too but some were paid officials of staff associations. The chair was taken by Sir Warren Fisher, Permanent Secretary of the Treasury, who was also leader of the Official Side. G. H. Stuart-Bunning, the leader of the Staff Side, became Vice-Chairman of the Council. There were four secretaries, two from each side. Both Official Side secretaries were provided by the Treasury. The objects of the Council, as set out in its constitution, were 'to secure the greatest measure of co-operation between the state in its capacity as employer, and the general body of civil servants in matters affecting the civil service, with a view to increased efficiency in the public service combined with the well-being of those employed; to provide machinery for dealing with grievances, and generally to bring together the experience and different points of view of representatives of the administrative, clerical and manipulative civil service'. The grievances dealt with must be collective, rather than personal: 'there shall be no discussion of individual cases'. The terms of reference were very broad: 'the scope of the National Council shall comprise all matters which affect the conditions of service of the staff'. In one crucial area, a monopoly was set up: 'the National Council shall be the only joint body to determine questions of remuneration affecting a class employed in two or more departments'. The Council was to be an executive rather than an advisory body: 'decisions . . . shall be arrived at by agreement between the two sides, shall be signed by the Chairman and Vice-Chairman, shall be reported to the cabinet, and thereupon shall become operative'.

The full significance of the new Council can be grasped only in the perspective of history. A major difficulty in writing about the past is that, once a system has developed to a certain point, 'it is difficult to imagine that things could ever have been otherwise'.[1] Had Whitleyism started from scratch, some of its basic features could have taken shape in a different way. In fact, of course, it had to be constructed from elements which were themselves the products of historical evolution. Three points are of special importance:

1. Within the civil service, as in other forms of employment, collective rather than individual bargaining was to be the rule. This underlies the provisions in the Council's constitution for the composition of the Staff Side: 'the Staff Side shall consist of persons of standing (who may or may not be civil servants) appointed by . . . groups of staff associations. . . . It shall be open to the authorities appointing the respective sides of the Council to vary their representatives.' This meant that a group of staff associations could withdraw its support from a representative who had forfeited its confidence and appoint someone else in his place. Now, had the architects of the Council been given *carte blanche*, it is easy to think of at least two other ways in which Staff Side 'constituencies' could have been drawn up. Either the departments, or the grades, could have been used. In either case, the larger ones could have been allotted two or more representatives, while the small ones could have been lumped together to elect a joint spokesman. In this way, a direct link between the rank and file and the National Staff Side would have been established.

2. Civil servants were normally to seek redress of their grievances within the administrative system. Industrial action and political pressure were not explicitly renounced. But the new procedure rested on the assumption that all ordinary problems could be solved within the family, as it were. Again, it is possible to imagine alternatives. The role of employer might have been enacted by commissioners nominated by the crown specifically for the duty, as the Civil Service Commissioners are for another purpose. Or ministers might have negotiated directly with staff representatives. A third possibility would have been a committee of Members of Parliament, since it is the House of Commons which votes the money. Each of these solutions may seem odd. But so did the notion of an Official Side, before it had been shown to be feasible.

3. On the Official Side, the major issues were to be the responsibility of the government as a whole, leaving only secondary questions to be settled at departmental level. The views of the departments would normally be co-ordinated at the official, rather than the ministerial, level. In this process, the Treasury would take the lead. As compared with the points dealt with in the two preceding paragraphs, it is not so

---

[1] Sir William Armstrong, 'Whitleyism in the Civil Service', *Whitley Bulletin*, Vol. xlix, 1969, p. 136.

simple to visualize optional courses of action. Given the traditional resentment of the Treasury, however, on the part of departments as well as staff associations, it is noteworthy that they accepted such a system.

COLLECTIVE BARGAINING

By 1919, the principle of collective bargaining was widely accepted in the civil service. It rested on the assumption that an official was bound by ties of common interest to those serving on the same level, in his own department and elsewhere, and that joint action would be more likely than individual action to bring benefits to individuals. A century earlier, a different mentality prevailed. At that time, the structure of British society was predominantly vertical. Men habitually looked to those above them for a betterment of their lot. Those who had a position acknowledged an obligation to assist their dependents. The relationship between patron and client was basic to such a society. 'When a man of rank and property had an appointment to make or influence, whether a Clerk of the Pells or footman, a bishop or governess, a colonial governor or workhouse master, an army contractor or a scullery maid, a Treasury agent or an insurance clerk, he looked first, and was expected and actively solicited to look, amongst his "friends".'[1] Patronage within the nascent civil service was only one aspect of the system which pervaded society. When an official wanted something, his impulse was to petition his superior for it. For example, in 1849, George Butler, Chief Clerk of the Board of Ordnance, expected to succeed Richard Byham as Secretary to the Board. But the post remained vacant for so long he began to feel uneasy, and put in a written claim. Characteristically, Butler sought to strengthen his case, not by looking at others on the same level, but by looking at those beneath him. 'It was not on my own account alone, but also as an encouragement to the fair and legitimate hope of promotion to which the other gentlemen of the office naturally look in the event of my elevation – an elevation which I covet far more for the honourable distinction it would bring with it than for any accompanying pecuniary advantage.'[2]

But within the patronage system, forms of joint action were beginning to develop. As officials became conscious, through working side by side, of common grievances, they drew up collective petitions to their superiors. The manuscript autobiography of Philip Hughes[3] provides an

[1] H. Perkin, *Origins of Modern English Society, 1780–1880*, 1969, p. 44.
[2] H. Parris, *Constitutional Bureaucracy: the development of British central administration since the 18th century*, 1969, pp. 65–6.
[3] A photostat copy of which was kindly lent me by Professor C. J. Hughes of Leicester University.

example. Hughes joined the office of the Commissary in Chief towards the end of the Napoleonic Wars. When the commissariat clerks were transferred to the Treasury in 1816, they 'were given to understand that they were not to expect any of the privileges or advantages of the office which they had thus joined: the Treasury establishment was composed of the relatives and friends of persons of rank, having high rates of pay, and very light duties, except the Secretaries and their Assistants; whilst it so happened that some of the clerks of the Commissary in Chief's office had been taken from a low rank in society' and, not surprisingly, the young Hughes took part in endeavours to improve the lot of the clerks. 'Remaining still a junior clerk with the maximum salary of two hundred pounds a year, and finding that the scale of salaries was inferior to that of surrounding public offices, I joined in several attempts to obtain an improvement of this scale by memorials to the Lords' Treasury Board: but all in vain.'

Many years later, Hughes played a more prominent role in a similar move, which was ultimately successful. 'In 1852, I was induced to draw up an improved scale for the clerks of the Commissariat Department of the Treasury, which I submitted to the Principal Clerk, expressing the hope that, as he had done so much in favour of the promotion of the Commissariat Officers abroad, he would draw forth the thanks of these clerks by obtaining an improvement in their position: this he promised to endeavour to accomplish.' But all that happened 'was that our application was left mixed up with other papers unnoticed by the Assistant Secretary and without further care by the Principal Clerk'. The formal approach having failed, Hughes tried informal methods. 'I consequently brought this slight to the notice of the Assistant Secretary's private secretary; the consequence was a discussion with these two gentlemen, the Chief Clerk and myself on the matter, when the Assistant Secretary promised to submit our claims for the favourable consideration of the Treasury Board. Afterwards a committee was appointed of Treasury officers to inquire into the government establishments, at which I attended, and a new scale of our salaries was recommended and approved, beneficial to the clerks.' From agitations of this kind, the first civil service staff associations developed in the second half of the nineteenth century. By the period the First World War, a considerable proportion of all civil servants were organized in one or other of the numerous bodies which had by that time come into being.[1]

KEEPING IT IN THE FAMILY

The growth of staff associations provided the means whereby represen-

[1] For further information, see B. V. Humphreys, *Clerical Unions in the Civil Service*, Oxford, 1958.

tatives of the employed were found. But they could not sit down with an abstraction. Who was to represent the employer? Of the three methods outlined above,[1] the third – consideration of staff demands by a parliamentary committee – would have been popular with many rank and file civil servants. There was a long tradition of action of this kind. As early as 1824, a petition was presented to the House of Commons by officers in the 'civil departments of the government' complaining about contributions under the Superannuation Act of 1822.[2] The debate made it clear that in addition to the petition, senior officers (who were mainly affected) had put pressure on individual Members. The result was a further Act which abolished contributions. Subsequently the contributory principle was re-introduced for new entrants only. But a fresh political agitation led to its complete withdrawal under the Superannuation Act of 1857. This measure was a triumphant demonstration of what civil servants could achieve by means of political pressure. A government supporter stated at the close of the debate that 'he must complain of the undue haste with which the Bill had been pressed forward, and the extraordinary zeal which the civil servants have exhibited in soliciting Hon. Members to support it. The measure, in short, was the result of an organized conspiracy on the part of the public servants, was unjust in its provisions, and based on erroneous statements.'[3]

In 1885 a petition from civil servants, signed by 120 Members of Parliament, resulted in a ministerial enquiry and the award of a special half-yearly bonus and a gratuity on retirement. When they sent a further petition in 1891 signed by 100 Members, a Treasury official commented that 'obtaining over one hundred signatures of MPs is a form of overawing the Treasury'.[4]

A petition to the Prime Minister in 1906, calling for an inquiry into the salary scale of assistant clerks, bore the names of 376 Members. The Treasury remained unmoved. There is little doubt, however, that the support of about 400 MPs was a leading factor in inducing Asquith to grant the demands of the staff for a Royal Commission in 1911. Once civil servants had found that political agitation could succeed, it was a logical step to seek a standing committee of the House of Commons to act as a court of appeal for their grievances. This is what associations in the Inland Revenue resolved to work for in 1906. The Civil Service Federation, founded in 1911, adopted the policy. Within a year, its executive council was recommending:

1. That there should be an inquiry by select committee of the House of

[1] See above, p. 16.
[2] M. Raphael, *Pensions & Public Servants: a study of the origins of the British System*, Paris & the Hague, 1964, p. 141.
[3] Raphael, p. 158.   [4] T1/8572C/10093/1891.

Commons into matters general to the whole civil service once every five years. This to include such matters as method of recruitment, superannuation, civil rights, principles of establishment, and anything absolutely general to the civil service.

2. That the civil service departments be divided into four groups, and that an inquiry into each group take place at intervals of not more than five years. The inquiries to be by select committees of the House of Commons, and to deal with pay, hours, conditions of working, and any other matters special to the department concerned.

In the event of both a particular group and the associations connected with it not being desirous of an inquiry at the expiration of five years, we recommend that there should be power to postpone the inquiry for a period of not more than two additional years. We are, however, of opinion that either side should be able to demand inquiry at the end of five years.

The statement was seen by the Chancellor of the Exchequer and discussed in the Treasury. The proposed select committees were taken to indicate 'the desire of the Federation . . . to get a sympathetic tribunal rather than an exhaustive investigation'.[1]

The first conference of the newly founded Civil Service Alliance, held in April 1917, called for a new controlling authority for the civil service which should be outside the Treasury. At its second conference, later in the same year, and after the publication of the Whitley Report,[2] the idea was elaborated. 'The controlling authority of the civil service should be a board under the chairmanship of a member of the ministry, and composed of equal numbers of (a) persons appointed by the government, and (b) representatives of employees nominated by associations of civil servants.'[3]

As late as September 1918, W. J. Brown, of the Assistant Clerks Association, argued that 'Members of Parliament and persons of public eminence' as well as 'Treasury men' should represent the government on the proposed Council for the civil service. Most of the good results of Whitleyism would be lost if control remained in the hands of the Treasury. The Council, or Board of Control, should take over all responsibility for the management of the civil service from the Treasury, and from the Civil Service Commission. There would be a separate department under a minister, but he would be guided in policy matters by the Council's advice. Two months later, a staff deputation gave oral evidence to the Heath Committee, which had been set up to consider the application of the Whitley Report to the administrative departments of the civil service. G. H. Stuart-Bunning was the spokesman. They

[1] T1/11783/1641/1915. [2] See below, p.25.
[3] *Red Tape*, Vol. vii, no. 75.

urged that the Official Sides, even of departmental Whitley Councils, should not be composed exclusively of officials. They might include ministers, Members of Parliament, and prominent businessmen.[1]

Thus, within a year of the first meeting of the National Whitley Council, the leaders of the staff were aiming at something of a very different kind. They wanted a recognized means by which disputes could be removed from the administrative to the political plane. It is all the more remarkable, therefore, that they should have accepted in 1919 a supreme negotiating body in which the role of employer was to be played by permanent officials. The clause in the constitution which states that 'members of the Official Side of the Council shall be persons of standing (who may or may not be civil servants)' was a concession to staff feeling on the point. But although it opened the way to non-civil service members of the Official Side, none were in fact appointed until 1922.

THE TREASURY TAKES THE LEAD

If a supreme negotiating body in which the role of employer was allotted to senior civil servants was only one of various possibilities, even less inevitable was it that Treasury officials should dominate the Official Side. For representatives of the staff in (say) the Ministry of Labour to negotiate with the Treasury appeared to contradict the constitutional doctrine of the minister's individual responsibility for his department. At an early date, staff leaders realized the desirability of doing so, for after all, it was the Treasury which held the purse strings. If one's minister made a concession, it was of little value until the Treasury confirmed it. If on the other hand, the minister said no, he might very possibly be voicing the Treasury view rather than his own, or using the Treasury as a scapegoat to hide his own opposition to the demand. But when staff representatives tried to approach the Treasury direct, they were told to do so through their departmental heads. The traditional attitude was stated in a Treasury Minute of 1866 'relating to the submission of memorials to the Treasury by subordinate officers in the civil service without permission of the heads of their department'.[2] It was 'far from the desire of Her Majesty's government that any classes of public servants or individuals should be debarred from making a respectful representation in regard to any matter in which they may feel aggrieved and My Lords will always be prepared to give every such representation their full consideration'.[3] Nevertheless with limited ex-

[1] F. Stack, 'Civil Service Associations and the Whitley Report of 1917' *Political Quarterly*, Vol. xl, 1969, pp. 290–1.
[2] E. N. Gladden, *Civil Service Staff Relations*, 1943, p. 15.
[3] Ibid. p. 16.

ceptions in the case of departments subordinate to the Treasury such as the Inland Revenue, all such representations must come through the head of the department.

As Treasury control of establishments extended in the latter part of the nineteenth century, action limited to one department became increasingly inadequate. The consequences were, firstly, the growth of staff associations cutting across departments, and secondly, claims by the associations for direct negotiations with the Treasury. Giving evidence before the Playfair Commission on the Civil Service in 1875, Robert Lowe admitted the link between Treasury control and the growth of staff organization. 'One thing which we overlooked was the danger of collecting a very large body of persons together, having friends all over the country, having a particular interest, and that interest being to obtain better terms from the government. I think that we overlooked the political aspect of the question. . . . I now think that it is a pity that there were collected some 3000 persons, or something of the kind, for this sort of employment, all having a common interest to press upon the government – the raising of their wages.'[1] The Lower Division clerks, who had become an all-service class in 1876, recognized the logic of the new situation when they petitioned the Treasury direct in 1880. Their memorial asked for an adjustment of salary increments, and bore 660 signatures. The Treasury made one small concession, justifying its departure from the normal rule in terms which were a portent for the future: 'the uniform character of this branch of the service . . . explains why the memorial . . . has been presented to the Treasury, and why My Lords have consented to receive it, and to deal with it directly'. Nevertheless, it was not to rank as a precedent. Further moves of a similar kind over the next forty years were occasionally successful, but more often not.

Nevertheless, the trend was clear, especially as government control of the Commons increased. In the middle of the nineteenth century, as at other periods, it was desirable to have the Treasury on one's side. Yet there was a limit to the value of its support, since it was always possible that MPs might reject, or reduce, its estimates. By 1900, however, such a possibility had become remote. Staff associations found it very difficult to wring concessions from the Treasury. But they could, at least, assume that, for any agreement they might reach, the money would be forthcoming. For this reason alone, it seems almost certain that, even without the war, the function of negotiating with the staff would have become increasingly centralized in the Treasury. The war greatly accelerated the process. There was for example the problem of adjusting rates of pay to meet inflation. In 1915, postal employees receiving three pounds a week

[1] Humphreys, p. 27.

or less secured a cost-of-living bonus. Naturally, civil servants in other departments felt they should be treated similarly. The universality of the problem caused the doctrine that claims should be considered department by department to wear thin. Eventually, in September 1916, the Financial Secretary to the Treasury received a deputation headed by W. J. Brown of the Assistant Clerks Association. Brown argued that the claim was based solely on the effect of increased prices – a trend which affected officials in all departments equally. The Financial Secretary admitted that the staff had a good case. Soon afterwards, the Treasury announced a general war bonus to civil servants in receipt of less than three pounds a week.

Another issue tending towards centralization was the length of the working day. The story may be told in the words of W. J. Brown himself. 'Under the terms of the Order-in-Council of 1910, the hours of civil servants were fixed at seven per day. This did not mean that officers were restricted to seven hours per day. In 1916 they were, in fact, working anything up to twelve hours a day in the pressure caused by the war. It did mean, however, that for all hours in excess of seven per day, overtime was payable. In 1916 we received information, by means I had better not disclose, that the Treasury had drafted a new Order-in-Council extending the seven-hour day to an eight-hour day. . . . The effect of the Order would have been to deprive civil servants of an hour's overtime pay per day while the war lasted, and to condition them to a permanently lengthened working day in time of peace, without any compensation whatever. The news caused great indignation amongst all grades. It was plain to everybody that the Treasury were using the exigencies of war as an excuse permanently to worsen civil service conditions.'[1] Staff agitation was successful and the Treasury withdrew its proposal.[2]

Increased pressure from staff associations led to a strengthening on the official side. The logic of the process has already been recognized in the Post Office. In 1907 it had asked for more clerks specifically to deal with the rising volume of staff association business. The Treasury wished to see a reduction in the amount of business rather than an increase in the number of clerks. Failing this, 'there must be a continuous and serious growth in the cost of clerical establishments in proportion to the practical work which is done'.[3] To which the Post Office returned the revolutionary reply: 'Mr Buxton would observe that a public service must necessarily devote more time than would be given in a private business to individual or collective complaints from the staff. A civil servant, or associations of civil servants, are fully aware that an alleged grievance can be brought to the attention of the Postmaster

[1] W. J. Brown, *So Far*, 1943, pp. 80–1.   [2] Humphreys, p. 91.
[3] T1/11057/15657/1909.

General, or under public notice, through Members of Parliament by means of a question in parliament or by correspondence. Mr Buxton regards it as greatly conducing to the good conduct of the service that the staff should have confidence that any complaints they desire to make are as fully enquired into on direct applications as through the indirect method of parliamentary publicity or pressure.'[1]

The Treasury disliked political pressure on staff matters just as much as the Post Office did. A petition from civil servants, which bore also the signatures of politicians, elicited from an official the comment: 'If the Treasury accept this memorial it is clear that ... in future we are to accept political influence put forward in its crudest form.'[2] Part of the answer was an improvement in Treasury machinery for dealing with such problems. The fact was that, in control of establishments, the Treasury's bark was a good deal worse than its bite. Indeed, 'the evidence strongly suggests that its control was very ineffective up to the 'nineties.'[3] From then on, there seems to have been a gradual increase in strength. 'Treasury control became increasingly a more effective restraint upon expenditure as the Treasury armed itself with the authority of Orders in Council, and made greater use of general Minutes and Circulars to regulate more uniformly the organization and administration of the departments. At the same time, departments appear to have become more susceptible to Treasury example and suggestion, and more willing to acknowledge its role as a co-ordinating department and to seek its advice.'[4]

The MacDonnell Commission (1912–16) emphasized the limitations of the Treasury in controlling establishments. It was inadequately informed about departmental practice, and in a very weak position to initiate reforms. It placed excessive reliance on certain traditional techniques, such as the *ad hoc* committee of inquiry, appointed at official level to deal with each problem as it came along. MacDonnell argued that this was no longer good enough. 'Such occasional committees ... are probably constituted every time they sit. They deal at each sitting with different matters, not with the same matter in different phases; they can never accumulate and transmit to their successors that knowledge of men, of official practice, and of service capacities, feelings and aspirations which it is essential that the controlling authorities should be enabled to draw upon if service administration is to be equable and prescient.'[5] A new section should therefore be set up within the Treasury to deal solely with establishment questions, as a means of strengthening Treasury control. It would have the task of watching over the general

---

[1] T1/11057/16134/1909.   [2] T1/8572C/10093/1891.
[3] M. W. Wright, *Treasury Control, 1854–1914*, mimeo, 1969, p. 24. See also the same author's *Treasury Control of the Civil Service*, Oxford, 1969.
[4] Ibid.   [5] Cd. 7338, para. 95.

conditions of the service, making inquiries, bringing their recommendations to the notice of heads of departments, and facilitating transfers between departments.

This proposal was carried into effect at the end of the war when, in 1919, an Establishments Department was created within the Treasury, under Sir Malcolm Ramsay as first Controller of Establishments. Its functions were to sanction rates of pay, to control salaries, and to issue general regulations relating to the conduct of the service. Each of the larger departments appointed at the same period an Establishment Officer who was made responsible for dealing with all questions of personnel. A Standing Committee of Establishment Officers, with the Controller of Establishments as its Chairman, was brought into being to advise the Treasury on all general matters concerning the staffing and organization of the service, and to ensure co-operation between the Treasury and the departments on establishment matters.

Whether or not Whitleyism in the civil service was desirable in 1919, it was at least possible. This was the result of three processes stretching back some decades. Staff associations had evolved to the point where they could effectively represent the great majority of civil servants. Civil servants had achieved enough by negotiation within the administrative system for them to be prepared at least to try a procedure which contained no provision for appeal to the political level. The establishments side of the Treasury had developed in such a way that it was competent to take on the task of leading the Official Side. The application of the Whitley philosophy to the civil service had the effect of fusing these three developments into one.

THE ORIGIN OF WHITLEYISM

To see how this came about, it is necessary to go back to the year 1916. At that time, widespread industrial unrest was hampering the war effort. In 1915, two million working days had been lost in strikes, rising to two and a half million in the following year. To investigate the problem, the government set up a sub-committee of the Reconstruction Committee, under the chairmanship of the Rt Hon. J. H. Whitley MP. There ensued a series of reports, of which the first appeared in March 1917, and the last in July 1918.[1] They recommended the introduction into industry of machinery to regularize relations between employers and employed, and the joint co-operation of employers and employed in the functions of management and control. In each industry there was to be a national joint industrial council on which employers and workers would be equally represented, supplemented by district councils and works com-

[1] Cd. 8606, 9001, 9002, 9085, 9099, and 9153.

mittees. But nothing was said at first with relation to clerical and administrative work either in the private or the public sector.

In June 1917, the Minister of Labour formally communicated the first report from the Whitley Committee to a large number of employers' associations and trade unions. It was not, however, sent to the civil service staff associations. The Civil Service Clerical Alliance wrote, therefore, to the Minister, explaining that they represented 150,000 civil servants, and asking that the invitation to consider the report be extended to them also. The Permanent Secretary of the Ministry of Labour told them in reply: 'It is not contemplated that its application should be extended to occupations of a purely commercial or clerical nature.'[1] In August 1917, the Civil Service Federation, speaking for some 125,000 civil servants, raised the matter with the Chancellor of the Exchequer. The Federation 'assumed . . . that if the principles of the Whitley report are approved by the House of Commons, they will be applied to government servants'. An invitation to the Chancellor followed. 'If you would be good enough to appoint three or four of your officers to consult with members of my committee, it will probably be possible to arrive at some understanding, which will permit of a smooth and easy working of any schemes mentioned in the above-mentioned report.'[2] In its reply, the Treasury followed much the same line as the Ministry of Labour had adopted towards the Alliance. Not unnaturally, the Federation was unwilling to let matters rest there. They retorted that they did 'not understand your statement that it is not contemplated that the application of the Whitley report should be extended to occupations of a purely commercial or clerical character. We find nothing in the report to justify this conclusion, and I am also to remind you that the civil service consists of a number of classes, many of whom come under neither designation.'[3] To this the Chancellor's private secretary replied: 'I am desired by the Chancellor of the Exchequer to say that he would certainly deny that the civil service could be regarded as an "industry" or as being included in the "main industries of the country" to which reference is made in paragraph 3 of the report in question. Mr Bonar Law regrets that he can add nothing to the answer given in his letter of 27 August, to which he fully adheres.'[4]

Since the government had adopted the Whitley recommendations and was urging them on industry, it was perfectly natural for civil servants to ask why they should not be applied within government departments also. As W. J. Brown recalled, 'The service associations . . . jumped to the opportunity. Wherever a government speaker appeared to commend the scheme to employers and employed, there was a pertinacious civil servant blandly inquiring why, if the ideas was so good, the government, which was the biggest employer of all, did not apply it in its own

[1] Armstrong, p. 137. [2] Ibid. [3] Ibid. [4] Ibid.

26

house ?'[1] Stuart-Bunning got in touch with Whitley himself, and it was probably this approach which the latter referred to in an address to the Society of Civil Servants in 1920. 'When my committee had issued its first report, the people in the civil service were among the first to prick up their ears, and I had, very speedily, an inquiry from ranks of the civil servants as to whether or not what we had said was meant to apply also to the civil service. . . . When I brought the matter before my Committee . . . we were unanimous in the opinion that the general plan we had suggested . . . ought to be applicable to the civil service . . . as well as industrial life. . . . There was, I am aware, a certain amount of impatience amongst some people. They said, over and over again. "Well, if the government has approved of this method as applicable to the private employer, how much more ought they to put it into operation themselves, and not wait for the private employers to make a beginning." '[2] At any rate, a further report from Whitley's group appeared in October 1917, in which they said: 'In considering the scope of the matters referred to us we have formed the opinion that the expression "employers and workmen" in our reference covers state and municipal authorities and persons employed by them. . . . We understand that the Ministry of Labour has up to the present circulated our first report only to employers' and work peoples' associations in the ordinary private industries. We think, however, that both it and the present report should also be brought to the notice of state departments and municipal authorities employing labour.'[3] By December 1917, the Chancellor had so far shifted his position as to say, in reply to a parliamentary question, that 'the government fully realize the importance of its setting an example in this matter'.[4]

The most obvious application of the Whitley principle was in those departments which employed considerable numbers of industrial civil servants, such as the Admiralty. In May 1918, Stanley Baldwin, as Financial Secretary to the Treasury, held a conference of the departments concerned, as a result of which a memorandum was put before the War Cabinet. The first question raised was whether the government would implement the Whitley recommendations in government establishments where the conditions were closely analogous to those in industrial concerns outside the public service. If so, the memorandum went on to suggest how it could be done. The most important point was that any joint committees should be consultative rather than executive. The government then set up an inter-departmental committee under the chairmanship of G. H. Roberts, the Minister of Labour, with

[1] Brown, p. 90.
[2] L. D. White, *Whitley Councils in the British Civil Service: a study in conciliation and arbitration*, Chicago, 1933, pp. 4–5.
[3] Cd. 9002. [4] Armstrong, p. 137.

instructions to consult Whitley. This committee reported in October 1918, recommending that, in government industrial establishments, there should be consultative councils, and that the Ministry of Labour should call a conference to secure the agreement of the trade unions concerned. The recommendation was accepted by the government, and a joint conference took place on 20 February 1919.

One of the speakers was Sir Malcolm Ramsay who had just been appointed to the new post of Controller of Establishments at the Treasury.[1] He was anxious to remove any misconception there might be about the role of the Treasury in the new scheme of things. 'What I think you are afraid of is that, where there has been a meeting of the Joint Council, if there is a dispute, the position may arise by which some clerk or official of the Treasury can hold up the whole thing. Is that not so? That I can assure you is a misunderstanding. The officer who will speak for the Treasury will have power to agree within certain limits. If he cannot agree the departmental Treasury is not going to turn the matter down without reference to the Treasury ministers. . . . If by any chance a proposal is turned down it will not be by the action of the departmental Treasury. The Treasury would have to send the matter to their ministers, who would have to consult their colleagues in the cabinet, who would have to decide if it is to go before parliament or not. That, as I understand it, will be the position of the Treasury in future, and I think that is the principal point on which you wish to hear me.'[2] This conciliatory tone had considerable effect, and it may be assumed that it helped to allay the traditional fears of the Treasury common among staff association leaders.

Meanwhile, the Roberts Committee had, in October 1918, set up a sub-committee to consider whether the Whitley principle could be applied to the non-industrial civil service. Its chairman was Sir Thomas Heath, Joint Permanent Secretary to the Treasury, and the Permanent Secretaries of the Ministry of Labour and the Post Office were among the departmental representatives. Having taken evidence from the departments and the staff associations, it reported in March 1919. It recommended a scheme for a National Joint Council, with joint committees in the departments and at local level. Thus it anticipated several features of the scheme which was eventually established, but with one significant difference. The system was to have only consultative and advisory, as distinct from executive, functions. This was because 'a minister would be placed in an impossible position if he were bound in any way by a decision to which his subordinates were parties even though he felt unable to defend it'.[3]

---

[1] See above, p. 25.   [2] Armstrong, p. 138.
[3] *Report on the application of the Whitley Report to the Administrative Departments of the Civil Service*, 1919, Cmd. 9, para. 9.

The Heath Report was accepted by the government, and sent to the staff associations, with an invitation to a joint conference to be held on 8 April 1919. Staff leaders were disappointed by the recommendations. Stuart-Bunning complained that 'the precise effect of this paragraph will be to prevent an appeal to parliament because a Whitley Council has been set up, and then leave matters just where they are now, that is to say, in the hands of the minister.'[1] Years later he put it more pungently: the scheme 'looked like Whitley, smelt like Whitley, almost tasted like Whitley, but it was not Whitley'. He and the Civil Service Federation set to work, in the short time they had, to get a united front among the associations. Since there were over 200 of them, this was no light task. The tactical position was difficult. They had to find a way of making clear their objections to some parts of the report, without giving anyone a pretext for saying that the rank and file had spurned the offer of a Whitley system. The Heath Report had suggested the setting up of a provisional joint committee to consider the details of the proposed scheme. The staff leaders decided to centre their attack on this point, by moving an amendment that the original Whitley Report, as well as the Heath Report, should be referred to the Provisional Joint Committee. This would make possible a reconsideration of all those points where the staff preferred the Whitley to the Heath proposals.

The Chancellor of the Exchequer, Austen Chamberlain, took the chair at the meeting, which took place on 8 April 1919. In opening the proceedings, he declared his belief that Whitleyism would 'make the task of the Treasury much lighter. . . . When you know us better you will think us more reasonable than you have thought us in the past. You have been told that "My Lords refuse." . . . But even where their decisions . . . would have been maintained by any impartial authority, and I venture to think approved by you, if you had had all the facts open to you, there was no machinery by which these facts could be brought home to you. There was no method of explaining to you and you were left in many instances quite in the dark. I know the feeling was that when you had been non-suited they had given no time to your appeal. The new machinery will remove any grievances, real or fancied, of that kind, and I believe that in many cases out of that discussion there will come agreement and satisfaction whether the answer be favourable or not to the petition.'[2]

Stuart-Bunning rose to thank the government for accepting the Whitley principle, but criticized it for departing from the spirit of Whitleyism, which was equality. This was a reference to the fact that, although the staff had had the opportunity to submit their views to the

[1] Civil Service Federation: memo. on the Whitley Report on the civil service. Union of Post Office Workers, file 120.
[2] Armstrong, p. 139.

Heath Committee, their representatives had not been invited to join in its deliberations. He then moved that conference adopt only paragraph 45 of the Heath Report, which recommended the setting up of a *joint* committee to prepare a detailed scheme for the National Council and to formulate the main principles on which departmental and local Whitley bodies should be constituted. All reports dealing with the scheme, and not merely the Heath Report, should be referred to the Provisional Joint Committee, which was to report to a further staff conference not later than 31 May 1919. The motion was seconded by F. J. Payne, secretary of the Staff Clerks Association and a member of the Society of Civil Servants. There followed a period of silence, which must have been extremely anxious for Stuart-Bunning and his supporters. If any staff spokesman had broken the ranks by putting forward an alternative proposal, the agreed tactic would have been endangered. But no one intervened, and the chairman replied simply and to the point: 'I want to say that we gladly accept the resolution which has been put today.'[1] After prolonged applause, the resolution was carried unanimously.

The Provisional Joint Committee was then set up, with fifteen representatives from each side, with Ramsay as chairman, and Stuart-Bunning leading the staff representatives. They worked very fast and presented a unanimous report on 28 May 1919. It followed Whitley, and sections of Heath, very closely. Its definition of the functions of the National Whitley Council has been permanently enshrined in the constitution of that body. Its recommendations differed, however, from those of the Heath Report, in one respect which seemed very important to the staff. Whereas Heath had indicated only a consultative and advisory role for the Council, Ramsay-Bunning favoured an executive function: 'The decisions of the Council shall be arrived at by agreement between the two sides, shall be signed by the Chairman . . . and the Vice-Chairman . . . shall be reported to the cabinet, and thereupon shall become operative.'[2] These words, too, were subsequently incorporated into the constitution of the Council. The report was accepted by the War Cabinet on 13 June 1919.

A conference of heads of departments, presided over by Sir Malcolm Ramsay, met at the Treasury on 30 June 1919. Ramsay admitted that the committee had started badly. 'I must say that at the first meeting my heart sank. The atmosphere was very frosty. It was full of mistrust and suspicion which was directed mainly, but not exclusively, against the Treasury. We used, of course, every effort to thaw the frost and to dissipate the suspicion, and I am glad to say that as the proceedings progressed the relations between ourselves and the staff became more and more cordial. They came out into the open. They were much more disposed to listen to what we had had to say, and to believe that we were reasonable human beings.'[3] The Treasury meant to make the new system

[1] Armstrong, p. 139. [2] White, pp. 7–8. [3] Armstrong, p. 152.

30

a success, and believed it would succeed. 'But I am perfectly sure that
. . . if after trial the system is found wanting and does not satisfy the
legitimate – I say "legitimate" advisedly – aspirations of the staff and
the reasonable hopes which they undoubtedly found upon it, we shall
find ourselves embarked upon a sea of troubles far more stormy than we
have yet had to navigate and we shall be in great danger and disaster.'[1]
In the subsequent discussion, it became apparent that some had mis-
givings about the new system. On the other hand, support came from
such Permanent Secretaries as Sir David Shackleton, Sir Warren Fisher,
and Sir Claud Schuster, of the Ministry of Labour, the Treasury and
the Lord Chancellor's Department respectively. It was left to the Treasury to arrange the composition of the Official Side in time for the first
meeting of the National Whitley Council. The outcome was something
of an achievement for Ramsay personally. He had persuaded a group of
men, most of whom were senior to himself and much more experienced
than himself in establishment matters, and some of whom were suspicious of the new system, to give it a fair trial. A second joint conference
was held on 3 July 1919. Caxton Hall was packed with civil servants,
many of whom had queued to get in since early morning. Some had
come from places as far away as Edinburgh and Dublin. Sir Austen
Chamberlain once more took the chair. This time he was flanked by
Ramsay and Stuart-Bunning. Chamberlain recommended the adoption
of the report. The proceedings were marked by good humour, and no
one felt the need to speak at great length. The report was adopted unanimously and the way was clear for the first meeting itself – the event
with which this chapter began.

Ramsay had given a warning that if the venture did not succeed, the
alternative would not be a reversion to the *status quo ante*, but something
very much worse. A staff journal of the period saw things in much the
same terms. 'The establishment of a National Whitley Council for the
civil service is an event of first importance. . . . Civil servants have
acquired a new status. . . . The organization and control of the civil
service will henceforward be the joint task of representatives of the staffs
and representatives of the state. . . . We have won rights but we have
also accepted responsibilities. . . . We have pledged ourselves to a full
share in this vast work of reconstruction. . . . We know that the responsibilities [Whitleyism] imposes are at least as great as the advantages it
offers. . . . The Whitley Councils represent the final attempt to settle
civil service problems by conciliation. If they fail, there will remain to
the service only two alternatives – acquiescence in existing evils, or
failure of Whitleyism . . . depends, more than on any other factor, upon
the spirit in which the two sides meet.[2]' What that spirit was to be, the
next chapter will indicate.

[1] Ibid.
[2] *Red Tape*, Vol. viii, 1919, p. 124; White, pp. 8–9.

CHAPTER 2

STARCH AND DYNAMITE

The meeting of 8 April 1919, has usually been represented as a staff victory. It is easy to see why. An executive body had been secured in place of one which would have had consultative and advisory status only. It may well have been, however, a hollow victory. A form of words does not change the realities of power. Most decisions of the Council would cost money – money which would have to be voted by parliament, on the motion of a minister of the crown. It followed, therefore, that the Official Side would never agree to anything ministers would not accept. On the government side, the point was quickly grasped. The Minister of Labour commented: 'it should be understood that in the course of the discussion of the subject upon the National Council the representatives of the government will necessarily have to take the instructions of the minister or ministers concerned, and will not agree to any settlement except in accordance with these instructions. The effect of this will be that the government will in fact have agreed to the decision being taken before the matter is settled upon the National Council and consequently the decision can become operative.'[1]

Since there was no voting on the Council, only agreement or disagreement could be registered. A disagreement over pay could be referred to arbitration. But in many cases, disagreement could be broken only by executive action on the part of the government. Not surprisingly, the Staff Side objected strongly to executive action following a disagreement. They held that the Official Side were not free to use the Council only when it suited them. Yet it was hardly to be expected that the Official Side would undertake never to act except through Whitley. It became urgently necessary to clarify the position, lest it develop into a stalemate. In December 1920, the Official Side secretary reported his inability to find any evidence 'that it was made clear at the time that the use of the Whitley Council was optional. . . . The official view is that Whitleyism provides an opportunity but does not impose an obligation.'[2] Nevertheless, it should be used whenever possible. 'I should be inclined', wrote Sir Russell Scott, 'to tell the Staff Side that we on the Official Side hold the view that the government has bound itself by a declared inten-

[1] G247. Memo. to the Cabinet. [2] WC 8/12.

tion to make the fullest use of Whitleyism in all matters affecting the welfare and conditions of the staff; but that this pledge cannot be held to relieve ministers of their primary responsibility for taking whatever action may be deemed to be right in the public interest; and that, in particular, it may be necessary for the executive to act independently in case of urgency, in matters of general policy and in cases of disagreement between the Official and Staff Sides.'[1] In January 1921, at the suggestion of the Official Side, the Council appointed a committee to consider the relationship between the Whitley Councils and the executive. After two meetings it agreed that 'while the acceptance by the government of the Whitley system as regards the civil service implies an intention to make the fullest use of Whitley procedure, the government has not surrendered, and cannot surrender, its liberty of action in the exercise of its authority and the discharge of its responsibilities in the public interest.'[2] By the time this was published the government had taken their action in the 'supercut' case.[3]

At the first meeting of the Council, Sir Malcolm Ramsay of the Official Side was elected Chairman and G. H. Stuart-Bunning of the Staff Side Vice-Chairman. Ramsay, Controller of Establishments was, like all but one of his successors, a Treasury Official. The Permanent Secretary to the Treasury, Sir Warren Fisher, was a member of the Official Side, but he left it in 1920 and the Permanent Secretary was not a member again until 1939. Sir Malcolm Ramsay was succeeded by Sir Russell Scott because 'the Chairmanship of the Council cannot be divorced from the post of Controller of Establishments who is concerned with the day to day control . . . of the civil service'.[4] However ten years later Sir Horace Wilson, who was Chief Industrial Adviser to the Ministry of Labour, became Chairman. He resigned in 1939 when he became Permanent Secretary to the Treasury but remained on the Official Side. The Chairman of the Staff Side, Stuart-Bunning, remained Vice-Chairman of the Council until 1925, when he was succeeded by George Middleton, of the Union of Post Office workers. From 1928 to 1939 W. E. Llewellyn held the post which was then taken by A. J. T. Day, of the Society of Civil Servants. The Chairman presided over meetings of the National Council, and was also the main spokesman for the Official Side. In the early years, when the Chairman was absent, Stuart-Bunning occasionally took the Chair, but he remained the Staff Side's chief spokesman.

General discussion at Council meetings was exceptional. The normal practice was for each side to present a single case. This was particularly true of the Official Side who worked within the framework of government policy. Despite arguments beforehand, the Staff Side presented a united front at the Council. But because they represented so many

[1] WC 8/12.   [2] E 6599/01.   [3] See below, p. .85-7   [4] WC 1/30.

C   33

interests, each member was anxious to present his side of the case. In fact, general discussion was impossible in so large a body. The Official Side wanted to reduce the size of the Council, at one time even allowing their strength to drop to sixteen, but the Staff Side needed the full representative capacity to satisfy all the associations. This was also a problem in committees and the Joint General Purposes Committee which was set up to speed Council business had to have an Official Side of six and a Staff Side of eight drawn from a panel of ten.

STARCH

'During the early years of Whitleyism,' wrote Sir Albert Day, 'relations between the two sides of the National Council were a blend of starch and dynamite. Each viewed the other with some distrust. . . . Some meetings of the Council were chilly gatherings of about fifty men and women brought from overloaded desks to sit, most of them, mute and idle while more or less formal business was transacted; others were red hot rows.'[1] There is ample confirmation of the starchiness of proceedings. Lord Bridges remembered 'tremendous meetings attended by large numbers of . . . very distinguished people but . . . very few things were really ever settled at these great meetings. There were too many people, and there were too many points of view, and . . . it was a thoroughly ineffective form of organization. . . . At that time, . . . the organization didn't work well.' Others whose memories went back to that period generally agreed. Lord Crook recalled 'a time when everybody marched in from each side . . . and it was like a mass meeting of people glowering at each other in that long room at Montagu House.' (Montagu House, where the Council normally met, was then the headquarters of the Ministry of Labour.) One of his contemporaries recollected that 'we used to meet formally fairly frequently and the matter was all dealt with on a very rigid sort of basis and both sides had to take a firm stand and put their points of view and it was very difficult to break down the resistance on the two sides'. Sir John Simpson, who later became one of the Staff Side secretaries, was even more severe in his judgment of the pre-war Council. 'I always regarded it as a most unsatisfactory piece of machinery. You had the permanent secretaries of most of the departments there . . . but few of them ever made any contribution, the running was entirely in the hands of the Treasury representatives.'

From the beginning the work of the Council on specific subjects was delegated to committees and the Council discussed and ratified their reports.

Discussion on committees was freer than on the Council, but the two

[1] Sir Albert Day, *Whitley Bulletin*, Vol. xxxiii, 1953, p. 102.

sides still put forward single points of view, as agreed at meetings held prior to the committee sessions. In addition to committees on specific topics, there were two standing committees. The purpose of the first was to follow up the recommendations of the Reorganization Committee. The other was the Joint General Purposes Committee, first suggested in 1920 by the Official Side in an effort to streamline the operation of the Council. 'It would review critically, on behalf of the Council, all reports of committees, and any question which required detailed consideration, but was not itself of sufficient importance to require a special committee, would be referred to it for report. This committee, combined with the special committees appointed for particular subjects, would relieve the Council of all but purely formal business and the discussions of big questions of principle. It would thus save valuable time and would go some long way to prevent friction arising from misunderstandings.'[1] Scott anticipated that the Staff Side would not welcome the proposal, because they 'would not find it easy to select members for a General Purposes Committee realising as they will that this Committee will inevitably become a sort of inner cabinet'.[2] That is to say, no one would wish to be left off. His guess was correct, but the Staff Side did in the end agree, though not until October 1921. Even then it took a long time to reach agreement on the composition of the committee, and it was October 1923, before it met for the first time. The Committee did in fact carry out just the functions envisaged. In framing constructive suggestions for consideration by the Council, and in drafting statements and Treasury Circulars the two sides were also able to negotiate in a way impossible on the Council. As with the other committees the two sides established their general positions in prior meetings.

This committee system contributed, in the memory of participants, to the formalism of early Whitleyism. 'The National Whitley Council before the outbreak of war did its effective business by the committee system.' In addition to a joint General Purposes Committee, there were others some of which 'lasted quite a long time and presented report after report on different aspects of their terms of reference: There was a subsistence committee, there was a promotions committee. . . . Usually the chair was taken by a Treasury man, though not always, but he was reinforced by departmental officers, usually a rank or two below the permanent head.' The result was to reduce the amount of discussion of many topics at the highest level. 'The important decisions were taken . . . by rubber-stamping a committee report . . . which meant that the national Whitley Official Side representatives were involved.' The function of the departmental representatives resembled that of the witnesses to a medieval charter. They were there to lend weight and dignity to the proceedings, but not to discuss. 'The Treasury made the

[1] WC 5/43/01.   [2] Ibid.

35

running all the time! . . . It was very rare, unless it was something that affected his department in some particular way . . . for anybody else to open his mouth. . . . It was really absurd in a way. We were discussing with the same people [with whom] we'd had . . . preliminary discussions, and the matter had then been referred to the National Council, but in fact we were discussing with the same people.' As a result, many meetings were extremely short. Sir Albert Day remembered 'on one occasion turning up at a National Whitley meeting five minutes late and hearing the Chairman say, "Any other business ?" The constitution said that there was to be a meeting of the National Whitley Council . . . and there jolly well was a meeting!'

DYNAMITE

Some meetings, however, took a very different course. Sometimes the Council resolved itself, in Lord Bridges's words, into an 'enormous parliament, leading to torrents of rhetoric. . . . That great man, W. J. Brown, used to deliver the most tremendous oratorical speeches, making a great deal of play about a great many points, done very cleverly, but not all very relevant to the point at issue.' Muriel Ritson recalled Brown's interventions as 'the highlight' of Council proceedings. They gave the business a 'feeling of go' and 'lifted it from being stodgy'. But Staff Side representatives recalled no victories achieved in this way. An Official Side survivor from the twenties explained why, by quoting a Whitley proverb current in his day. 'The Staff Side, they say what they like, . . . but the Official Side . . . do what they like.' Hence, they were 'really rather phoney debates, when Brown would do his soap-box stunt, but it wouldn't make any difference. I mean, you simply registered disagreement, and that was the end of that.' The Council 'was . . . only then a debating gathering, not . . . a meeting that did business really. . . . Brown was the most effective debater that I've ever met. He could make mincemeat of any member of the Official Side in a set debate at meetings of the full National Whitley Council. . . . But it made no difference to the result in the end. The scales were so heavily . . . weighed on the Official Side . . . that mere cleverness, mere superiority in argument, or the weight of facts, just wouldn't alter things. . . . The official line . . . just automatically triumphed.' Discussions of this kind had a certain entertainment value. 'If it's to have a lively discussion of interest, like a bullfight or something of that kind, undoubtedly, Brown's your man! . . . [But] fireworks, [although] always pleasant . . . really don't help in the field of negotiation.' That was a Staff Side opinion: but a member of the Official Side held much the same view. Meetings of the Council were 'at times . . . formal slanging matches'. 'If you *really* want to negotiate, that may not be the ideal forum in which to do it.'

Outbursts from Staff Side members were, at the very least, ineffective. 'That was one of the objections to the formal Whitley system,' said Sir Albert Day. 'It was so terribly time-wasting – futile. All those ... heads of departments, with important public business to do, congregating there just to listen to some trivial point that some Staff Side member insisted on pursuing.' Lord Bridges went further, arguing that such tactics did positive harm 'Of course, the Official Side used to get angry about this. . . . They did feel [it] was a great waste of time, and it was just something that we were landed with. . . . The meetings really used to be an irritant which . . . made each side less content with the other than they were before. They didn't bring the sides together. They, if anything, tended to push them apart a bit.' A member of the Staff Side looked back on the years 1923–39 as a bleak age. There was hardly anything constructive done after about ''22–3 on the Whitley. I mean, they went through all the motions, and they had periodic meetings, they discussed this, that and the other, but it is extraordinarily difficult to find anything really effective'.

THE OFFICIAL SIDE

For this disappointing record, both sides must share the responsibility. 'The Official Side in the early days really comprised the heads of all the important ministries . . . plus one or two others who took a particular interest in personnel matters. . . . In '22 there were two representatives of the Ministry of Health; Sir Arthur Robinson was the Permanent Secretary, and Sir Alfred Woodgate . . . was their establishment officer. He was tremendously interested in personnel questions and a very, very wise man in that respect, and that's why you get the odd one added like that. But broadly speaking [the Official Side comprised] the heads, or the deputies, – generally the heads – of virtually all the important government departments. . . . So there wasn't really an enormous amount of selection. . . . Membership was, . . . at any rate, quasi-automatic.'

Still, some selection had to be made. How was it done? There had to be at least one representative of the Treasury and one of the Ministry of Labour; in fact these secured five places on the first Official Side between them. The Ramsay–Bunning Report intimated that there should be women on each side of the Council although it 'refrained from making any definite recommendations as to the direct representation of women by women'. The Official Side included two women, one of whom, the Hon. Maude Lawrence, was Director of Women's Establishments. It also included two representatives of Scotland, two of Ireland, and one of Wales. Muriel Ritson was put on because she was experienced in establishment work, because she was a Scot, and because she was a woman!

Treasury policy in choosing the Official Side was clearly stated by Sir Malcolm Ramsay in a letter to the Air Ministry, which had complained of not being represented, although a large department. 'Although we could not disregard the big departments in choosing the members, we were mainly interested to see that the whole service as far as possible was properly covered and represented on the Council.'[1] A little later, however, the Air Ministry did get a place. The power of selection belonged exclusively to the Treasury. In March 1920, the Permanent Secretary to the Ministry of Labour resigned under pressure of work and nominated his Second Secretary to replace him. The latter was not appointed. Yet when the Admiralty representative resigned for the same reason in 1925, he was asked to suggest someone else from his department to fill the vacancy.

Official Side members were representatives of the government, not of their departments. The appointments were personal and a member normally left only when he left the service. In May 1946, when Sir Arthur Street was transferred to the National Coal Board, there was some discussion as to whether he should remain on the Official Side, but it was decided to maintain the rule that members should be civil servants. At the meeting of the Official Side on 26 September 1919, the Chairman made it clear that, since membership was personal, substitutes might be sent only when departmental specialist knowledge was absolutely necessary. In June 1924, the First Civil Service Commissioner was allowed to send a substitute to a National Council meeting which he could not attend himself but in which the Commission was closely involved, since recruitment policy was to be discussed. The rule ensured that members of the Official Side, who frequently complained of pressure of work, attended meetings in person and that these meetings which were intended to be authoritative did not become groups of substitutes at a lower level.

The first Official Side was selected by the Treasury, approved by the cabinet and announced by Treasury minute, but the cabinet agreed that thereafter the appointments should be made by the Chancellor of the Exchequer on behalf of the government. A Treasury memo. of November 1944, summarized the development. The original 'procedure was soon abandoned. Thereafter changes were simply approved by the Chancellor of the Exchequer; later they were not submitted to the Chancellor, but approved by the Permanent Secretary to the Treasury; and later still they often did not go even to the Permanent Secretary, but were approved by the Controller of the Establishments Department.'

In presenting for cabinet approval the names of the original Official Side, the Treasury had argued the case against including non-civil servants. 'The presence of outside representatives would seriously im-

[1] WC 1/2.

pair the authority and influence of the Council. Apart from minor objections, such as the technical nature of most of the questions which will come before the Council and which call for a highly specialized experience and knowledge of civil service conditions it is felt[1] – that the presence of an outside element would be quite foreign to the spirit of Whitleyism, which contemplates direct negotiation between employer and employee without the presence of a third party.... And[2] certain important features in the approved Report such as the machinery for arriving at agreements pre-suppose that the members of the Official Side will always act together as a side. This can be readily secured if the members are all civil servants acting as the representatives of and spokesmen for ministers and with their powers and responsibilities clearly recognized and defined. The state can always exercise effective control over the civil service members. The position of an outside member would be entirely different.'[1] Three government MPs were however asked to join the Official Side on 28 March 1922. A Treasury memo. was firm about their position. 'The Members so appointed will of course definitely form part of a body responsible to ministers and exercising such responsibility and authority as may be delegated to it by the Chancellor of the Exchequer.'[2] The Members should have a capacity for teamwork, and one or two of them should be interested in the problems of big business and be able to appreciate the points of similarity and difference between business and the civil service. Finally they should not have large numbers of civil servants in their constituencies. The Members always came from the government side and resigned on a change of government: some therefore served for two periods. There is no evidence that any of them made a significant contribution to Whitley discussions. A Treasury memo. in 1929 argued that since there were three Members on the Staff Side (Bowen, Brown and Middleton), there should continue to be Members on the Official Side. But the Tomlin Commission, recommending that the size of the Whitley Council should be reduced, advised that the Members of Parliament should be removed from the Official Side. They resigned in October 1931.

Among respondents whose memories went back to that period there was general agreement that the experiment was a failure. Sir Harold Parker did not 'think that they really contributed very much. . . . That was not because they were bad appointments. . . . Ralph Glyn . . . was very interested in it. Eustace Percy was very interested in it.' Lord Bridges was more severe. 'I think the addition of Members of Parliament to the Official Side really made it, if anything, more difficult. It was a bit of muddled thinking, I think, putting Members of Parliament on it.' Staff Side respondents agreed. The practice 'was a complete waste of

[1] G 256 Treasury memo. to Cabinet, 14 July 1919. [2] WC 1/30.

everybody's time and a handicap on doing work. To have outside interests involved in . . . things is hopeless.' A colleague, whose membership of the National Staff Side began in the twenties, agreed. 'They were not a success. . . . I don't think they were really very effective neutrals. Sort of watchdogs, I think they were intended to be. . . . Benevolent neutrals. But I don't think they were. I think they became rather yes-men on the Treasury side. I don't think there was any regret when they went.' One of his contemporaries went further. The MPs 'never made any contribution. I'll tell you the funniest episode that I recall of these MPs. The Council . . . always met in the conference room of Montagu House, which was then the headquarters of the Ministry of Labour. . . . Quite often, the meetings were just formalities – minutes of the last meeting, formal reports of a few committees. . . . On one occasion . . . this row of permanent heads assembled . . . and Sir Russell Scott was in the chair, there was really no business at all, and we ran through the agenda in less than fifteen minutes, and almost at the very moment when the chairman declared the meeting closed, in walked Patrick Hannon, to play his part in this important gathering. . . . That was about the measure of the contribution of any of them. It was pure political window-dressing, of no value to anybody. . . . [They] had neither knowledge, nor real interest in the business. They were there just as political figureheads.'

HIGHER CIVIL SERVANTS ON THE COUNCIL

Typical higher civil servants of the period, chosen as they were, found themselves for the most part quite unprepared for the roles Whitleyism required them to play. Sir John Simpson, a Staff Side secretary who subsequently became a Department Official Side Chairman himself, thought that 'the Official Side were not anything like as co-operative as they might have been'. One of his colleagues described most Official Side nominees of the period as 'stiff stooges' and one of the Council's chairmen as 'a man without any ingratiating qualities to people who differed from him fundamentally'. He also recalled a distinguished Permanent Secretary who appeared to make a point of always arriving late for Whitley meetings – which the Staff Side took to be a sign of the small importance they had in his scheme of life. 'Members of the Official Side to a man had never dreamt of being required to meet face to face on equal terms and discuss rationally with either members of their own staff or – almost worse still – outside representatives of their staff.' It is not surprising that 'the idea of the Official Side really consulting with the Staff Side' developed slowly. 'Despite the terms of the Whitley constitution, it just didn't happen. You were always going along and sobbing on somebody's shoulder that you hadn't been talked to about whatever it was that was developing. One got consultation only by continually hammering away.'

The formal atmosphere of Council meetings did little to break down the image of Official Side members as cold, remote mandarins. Sir Claud Schuster, permanent secretary of the Lord Chancellor's department, was one who 'intervened most effectively at times, and didn't hesitate to intervene on any provocation. . . . He was, in a sense, comparable with W. J. Brown – willing to take on anybody, at any time, in debate.' Of course, he always defended the official line, though he had his own way of doing so. Yet there were times when a man 'like Sir Arthur Street obviously was not echoing anybody else. I mean, if he had any views to express, he expressed them and done with it.' But even so slight a gesture was unusual. At the other extreme were members like Muriel Ritson, who could not remember speaking on more than two occasions during all the many years she sat on the Council. 'It was the rarest of rare occasions for anyone to open his mouth on the Official Side but the chairman', recalled Sir Albert Day. 'So you couldn't tell who among them were your friends or adversaries.'

From 1919 to 1939, the Official Side held regular meetings before those of the National Council, and sometimes, but not very frequently, in between. Russell Scott said at the meeting on 19 February 1920, that they 'should not show the other side the chinks in our armour',[1] and if they were not all of one mind they should not reveal that to the other side. At these meetings therefore it was intended that the Official Side should settle their differences so as to present a single case at the Council meeting. But in May 1920, the question was raised, with regard to the Cost-of-Living Report, of how much members of the Official Side could in fact discuss when the decision had already been taken by ministers. 'Sir Claud Schuster inquired to what extent a member of the Official Side of the Council accepted responsibility for a report of this kind. Was he in the position of having merely to record formally the decision of ministers, or was he entitled to object to the report in whole or in part ? . . . It was explained in reply that, although it was not anticipated, in this instance, that members of the Official Side would wish to modify the report, the meeting of the Official Side then in progress was the proper opportunity for any points to be raised. If the Official Side would not agree, the matter would have to be adjourned for further consideration and, if necessary, reference to ministers.'[2] Evidently the Official Side members continued to feel diffident for later in the year Sir Malcolm Ramsay noted that 'So far the members of the Official Side, with certain conspicuous exceptions, have shown an imperfect disposition to address their minds to the questions involved (or have had an adequate opportunity of so doing), and some of them have used to me

[1] WC 8/1.   [2] WC 8/7.

language to this effect – "After all the ultimate responsibility is really with the Treasury, and with the best will in the world we cannot do much to lighten it".'[1]

This was listed as one of the reasons why the Treasury dominated the Official Side, the other two being that the Chairman was a member of the Treasury and that the subjects dealt with had formerly been the province of the Treasury. The Official Side secretary (after 1920 there was only one) was also a Treasury Official. He was responsible for calling Official Side meetings and taking the minutes, and in conjunction with the Staff Side Secretaries for drawing up the agenda and taking the minutes of the Council meetings. But it is clear that he soon became closely involved with the Chairman and the Permanent Secretary to the Treasury in clarifying the position to be taken by the Official Side on particular issues. When questions were put up to ministers, it was the Chancellor of the Exchequer or the Financial Secretary who decided them. Thus the Treasury retained its dominant role in the determination of civil service questions.

This is not to say that it could ride roughshod over the other departments. The silence of the Official Side at Council meetings was *le silence de la mer*. Beneath the surface, a good deal was going on. Sir Harold Parker was secretary of the General Purposes Committee of the Council between the wars. Speaking in 1968, he gave it as his view that 'in the early days, heads of departments took a good deal more personal interest in the National Whitley machine than probably they do now.[2] . . . 50 per cent . . . rarely attended meetings of the Council, but the other 50 per cent not only attended but took quite a prominent part.' In addition to Schuster, other examples were Sir John Anderson, Sir Thomas Gardiner, and Sir Horace Wilson, even before he became Chairman of the Council. Muriel Ritson confirmed this account. Official Side meetings during Sir Horace Wilson's chairmanship were, in her recollection, conducted very fairly. Everyone had ample opportunity to say what they thought before meetings of the full Council. Proceedings were not dominated by a few personalities, and the Treasury people did not stamp on discussion. With individuals of higher calibre forming the Official Side, it is not to be expected that they would be mere pawns in the hands of the Treasury.

At the same time, it is true that, in the words of Lord Bridges, 'on the Official Side there's always been a strong sense of working together as a team'. How was the team-work co-ordinated? Minor questions were normally settled by the Treasury. 'On matters of lesser importance, the probability is that the Treasury view normally carried the day. . . . They were the experts. If it's not a matter of first importance, you usually fall in with the view of the expert unless you think it's nonsense.' More serious matters were dealt with at establishment officer level. 'The

---

[1] WC 5/43/01.   [2] But see below, p.54.

people dealing with staffing matters in all departments realized that there was a sort of general picture and that their problems fitted into this picture. And they would know that . . . they wouldn't get approval from the Treasury for something that completely upset the whole picture, and so they would naturally come along and talk about things.' When major issues arose, however, there were always a number of heads of departments on the Official Side who 'would find means of making their views known and felt. . . . On the major issues, the Treasury view carried considerable weight but it was influenced by strongly expressed views by a certain number of other heads of departments.' Meetings of the Official Side prior to sessions of the full Council gave an opportunity for such representations. But usually they had been put forward earlier. 'Discussion at the preliminary Official Side meeting wasn't the only way of doing business. . . . If a head of a department had very strong views on something, and wasn't sure whether those views entirely commended themselves to the Treasury, or vice versa, wasn't sure whether the Treasury views entirely commended themselves to him, they would probably meet and talk it over before the meeting and . . . probably reach some compromise. I've no doubt much the same thing happens on the Staff Side. . . . You don't have all your rows or all your arguments in public! In other words, by the time you got to the position of the preliminary Official Side meeting, you'd probably get a very nearly agreed point of view amongst the members of the Official Side.'

But what of questions of a higher level still, questions involving ministers? Lord Bridges admitted that 'officials don't like going into a meeting without some kind of a brief. . . . We're cautious animals.' The point to emphasize is that the brief was rarely, if ever, formulated in advance by ministers and handed down to civil servants on the Official Side. In practice, policy evolved from below. 'I don't think it presented any difficulty', Lord Bridges continued. 'It's so much part of the general civil service practice – knowing how far you can go yourself, and at what stage you've got to get approval, first of all from a higher civil servant, and then from a minister.' The criteria applied in Whitley business were the same as those used in Treasury business generally. 'If it was obvious from the outset that some big political question was involved, you wouldn't go to the discussion without mentioning it . . . probably to the Financial Secretary. . . . It would depend on the type of question and the stage in negotiations reached. . . . It doesn't simply apply to Whitley. If a civil servant knows that a matter which he's dealing with, . . . will cost a certain amount of money or attract a certain amount of attention, his natural tendency is to consult the minister who would have to answer the question beforehand and say, "We look like reaching agreement on these lines. I think it would be justifiable to go this far but not beyond. . . . What about it?" and see what he says.' Lord Bridges went on to explain that such issues were not always intrinsically the most important

'You can never define that, you know. . . . One of the things which you get to know when you're in the civil service is whether something is something which has got to go to a minister or, even more, when it is a cabinet matter and . . . it's not only the size of a thing, it's the smell of a thing. . . . There are some things which are really not important, but which have got to go to ministers because they excite political interests'.

THE STAFF SIDE

Paragraph 3 of the constitution laid down that the Staff Side should, like the Official Side, be composed of 'persons of standing' and named the groups of associations which were to appoint them. No mention was made in the Ramsay–Bunning Report of the representation of unorganized civil servants, and in August 1919, the Treasury sent a memorandum to departments with reference to the establishment of Departmental Councils pointing out that 'as the scheme is based on the principle of representation by association, and as only those members of the staff of the department who are members of associations will obtain representation on the Departmental Council, it will be necessary for officers who have not yet joined associations to consider whether they will become members of an association'.[1] If they did not see things in this light of their own accord, they might be brought to do so by the reasoning of association activists. F. A. A. Menzler recalled: 'I did an awful lot of speaking [and] organizing meetings to get . . . people to join the IPCS. One of my . . . arguments was, "Whether you believe in associations or trade unions or not, the government has set up this machinery. To work it you've got to have associations. You can't have a mass meeting of people coming along . . . and representing your case. It's got to be done in an organized way."' In December 1925, the Staff Side asked the Treasury to issue a circular reiterating this principle but they refused to do so, for as Sir Russell Scott wrote in a memorandum to Sir Horace Wilson, this could not be done 'without creating a widespread impression that the government was endeavouring to force civil servants to join associations'.[2] About two hundred associations sought representation on the Staff Side. Most of them were organized into groups. Some of these (the National Joint Committee, Civil Service Federation, and Civil Service Alliance) had been in existence for some time, but the Institution of Professional Civil Servants was formed only in 1919, thus enabling a number of specialist and professional associations in the departments to be represented on the National Council.

Paragraph 40 of the Ramsay–Bunning Report noted the distribution of the seats among the associations:

[1] WC 7/129.   [2] Ibid.

Post Office Associations	10
Civil Service Federation	6
Civil Service Clerical Alliance	5
Society of Civil Servants and First Division Association	2
Institution of Professional Civil Servants	2
Temporary Staff Associations	2.

Although the professional classes and temporary staff were specifically represented, women and ex-service civil servants were not. The Association of Ex-Service Civil Servants was part of the Temporary Staffs Group and the Federation of Women Civil Servants was part of the Alliance. A member of the latter was one of the representatives of the Alliance on the National Staff Side and when the Federation resigned from the Alliance it applied to the Staff Side to retain its seat. It was informed that the question was one for the Alliance to settle.[1]

New groups came into existence to strengthen the representation of various categories. In 1920, the Union of Post Office Workers emerged as an amalgamation of a number of Post Office organizations. In the same year, the Federation and the Alliance merged to form the Confederation. These two groups were to dominate the Staff Side during most of the interwar period.

The composition of the Staff Side, like that of the Official Side, was criticized in the early years. As soon as the constitution was published, the executive grades complained (without justice) that as Staff Side representation was based solely on the numerical strength of the associations they had not the weight commensurate with their position in the service. This was a problem since voting at Staff Side meetings was by simple majority. In September 1920, the Society of Civil Servants proposed that, if a question concerned a particular grade, no decision could be arrived at without the consent of the representative of that grade, this being 'merely an honest attempt to put the question of minorities on a clearer footing without interfering with the majority rule'.[2] The Standing Orders were amended in June 1922, so that policy decisions could only be passed by a two-thirds majority or fourteen, whichever was the greater.

Members of the Staff Side may be divided into two categories. At the outset, the majority were serving officials. Within a year or two, however, full-time officers of staff associations became dominant. 'All these people gradually saw the need for a full-time man as distinct from a part-time man. The work began to grow, and it . . . became national, and you had to develop and get your full-time officers to cope.' W. J. Brown considered that the advantage of a full-time officer was that he 'could negotiate with or fight the enemy without being hampered by the feeling, from which no serving civil servant could be wholly free, that it was in the power of these he was fighting to wreck his career.'[1] Nevertheless, some associations took the step only with great reluctance. C. L. Leese became the full-time, paid secretary of the Institution of Professional Civil Servants in 1925. But, on the National Whitley Council and elsewhere, he had to play second fiddle to the Institution's distinguished Honorary Secretary, F. A. A. Menzler. This was because prominent members of his own organization took much the same view of full-time trade union officers as did some members of the Official Side. 'Many of the leaders . . . were of the same generation and the same outlook and they were extremely nervous and suspicious of the "paid agitators" within the civil service and associations. I'm sure they hated having to appoint . . . a person to such an office among their crowd.'

The Staff Side, like the official Side, held meetings before those of the Council in order to define their position. The first one, on the morning of 23 July 1919, elected the Chairman and Secretaries and set up a committee for Standing Orders. These laid down that the Staff Side should meet in the first week of each month, and at such other times as were thought necessary by the Chairman and Secretaries.

In the early years they met very frequently because there was so much to be done and because it took time to decide what line to take, given the divergent and sometimes conflicting views of the associations. The meetings agreed the Council agenda and established the position to be taken on each point in it, supervised committees and where necessary resolved issues for them. Voting was by show of hands and decisions were taken by simple majority, except for those on policy which after 1922 required fourteen votes or a two-thirds majority, whichever was the greater, and for those on extra-Whitley matters which after 1926 required the agreement of all members. Each of the groups of voting was in blocks. The dissentients were those groups with small representation – the Temporary Staffs Associations which left the Staff Side in 1920, the Federation of Women Civil Servants which also left in 1920, and the Joint Consultative Committee which left in 1926. However even during the heated arguments over reorganization which led to the withdrawal of the Temporary Staffs, the Staff Side preserved a united front at the Council; the groups realized that they could achieve nothing for themselves and would embarrass the Staff Side by expressing their divergent opinions there.

STAFF SIDE OFFICERS

The officers of the Staff Side were elected from among their own number. The first chairman was G. H. Stuart-Bunning, a natural choice

[1] W. J. Brown, *So Far*, 1943, p. 85.

in view of his skilful leadership during the campaign to persuade the government to implement Whitleyism in the civil service. When he resigned in 1925, the Union of Post Office Workers nominated George Middleton to succeed him, while the Civil Service Confederation put forward W. E. Llewellyn. Each was assured of a substantial block vote. The Society of Civil Servants decided to support Middleton and this tipped the balance in his favour. Llewellyn again opposed Middleton in 1927. By this time, the Society had withdrawn from the Staff Side, as a result of events during the General Strike. With the combined support of the Confederation and the Institution of Professional Civil Servants, Llewellyn defeated Middleton. He remained chairman until the eve of the Second World War.

The first two secretaries were D. J. Milne and George Chase, neither of whom belonged to the Post Office. Milne resigned in 1920, however, and his place was taken by A. C. Wynyard, of the Union of Post Office Workers. This established a pattern which continued until after the Second World War, in which one of the secretaries came from the Confederation and the other from the Post Office. The two groups appear to have regarded it as almost their prerogative to nominate their man for the post. Ross Wyld took over from Chase in 1933, to be succeeded in turn by John Simpson in 1938. Thus the two secretaries at the outbreak of war were Wynyard and Simpson.

The officers had a good deal of work to carry out but for many years it was of a routine nature which did not conflict with their positions as Staff Side representatives of their groups. In 1937 after one of the Joint Secretaries, Ross Wyld, failed to be re-elected as a Staff Side representative of the Confederation, the officers were made *ex officio* members of the Staff Side. They were also association officials: Stuart-Bunning was President of the Confederation; Chase was Secretary of the Confederation; Wynyard was a member of the Executive Council of the Union of Post Office Workers. When the Staff Side acquired its own offices at Parliament Mansions, they sublet part to the Confederation.

The two Secretaries were at the same time serving civil servants. By the constitution, Staff Side members who were also civil servants were given special leave with pay to attend meetings of the Council, but this did not cover the special work of the Secretaries. Chase raised his position with the Treasury. The Treasury view was that 'the government having adopted this Whitley scheme, we must regard these people as working for the government and give them every facility'.[1] The two departments concerned agreed to do this. In 1923 Wynyard told a Staff Side Committee investigating the secretaries' work that the 'time given to Post Office work is so small that it is a negligible factor in this connection'.[2] And by 1924 the Admiralty was complaining that Chase was

[1] WC 1/6.   [2] NSS 337.06.

doing virtually no official work; he returned to full duty. But in 1929 the Post Office reported that Wynyard was doing ten days' work a year, and the Admiralty complained that even when Chase was there he was constantly involved with association and Whitley work through telephone calls. A similar situation arose with Ross Wyld and Wynyard in 1934 but no solution was found until after the war.

The two secretaries defined their work in 1923 as dealing with general correspondence, reception of deputations, relations with the press, daily scrutiny of Hansard for civil service questions, supervision of the work of the staff, and discussion of questions with Official Side officers. They were helped by four clerical staff. There was also from 1921 to 1925 a Co-ordination Officer, W. E. Llewellyn, who kept in touch with the Departmental Staff Sides and edited *Whitley Bulletin*, which started publication in 1920. A Statistical and Research Bureau was set up in 1934 by the Staff Side although constitutionally separate from it. It undertook work for the Staff Side, and, under contract, for the associations. It was run by a part-time officer and was concerned mainly with cost-of-living inquiries on which new bonus claims could be based. It undertook a large amount of work even during the war when its officer went into the civil service, but was never very active after the war because he was unable to work part-time again, and because there was a shortage of money. Under instructions from the Staff Side, the officers corresponded with the Treasury and had meetings with officials, but, although generally competent, they were never a dynamic force in the Staff Side until the war.

STAFF SIDE TENSIONS

During the first twenty years of Whitleyism, the Staff Side was no more able than the Official Side to realize the full potential of the system. To some degree, this was due to the mentality of its members. When he came to publish his autobiography during the Second World War, W. J. Brown could still write that the Treasury mind 'is indifferent to every criterion of right and wrong . . . and concerned only, if it is attacked for paying sweated wages, to be able to prove that somebody else is paying even lower rates! Lord, how I hate it!'[1] Another Staff Side leader still felt, when interviewed in 1968, extremely bitter about being sacked from the Ministry of Labour in 1923, which he had entered as a war-time temporary civil servant six years earlier. It 'constituted a damnable breach of faith [and] was one of the excellent reasons which led me eventually to take on the secretaryship of [a staff association] because I thought I would be able to get a bit of my own back on the Treasury in that way.' One of his colleagues told a story about a senior civil servant

[1] Brown, p. 208.

which recaptures the wary atmosphere in which early negotiations took place. 'I went to see him in his own room on some delicate question or other. In the middle of the conversation he got up rather noticeably, and stood with his back to the fire looking down on me. I distrusted a man who puts himself in a position in which he can look down on you. I think it's an interviewing trick. So I countered by immediately rising to my feet, and standing so solidly that he knew I was standing for a purpose. Whereupon he sat down.'

More important were tensions within the Staff Side itself. The more far-sighted members realized the importance of unity. W. J. Brown, for example, wrote: 'The experience I . . . had of dealing with the Treasury . . . had taught me that the Treasury never considered a claim in respect of any of our class without considering its effect . . . upon other classes of a related character. The Treasury was one closely organized unit. Opposed to it was a multiplicity of associations . . . which it could and did play off one against the other. . . . It seemed to me that, if it was to cope adequately with the Treasury, staff organization had to become as closely integrated and centralized as was the organization of the Treasury itself.'[1] This, however, failed to happen. 'The main difficulty', according to Sir John Simpson, 'was finding those topics on which there was a clearly recognizable mutual interest, and so very often, as subjects cropped up, you found that there were differences of opinion, and it wasn't easy to reconcile them and . . . associations felt "We've all got to be in it, we can't leave this to A and B and C because we can't trust them to ensure that the interests of our members are looked after."' This suggests two factors in Staff Side disunity: clashes of personality leading to mutual suspicion, and conflict of interests between different constituent groups. There is plenty of evidence that both factors were at work. What were their relative importance?

Of the Staff Side personalities, W. J. Brown was outstanding. Among his colleagues, there was no doubt that he 'did dominate the Staff Side'. Lord Geddes thought him 'the supreme egotist . . . in the trade union movement – certainly in the civil service trade union movement'. This was fully appreciated by the Official Side. Among the association leaders, 'Brown was the most dominating personality,' recalled Sir Harold Parker, who continued, 'I had a great admiration for Bill Brown. . . . I often got extremely cross with him but that didn't in any way alter my admiration for him.' Those who sat on the same side of the table as Brown also often got extremely cross with him. Lord Crook remembered a time when 'everybody decided they weren't having any more of Bill Brown on any committee, so it was agreed that nobody should nominate Bill Brown. But Bill Brown was good enough for that. Bill Brown nominated himself. He stood up in the meeting and said "I

[1] Ibid., p. 108.

desire to nominate Mr W. J. Brown as the best man to be on this committee." . . . And he got on the committee!'

A man who could so effectively confront his colleagues as a body naturally often came into conflict with them as individuals. Such clashes were made more acute by personal tensions. Take, for example, Stuart-Bunning, who was in the view of his colleagues 'a very able man'. 'He was not at all the ordinary postman of that day – or indeed, of any day. He was a man . . . who clearly stood out in his own crowd.' Brown, unlike Stuart-Bunning, 'was a very volatile man . . . who was always looking for a scrap, and Bunning was a rather different type and they just didn't hit it.' So fierce was the antipathy that at one Staff Side meeting, Brown threatened to throw Stuart-Bunning out of the window. The two men had to be held in their chairs. The antagonism was 'very terrible. . . . When I talked about fisticuffs and throwing out of windows, it really was a quite serious proposition. . . . They couldn't stand the smell of each other.' Brown freely admitted as much himself. 'It used to be suggested that in the many battles I had with Stuart-Bunning I was animated by personal feeling against him. This was untrue. I don't think I've ever in my life fought anybody except on the basis of what, to the best of my judgment, were the merits of the case. It is true, however, that in Stuart-Bunning's case personal feeling lent zest to the battles.'[1]

A little later, similar clashes developed between Brown and J. W. Bowen. The former's antipathy to Bowen was 'always because Bowen was one of these quiet, very reasoned, methodical [men] who would never be able to take to a man like Brown, with all his flamboyance'. Bowen was 'a good type to have, because he would think twice before he spoke once'. Personal bad feeling was deepened by political differences. Bowen adhered to the right wing of the Labour movement, while Brown was very much to the left. The two men 'couldn't stand each other'. One of their contemporaries remembers a time when 'it almost got to the stage of a fight and . . . people had to intervene between them. There was one occasion when . . . matters nearly came to blows and we had to separate them.' Another recalls a Staff Side meeting when Brown called Bowen 'a ponderous mediocrity and it was only the width of the boardroom table that prevented the argument continuing in fisticuffs'. There was another episode, with Bowen in the chair, when Brown told him 'to get to hell out of it'.

Yet, in spite of all this, it remains true that it was not 'terribly important. . . . When you have two strong personalities, you are bound to get clashes, and of course the Union of Post Office Workers had been in existence for a very long time, and had developed their own field of operations, and it was something new for them to have to co-operate with the other side of the civil service, of which Brown was the real

[1] Brown, p. 94.

strong representative. So that there was a certain clash of temperament, but I don't think it really militated against the efficiency of the organization.' Such were the words of P. H. M. Hoey, one of the shrewdest members of the National Staff Side in the period between the wars. Stuart-Bunning and Bowen both came from the Post Office. Brown was originally a clerk. The conflict of personalities was significant only because it personified a conflict of organizations.

Staff Side survivors from the inter-war period were candid about its weaknesses. 'The Staff Side worked together reasonably well . . . better than the TUC does, but . . . all the interests were not identical, and the Society [of Civil Servants] was always watching the [Civil Service] Clerical Association, and the Inland Revenue Staff Association . . . was always watching the Clerical Association, we were all suspicious of W. J. Brown, and . . . there was a very natural atmosphere of suspicion.' 'In its early years, the Staff Side was dogged by the misfortune arising from inter-union rivalries, which led not only to friction between the elements of the Staff Side, but a marked unwillingness to accept strong leadership, and this resulted in ragged negotiations when the Staff Side met on its own, and in unsatisfactory relations in the joint meetings, because the team lacked the cohesion that made for really first-class teamwork, and the situation was so bad that it could be said with a reasonable degree of fairness, that some elements of the Staff Side didn't trust one another, and the good faith of the Staff Side couldn't be sustained in joint negotiations because the Staff Side itself was unable to control these elements, who were out for their own interests and less concerned with the overall interest which it was the Staff Side's function to foster.'

The largest single group of civil servants worked in the Post Office, where the Union of Post Office Workers was the main association. But they were still a minority of the service as a whole. Most Staff Side members represented non-postal groups, of which Brown's Civil Service Clerical Association was the largest. Most of these groups were attached to the Civil Service Confederation. Here was the major split. 'I don't think anyone was ever happy about the balance of power between [the Confederation] and the Post Office side. . . . That was the clash always to get in your mind. Civil Service Confederation–Post Office.' 'The Union of Post Office Workers has always been a good bit outside, because of their different and peculiar gradings.' (The unconsciously patronizing use of the word 'outside' is significant.) This tension was, of course, something of which the Official Side was well aware. One of its most distinguished members traced it back to the initial decision to group postal workers in non-industrial, rather than industrial, Whitleyism. 'It was always a bit anomalous to have the Post Office Engineering Union, and indeed to a large extent the Union of Postal Workers, in the non-industrial Whitley Council at all, because you couldn't have anything very much more industrial than a Post Office linesman and . . . the impact of the Post Office unions on the Staff Side – their thinking and the balance of power within the Staff Side – has been profound. . . . You have had in a position of considerable power, because of their numbers, unions and blocks of staff within the non-industrial Whitley Council whose interests are not really very closely in common even with the humblest white-collar worker. . . . One was very conscious of this.'

The representatives of postal workers were also very conscious of it. 'Of course, we on our side', stated Lord Geddes, 'always had the feeling that as far as National Whitley was concerned we were to a very large extent merely fee-paying members, that we didn't get a lot out of it because we only participated in so far that we could influence the Staff Side, and we were always in a minority when it came to a question of voting. . . . In the pre-war years, this was the feeling in the Post Office unions, and in the Union of Post Office Workers, that we were a big battalion who had a very small number of votes, and who, against people like Houghton and Brown, really couldn't sufficiently sway the Staff Side in the direction in which the union wanted to go. . . . We were only allowed to advance as far as the others were willing to let us advance. . . . Therefore, National Whitley, from the union's point of view, was never looked upon as a body which could be effective.' The Union felt, moreover, that its attitude towards the Council was reciprocated. 'Before the war, we weren't of use to the Staff Side and therefore you had this antagonism, this feeling of frustration, as it were, on the part of the Union that Whitley was no damned good anyway!' Lord Geddes, whose memory of Union conferences went back to 1923, could recall no pre-war instance of the National Whitley Council report being discussed. 'It was put and carried. Nobody ever took the trouble to query it, because nobody had any interest in it. They weren't interested in what the National Staff Side was doing. As far as they were concerned, it didn't do them any good, and whatever it did, it was not in their interests. . . . This is an indication of the attitude of the Union towards the National Staff Side in those years.' Against such a background clashes of temperament, such as did exist between (say) Bowen and Brown, were of minor importance. 'It was [not] a question of Brown not appreciating, it was a question of Brown looking after his own – which is, after all, what every member of the Staff Side was doing. It was all looking after his own!'

Looking back, it would be easy to say that strong leadership would have put everything right. But that would be a superficial judgment. The situation was one in which strong leaders were extremely unlikely to emerge. Since they would probably lead in directions undesired by powerful constituents, care would be taken to choose people of a different calibre for the posts of chairman and secretary. A chairman from the postal workers would have difficulty with the clerical officers' representatives. 'George Middleton, of course, did his very best but was never a powerful man and, of course, being Post Office, he didn't have the influence of other people. The sheer fact that he was Post Office, he could have been as successful as you liked, and still they wouldn't have liked him.' A chairman from an association representing the higher ranks would encounter resentment from the leaders of the rank and file. Llewellyn had 'the executive taint round him, from the point of view of people like Bill Brown'. 'He hadn't the command of the Staff Side.' Monroe, of the Institution of Professional Civil Servants, who held the post temporarily after Llewellyn, found even greater difficulties. He was a 'very charming person indeed . . . a gentleman, well educated, cultured, but not a strong enough personality to lead a team as rough or as tough as a team composed of civil service staff associations. Gentlemanliness doesn't carry you very far against the buffets that you are likely to receive from large unions and Monroe wasn't really a strong enough personality to hold the fort.'

It would be interesting to speculate how long the Staff Side – and indeed, the Council as a whole – might have gone on in the same way in the absence of any external pressure making for change. Certainly it is not easy to discern in the years immediately before the Second World War signs of promising development from within. But the impact of external events was to achieve more in a few years than decades of quiet evolution might have done. Perhaps surprisingly, it was the Second World War which led to the great breakthrough in the growth of national Whitleyism.

CHAPTER 3

SINCE WORLD WAR TWO

In the year running up to its golden jubilee in July 1969, the structure of national Whitleyism had become something very different from that analysed in the last chapter. The Council itself had long ceased to meet. Almost two decades had gone by since it last came together to do business, though most of its members attended the annual sherry party. But even to assemble them for a jubilee photograph was not easy, 'a logistical feat of no small measure being achieved in getting all the members, save two, together at the same time'.[1] Yet, despite its not meeting, the Council continued to exist. A joint committee on the implementation of the Fulton Report was set up under its auspices in July 1968. The chair was taken by Sir William Armstrong, head of the civil service, and Chairman of the Council. It did a great deal of work, leading to the publication of an important report, *Developments on Fulton*, in February 1969 – in time for discussion at the staff association annual conferences in the spring and summer of that year. Thus it served to keep representatives of the rank and file in close touch with the progress made at national level. Meanwhile, the Joint Training Committee gave detailed consideration to the Fulton proposal for a Civil Service College and for a further increase in training programmes. Another joint committee began a thorough-going review of superannuation. Other joint committees could be mentioned, but enough has been said to show that, under the aegis of a Council which did not meet, its members were in frequent contact.

Those contacts led to a steady flow of agreements on points of importance to civil servants generally. Some were announced as such. For example, 'it is agreed between the two Sides of the National Whitley Council that temporary staff successful in open competition for the class in which they are currently serving will no longer be restricted to a mark-time rate of pay'.[2] A new scale was introduced with the words: 'the Official and Staff Sides of the National Whitley Council have agreed new rates of night subsistence allowances operative from 1 November

[1] Sir William Armstrong, 'Whitleyism in the Civil Service', *Whitley Bulletin*, Vol. xlix, 1969, p. 66.
[2] *Whitley Bulletin*, Vol. xlviii, 1968, p. 156.

1968'.[1] Similarly, 'the present general arrangements for special leave for local government work and for magisterial duties have been under review in consultation with the Official Side, and it has now been agreed that they should be extended to allow a measure of special leave with pay . . . in certain other cases where voluntary unpaid public service is relied upon for the fulfilment of statutory functions'.[2] But in other instances, decisions announced unilaterally might be agreements in disguise. For example, the Treasury issued a letter to Establishment Officers in 1968 which began: 'the Staff Side of the National Whitley Council and the Civil Service Council for Further Education have drawn attention to the need to try to help staff over the transition from their working life to the new way of living during retirement'. It went on to explain what could be done to meet this need. The *Whitley Bulletin's* caption fills in the background. 'The National Staff Side's Welfare Committee has recently been pressing the Official Side to introduce arrangements to prepare officers for retirement. As a result, the Official Side have agreed to introduce arrangements which will provide advice and guidance for people about to retire.'[3] Variations on this theme abound. 'Agreement has been reached with the Staff Side of the National Whitley Council on revisions in the rates of allowances for day absences.'[4] 'The rates of motor mileage allowance payable to officers who use their private motor vehicles on official business have been reviewed with the Staff Side of the National Whitley Council. It has been agreed that the rates . . . should be increased.'[5]

In all these examples the terminology implies that such agreements resulted from meetings between the entire Official Side and the whole of the Staff Side. Negotiations were not, in fact, carried on in this way. Had it been desired to do so, the simplest way would have been to revive the meetings of the Council itself. Instead, a variety of negotiating levels had come into being. In some cases, the forum was a joint committee. In others, the business was done at meetings between a number of representatives from each side, but under conditions less formal than those of a committee. On other occasions, an officer of the Staff Side (normally the Secretary-General) was empowered to work out the details with the Official Side – usually a single representative of the Official Side. One feature common to these various patterns of negotiation was the necessity for the spokesman on each Side to carry the whole of his Side along. On the Official Side, this meant consultation with the departments: on the Staff Side, with the constitutent associations. Where a negotiating team was formed, with representatives from the half-dozen principal associations, the risk of entering into a commitment unacceptable to the

[1] Ibid. Vol. xlix, 1969, p. 9.   [2] Ibid. Vol. xlix, 1969, p. 77.
[3] Ibid. Vol. xlviii, 1968, p. 176.   [4] Ibid. Vol. xlix, 1969, p. 30.
[5] Ibid. Vol. xlix, p. 31.

full Staff Side, or any substantial group of staff, was fairly small. But where discussions were carried on tête-à-tête between single representatives of the Sides, great care was necessary to secure the assent of the Staff Side as a whole before concluding any agreement. This could be done by placing the matter on the agenda for discussion by the Staff Side, or one of its committees, at a regular meeting. Alternatively, it might be possible to secure the necessary clearance by consulting the general secretaries of the major associations, personally or by telephone. Whichever approach was taken, the representatives of one or more of the associations might find it necessary to consult their executive committees before giving an answer.

As an example of this process, the aftermath of a meeting which took place on 2 May 1969 may be cited. The Staff Side expressed forcibly to the Official Side their dismay at the slow progress of their claim for a central pay increase. 'At this meeting, the Staff Side pointed out that civil service pay had fallen markedly behind outside pay rates. An increase in civil service pay had become an urgent necessity. Civil servants . . . were not in a mood to accept further delay. The Official Side were warned that annual conferences [of staff associations] would be bound to urge strong action to secure a pay settlement.'[1] The *Whitley Bulletin* went on to report that the Official Side was now considering the views expressed by the Staff Side, and a further joint meeting had been arranged. 'The Official Side's response will enable the Staff Side to consider, at their next meeting due early in June, what further action is necessary.' An offer was in fact received in time for the Staff Side meeting on 2 June 1969. Some associations were unable to accept then and there. But ratification from their executives quickly followed, and agreement was reached three days later.[2]

In the case of disagreement also, Whitleyism could still have a part to play. If the two Sides had failed to agree on a point covered by the procedure, either Side could go to arbitration. If, on the other hand, arbitration was ruled out, the Whitley framework was useful, to the Staff Side at least, as a means of concerting alternative action. As an example, the response to the publication of the Government's White Paper on *Productivity, Prices and Incomes*[3] in the spring of 1968 may be cited. It announced the new principle that large pay increases in the public sector would have to be achieved by stages. That is to say, the beneficiaries of a settlement would get their higher pay by instalments, but without retrospective payments to cover the interval between the date of the settlement and the date of its complete implementation. Not surprisingly, civil servants did not like this, and the National Staff Side provided a natural focus for the indignation of the associations. A meeting with the Chancellor of the Exchequer took place on 26 March 1968,

[1] Ibid. Vol. xlix, 1969, p. 81. [2] Ibid. p. 98. [3] Cmnd. 3590.

at which the Staff Side 'expressed . . . their view that the civil service should continue to be treated fairly under the government's incomes policy. It was stressed that pay research settlements are "catching up" exercises and that the civil service should receive the increases due with effect from the agreed operative date. It was emphasised that there would be bitter resentment if the civil service were discriminated against unfairly.'[1] The Chancellor promised to give careful consideration to the views expressed by the Staff Side. He replied at length by letter, dated 1 May 1968.[2] The Staff Side found little comfort in what he had to say, and a further meeting took place on 7 May 1968, at which their case was presented by the Secretary-General. He 'said that the government's decision to defer a part of the increases due under the pay research surveys would place the civil service at an unfair disadvantage. The government's decision would extend the time-lag which already existed in bringing the pay of the government's own employees into line with their counterparts in other employments and there was no assurance that they would catch up at a later stage.'[3] It would be particularly hard if the increase secured for lower paid workers in 1967 were to be deducted from the amount which they would otherwise receive in 1968. Once again, the Chancellor undertook to consider carefully the representations which had been made. This time he replied within three days. Although he made no positive concession, the point about the lower paid workers had clearly made some impression on him. 'On the particular point which you put to me very strongly about the effect of this decision on those low-paid civil servants who received increases from 1 August 1967, I am bound to say that I think, as I told you at our meeting, there are considerable difficulties about making an exception to the general principles on which 1 January 1968, pay research surveys will be implemented. But I am still thinking about this, and I will write to you later on.'[4] He did so ten days later, and this time his letter brought good news to the staff. 'I have thought very carefully about the points which the National Staff Side put so persuasively to me on 7 May, and I am glad to be able to tell you that in the light of what you then said, it has been possible for the government to agree that all civil servants affected by 1 January 1968 pay research surveys, including those who benefited from the increases of August 1967, should, provided that the evidence of the survey justifies this, receive from 1 January increases of 7 per cent over the rates of pay in issue immediately before that date.'[5] In other words, the interim increase would not after all be deducted from any increase payable as a result of the pay research surveys. It was not the sort of victory to lead to dancing in the streets around Whitehall. But it

[1] *Whitley Bulletin*, Vol. xlvii, 1968, p. 70.
[2] Printed in *Whitley Bulletin*, Vol. xlviii, 1968, pp. 85–6.
[3] Ibid. p. 86.   [4] Ibid.   [5] Ibid. p. 102,

was better than nothing. And it was almost certainly better than anything the staff associations could have secured without a concerted
strategy. The National Staff Side had become 'the civil service N.A.T.O.
as well as the civil service T.U.C.'[1]

THE NATIONAL WHITLEY COUNCIL
AND WORLD WAR TWO

How had the new structure come into being? The crucial turning-point
was the Second World War. In the summer of 1938 the representatives
of the two Sides began to discuss how the Whitley system could be
adapted to a war situation. The Staff Side General Purposes Committee
recommended that 'the existing formal arrangements for consultation
should not be abrogated in the event of war but . . . there should be
emergency machinery designed to act swiftly, and capable of formal
meetings, consultation with constituents, etc.'[2] A small joint committee
was set up and given plenary powers in the event of an emergency. The
Staff Side of this committee made it clear that 'if the Official Side would
arrange to consult with the Staff Side on any matters of importance, the
Staff Side, for their part, would make it as easy as possible for the
Official Side to get things done, and in particular they would not be
sticky on matters of procedure.'[3] A letter had been sent to Departmental
Staff Sides advising them to adopt a similar attitude, and the Official
Side gave an assurance that they would advise the departments of the
position. These initiatives hung fire for a time when the Munich crisis
passed, to be revived on the initiative of the Official Side in January
1939, when the rapidly deteriorating international situation provided
omens which could not be ignored. The Staff Side Emergency Committee now embarked upon virtually continuous discussions with the
Official Side. Emergency circulars covering a wide range of subjects
were agreed and sent to departments. They included detailed proposals
for the evacuation of essential staff from London and other areas thought
likely to come under aerial attack; compulsory billeting of evacuated
staff; air raid precautions; and injuries on duty. When war broke out in
September 1939, the benefits of this unprecedented joint endeavour
were realized. The numerous plans were smoothly carried out, and
dislocation of work reduced to a minimum.

    W. J. Brown's Civil Service Clerical Association protested against the
broad scope of the Emergency Committee's work, fearing that they
might find themselves committed more deeply than they wished to go.
But others on the Staff Side realized that if Whitleyism failed to adapt,
there was a real danger that it might simply be by-passed for the dura-

[1] Douglas Houghton, writing in *Whitley Bulletin*, Vol. xlix, 1969, p. 87.
[2] E 37560.   [3] Ibid.

tion of the war. The government would use its executive powers to the full. It was necessary to streamline methods of negotiation in order to maintain the Staff Side's right to be a party to decisions. A member of the Official Side stated that 'it was impossible to expect that heads of departments with tremendous war problems could really spare the time' for formal meetings of the traditional kind. A Staff Side representative said much the same thing. 'The old arrangements for dilatory discussions in committees, with long intervals between meetings, and all the paraphernalia of minutes, drafts, and approvals of minutes, and so on, and formal committee reports, and discussions of committee reports by full Councils – all that business couldn't continue under war conditions. . . . Bombs were falling and the situation was changing from week to week.' The question was, would Whitleyism simply be put away in mothballs, or would it take on a new form appropriate to the new circumstances?

On the outbreak of war, the Emergency Committee gave way to two joint bodies: Committee A to deal with all matters of urgency involving questions of policy and requiring prompt decision, and Committee B to handle less pressing issues arising out of the war and those which regularly came under review in peace-time. Committee A met every few days during the closing months of 1939 and the whole of 1940. For the first time a close working relationship developed between the representatives of the two Sides; the Official Side consulted the Staff Side, who in turn guaranteed co-operation in carrying out the new measures. Such guarantees show how the relationship between the Staff Side and its organs had changed. The old General Purposes Committee had never had any such power, and many of the associations were suspicious of delegating responsibility to it. But in wartime, decisions had to be implemented so quickly that it was often not possible to obtain the prior approval of the Staff Side as a whole. Since the half-dozen largest associations were represented on Committee A, they were generally satisfied with what was done. There were allegations that the Staff Side was no longer a democratic body, but in fact it continued to meet throughout the war at least once a month. Committees A and B kept the parent body closely and continuously informed of the results of joint discussions, and between meetings its members were kept in complete touch with everything done in their name. This pattern proved adequate to carry the whole burden. There was only one meeting of the full Council during the war. It took place in May 1941, for the purpose of reaching agreement upon the extension of the normal working week to fifty-one hours and drastically curtailing annual leave.

The new form of Whitleyism was being used before the war ended for the discussion of fundamental principle. It thus shifted Whitleyism out of the dead calm in which it had rested since 1923 or thereabouts.

A member of the Staff Side, speaking of the pre-war Council, put it in this way. 'One of the disappointments that I felt . . . was that one could never [persuade] the Council to get very much further than questions of pay, hours and that sort of thing. . . . You could never get them to discuss training, apprenticeship, . . . development and status. . . . That, I think, has been a fairly general defect of the growth of Whitleyism. . . . The early developments – [the] Reorganization Report . . . and the new bonus scheme, and things of that kind, went off with a terrific bang, for the first year or so, and then afterwards it settled down into the doldrums.' Now, in the middle of the war, the staff found themselves invited to take part in planning for post-war reconstruction. T. R. Jones, who was then secretary of the National Staff Side, has described its acceptance of this invitation as 'the most momentous step in the history of civil service Whitleyism'.[1] The proposed joint discussions were to be strictly confidential at the outset, and neither side was to be required to enter into commitments. Under pre-war conditions, the acceptance of an invitation on such terms would have been unthinkable. War-time experience, however, of close and effective working in small joint committees had shown how valuable they could be. Hence no objection was raised from the Staff Side. These informal discussions provided the groundwork for formal joint committees at a later stage to deal with post-war problems. The first and most urgent of these was the planning of a scheme of examinations for recruitment during the reconstruction period, taking account of the special needs of demobilized service personnel and civilians who wished to make the civil service their career. Plans to meet both short-term and long-term needs were evolved. When the time came, they went smoothly into operation, with a complete absence of the controversy in Parliament and elsewhere that marred the re-settlement of ex-service personnel after the First World War.

Work in joint committees was supplemented by frequent meetings between Staff Side officers and representatives of the Official Side. Sir John Simpson, who was Staff Side secretary when war broke out, recalled that 'in the early days of the war, . . . hardly a day passed when we weren't in the Treasury discussing something or other. . . . I don't suggest that we took any vital decisions, but we were able to make representations on a number of matters, . . . [We were] in almost continuous session with the Official Side.' Sir Harold Parker's picture of the period after Jones had succeeded Simpson is very similar. 'Day and Jones were always dropping in to see me, probably with the secretary of the Official Side. . . . Day saw me once, twice, or possibly more, a week on a vast mass of detail – how much should the billeting allowance be, should we in fact put the civil service on a seven day week, or a six day week,

[1] *Whitley Bulletin*, Vol. xlix, 1969, p. 103.

and . . . an awful lot of little things which were liable to go wrong and
. . . the machinery . . . worked pretty well. I don't say we solved everything, but I think we probably solved the majority of the day-to-day
problems which, if they'd been allowed to fester, might have developed
into rather nasty situations.'

How was it possible, not merely to keep Whitleyism alive in wartime,
but actually to improve it, under what seemed at first unfavourable
circumstances? Is the explanation to be sought in the character of those
involved, or in the social structure within which they worked? One
respondent, at least, would have preferred the first alternative to be true.
'Well, of course, one would like the answer to be that they were exceptionally sensible and able people!' Personalities were important. But no
one was consciously aiming at a reform of the system. Sir Albert Day
was quite explicit on this point. 'I wasn't conscious of any goal . . .
except what could be done in the first onrush of wartime emergency to
keep one's head above water. And for a long time after the outbreak of
war, the problems that faced me, representing the Staff Side' were so
overwhelming as compared with the time and trouble I could give to
them, [that] it was a long while before . . . I could begin to think about
looking forward. Until then it was a fight for survival, so to speak.'
Nevertheless, it was fortunate that the emergency found men in the
crucial positions who were capable of rising to its challenge. They might
all have been like a Staff Side Officer described by a member of the
Official Side as 'a dear old boy . . . a very nice old boy'; and by one of
his colleagues as one who 'played no real part in policy making. He had
his own little pitch where he was something of an authority, an expert,
but he didn't really play any part in major policy discussions. . . . He
wasn't really qualified.' Could such a man have shown the initiative that
was called for? Had he done so, would the Official Side have responded?
And could he have carried the Staff Side with him?

At the same time, external factors were far more important than
personalities. In the words of Lord Bridges, 'war presented all sorts of
. . . real problems for the staff and real problems for the country and
for the administrators. People had to be moved from [one department]
to another, and from one part of the country to another, and it became
evident that there were an awful lot of real problems which affected
individuals, and because of the individuals, the organizations, very
acutely. This . . . brought the two sides together, and they started
having small meetings of . . . three or four people on each side, getting
together to see how these problems should be faced.' One of his colleagues spoke in similar terms. 'One is bound to recognize . . . that the
war atmosphere had a good deal to do with it. . . . Many differences of
view . . . were submerged and suppressed by the needs of the time and
. . . [Staff Side leaders] were extremely easy to work with and sensible,

co-operative, helpful – pressing, of course, but never unreasonable, never taking undue advantage of the situation. Of course, we had plenty of differences of view [and] some arbitration cases, but the atmosphere in this as in so many other activities of life in those days was materially influenced by the common desire to get on with things in the most sensible way. . . . You don't win the war by conducting civil service Whitleyism well, but you don't help the war by conducting it badly.'

Staff Side respondents confirmed this view. As Sir Albert Day put it 'under wartime conditions . . . compulsion of events helped to produce an atmosphere in which sectional sacrifices of interest were readily made'.

THE POST-WAR PERIOD

When the war ended, there was little inclination on either side to revert to the old pattern. The 'experience of working together under the pressure of wartime needs carried on into the post-war period with the almost day to day contacts between the [Staff Side] officers . . . and the Treasury'. The Staff Side found that the innovations of wartime had brought distinct benefits. 'We found that informal negotiation produced much better results and . . . and it also was a great saving in time. All these people were busy, either as union leaders or as senior civil servants, with responsibilities for their ordinary jobs, and people began to realize that they could not spend a great deal of time on formal discussions.' In the recollection of Sir Thomas Padmore, 'contacts and discussions took every kind of form [from] very private talks between Albert Day and myself to little groups with two or three on each side to more formal meetings of a larger character'. The sheer difficulty of getting people together, however, continued to militate against gatherings of the latter type. To quote a Staff Side secretary, 'the claims on man-power, both on our side and on the Official Side . . . made it obviously difficult to convene formal, full, committees'.

Among the relatively small number of people involved an extraordinary degree of mutual confidence soon developed. In the words of one of those who led the Official Side, with men like those who represented the Staff Side in wartime, 'you know quite well that if you say, "This is off the record", then off the record it is. If you say, "Well, I'm just sounding you out, I can't commit [myself]. We may be able to do this, we may not", . . . this way of doing business will be respected. You knew quite well you could depend on them. . . . Their aye was their aye and their nay was their nay, and there was never any fear that you were going to be trapped, or that either side was digging a pit for the other. The mutual trust and confidence which comes from daily dealings with good and sensible people is really the secret of the whole thing.' One who played a similar role a little later spoke in very similar terms. 'Everything was done . . . with a high degree of . . . friendliness between the two sides, and . . . all the sense of caution on the part of the Official Side had gone. The general feeling was, "Well, these fellows are in the game with us, and let's sit down together, and let them say what they think." . . . I don't mean to say there wasn't a great deal of controversy from time to time, but the spirit was very good. . . . We knew one another very well. . . . On both sides we became personal friends. And although we never, I hope, on either side forgot that we represented on the one hand, the government, and on the other, the staffs, we did get into a very effective . . . system of co-operation. And this depended a great deal on a few of the key personalities on either side.' Staff Side speakers said much the same thing. 'The relations between the two Sides developed very rapidly on a personal basis. You got people you could talk to, who would respect your confidence, and you could respect theirs, and to be able to talk as we did, . . . with the hair completely down, and then do your formal business afterwards . . . – "We will agree afterwards what we put down on paper" . . . has quite transfigured the negotiations.'

THE OFFICIAL SIDE

An early consequence of the wartime changes was that the Official Side lost its corporate existence. There have been only two meetings of the Council since 1945. These took place in 1949 and 1950, and were called at the request of the Staff Side to discuss the Masterman Report.[1] There were a few meetings of the Official Side after the war but these soon lapsed, as did Joint Committees A and B. There have been both standing joint committees and joint committees for special purposes. But they have, of course, brought together only a minority of Official Side members. As a result, Treasury officials have conducted most of the day-to-day negotiations. By 1945, according to one respondent, 'the real working of the Whitley machine had come to be . . . – not wholly, but preponderantly – a thing that was done between the Staff Side and the Treasury.' In 1967, immediately prior to the setting up of the Civil Service Department, there were eight members of the Treasury on the Official Side – 'people who are, so to speak, professionally on it as being concerned with these things in the Treasury', as one respondent put it – as compared with only one each from the other departments represented. By 1968, an Official Side respondent could say that 'although it always quite obviously played a very prominent role, . . . the Treasury is probably playing a bigger role now than it did' when Whitleyism began. That role has now passed to the Civil Service Department, which provided eight members in 1969.

[1] See p. 128–30.

The Chairman of the Council has only taken a personal interest when he wished to, or when called upon to do so.[1] This did not represent any profound change as compared with the inter-war period. Even when the Council was meeting regularly, the Chairman's role was to express Official Side policy, not to dictate it. As a member of the Staff Side recalled: 'these people were Chairmen but they played little part in the actual negotiations. They presided over the meetings of the full Council, but this was a very formal business, and whilst I've no doubt that they exercised a good deal of power behind the scenes, we really didn't have a great deal to do with the actual Chairmen of the Council. Our work was done with the senior officers of the Treasury below the rank that Horace Wilson and so on held.' In much the same way, a postwar Chairman, Lord Bridges, recalled that he used 'to get brought in now and again. . . . I, as Chairman, would only be brought in really when there was something that had been brought up to the boil. . . . The work would have been done down below.' Sir Thomas Padmore, as Second Secretary to the Treasury, wrote to Sir Norman Brook about the Chairmanship in 1956: 'This will not involve you (unless you should ever want to) in taking any part in Whitley meetings. I took all the meetings on Priestley (a topic as important as any we are likely to handle) without anyone saying that the Chairman of the Council ought to be doing it. On the other hand, if anything arises which you *want* to handle (as your predecessor Masterman did) your Chairmanship makes it easier. And on other matters you are there as a final court of appeal short of ministers.' When, however, Sir William Armstrong became Chairman in 1968, an important change ensued. Sir William has been a far more active Chairman, particularly in the complex and important negotiations arising out of the Fulton Report, than any of his predecessors for many years.

The centralization of negotiations in the Treasury did not enhance the office of Official Side secretary. Other Treasury members of the Official Side have been closely and continuously involved, as well as relatively junior Treasury officials who had no ostensible connection with the Council at all. As one of them recalled, 'long before one went on to the formal Whitley, one had had a great deal of discussion, both on the committees and informally, with the Staff Side representatives.'

Among Staff Side respondents, there was general agreement that from the period of the war there was a marked change for the better in the attitude of the Official Side towards them. One explanation offered was that they 'were people who had grown up with civil service . . . staff

---

[1] The post was held, 1939–48, by Sir Alan Barlow, Joint Second Secretary in the Treasury. Since that date it has been filled by successive Permanent Secretaries of the Treasury and Civil Service Department.

organization and Whitley machinery almost from the time when they joined the civil service. . . . It was not a novelty to them. . . . It was part of the furniture almost. . . . They were therefore willing rather than reluctant parties to contributing their share.' There were people of whom this was absolutely true: Sir Bruce Fraser, for example. 'From my earliest days – I think I can say "days" literally – in the service I began to get an acquaintanceship with establishment problems and, of course, that very soon introduces you to Whitley problems. . . . I was brought up with [Whitleyism] from my earliest days.' At a later stage, he became private secretary to Sir Horace Wilson, an experience which, 'given his own particular cast of mind and experience, . . . helped with my Whitley education'.

Sir Bruce realized however that the type of apprenticeship he served set him apart from his peers. 'I don't think the ordinary cast of mind, certainly in those days, of a young member of the administrative class was terribly interested in that sort of thing [i.e. Whitleyism]. It was more interested in getting on than in agitating for better conditions.' A colleague went even further, in speaking of the attitude of the administrative class towards Whitleyism. 'Before the war, in so far as they were conscious of it at all, most [of them] . . . regarded it as just a chore – a thing that had to be gone through. You obviously had to have discussions about pay, conditions of service, and this sort of thing, and this was the machinery appointed and, fine, you hoped . . . not to have to be bothered with it. But then this was rather the whole attitude, I think, to staff management and staff relations. It was really a bore.'

It was more typical, therefore, for Staff Side representatives to find themselves negotiating with men and women to whom staff relations were an unfamiliar field. In the words of Sir John Simpson, 'whenever a new man came along, we had, as it were, to try and educate him'. Sir Thomas Padmore gave an account of what it was like to be 'educated'. He had no direct connection with Whitleyism prior to 1945. 'Like most of my fellow civil servants, I was aware of its existence and paid no attention to it whatever. I knew that there was a series of associations, including the First Division Association, which I joined automatically when I came into the service, and did absolutely nothing about it, and I think this was very common, particularly perhaps with the First Division Association. I don't think it was unusual in any sense. I was aware that there was this association, which was no doubt occupying itself busily with looking after my interest, and I left it at that!' Then, suddenly, in 1945, he found himself 'plunged up to the neck in Whitleyism and all that it involved and was closely involved from that time onwards. . . . I came absolutely as a tyro. I'd never done this kind of work before. I knew nothing about it.' In this situation, how would the Staff Side leader react ? Would he exploit his temporary advantage for short-term gains? 'Albert Day was by this time the highly experienced chairman of the Staff Side. . . . While I was feeling my way in, I used to see him from time to time behind the scenes and talk to him very freely about what I ought to do. And he would tell me absolutely frankly what were the difficulties from my point of view. . . . He and I established . . . a very remarkable situation of mutual confidence in which I knew that he wouldn't for a moment attempt to exploit my inexperience in order to score points off me, or get me to agree to things that he knew I oughtn't to agree to, and [he] was – I say this in tribute to him, though I don't for a moment pretend that . . . it was wholly a matter of altruism on his part – he was sensible enough to know that if he exploited my inexperience to take me for a ride, a time would come when I should find out what had happened, and he would suffer for it.' The key to this remarkable statement is the phrase 'behind the scenes'. Sir Thomas was not an employer. Sir Albert was not his employee. But those were the parts for which they had been cast.

The idea of 'growing up with Whitley' does not, then, entirely explain the more positive attitude adopted by members of the Official Side during and since the Second World War. Earlier, and even more important, came their realization that Whitleyism is of value, not only to the staff, but to management also. Faced with the difficulties of wartime, as Lord Bridges recalled, 'the Official Side recognized that in handling these problems they would get tremendous help from discussion with the representatives of the associations who represented all the people concerned and who would tell them what was acceptable and what would work and what wouldn't. . . . From that moment . . . the Whitley machine in the civil service as a whole really began to tick.' Of course, the relative importance of the two factors has tended to equalize over time. At the end of fifty years, a typical member of the Official Side has both grown up with Whitley, and is (largely for that reason) very well aware of its value to management.

FORMULATION OF OFFICIAL SIDE POLICY

As mentioned above, Official Side meetings lapsed in the late forties. How, then, has Official Side policy been made? It would be easy to imagine the minister, at the outset of a negotiation, summoning the little group of officials to whom it was to be entrusted, and laying down the policy they were to follow. It would also be extremely misleading. 'We didn't have a brief in the sense that there was something that was provided from any outside source. . . . We were both the negotiators and the briefers.' 'I don't ever remember being restricted by my superiors saying "You can't go further than this." . . . It must have happened sometimes: they [must have] said, . . . "You can take it up to half-a-crown an hour . . . but you can't go any further", or something like this. But my general recollection is that one went in with a free hand.' The first stage was to study the problem within the confines of the Treasury. 'We would prepare ourselves for joint discussion . . . in the ordinary way by having talks among ourselves, by writing papers, and briefing ourselves. In very large degree we were self-governing in the sense that the extent to which either the permanent secretary or ministers concerned themselves with these matters was pretty limited.' Further consultations of a similar kind punctuated the negotiations themselves. Since a rule analogous to 'Pas devant les domestiques!' had to be observed, they were often conducted under the conditions of some difficulty. 'One of my chief recollections of the committees between the official representatives and the staff, is that one side or the other used to scuttle out into the corridor, or somewhere, and have a hasty confabulation. . . . I can see [X] and me in the corridor more than once saying, "Well, look here, we'd better try and meet this, hadn't we? . . . Let's push this up."' But, in the vast majority of cases, no reference outside the Whitley circuit was necessary. 'When you were in the Treasury, you were the master.'

There were two limits to this autonomy. An official entrusted with staff negotiations was, of course, in 'the usual position of a civil servant, that you reckoned that beyond a certain point . . . you would have to put the thing up.' 'If I, as the principal official engaged on this work, was embarking on a course which had political implications, whether financial or other, or very important service implications, naturally I would seek . . . instructions and guidance from either Sir Edward Bridges . . . as the permanent secretary, or from ministers, or from both. But in large part, both ministers and Sir Edward Bridges, who had a great many other things to do, trusted us to get on with it, and . . . we were both our own negotiators and our own instructing solicitors, as it were.'

The other limit was the need always to carry the other departments along. The Staff Side had a proper interest that the Treasury should do so. Sir Albert Day had experience both of the old regime, in which the presence of permanent secretaries at full Council meetings was a guarantee that Whitley decisions were acceptable to departments, and of the new, in which Official Side policy was often voiced by Treasury officials alone. Sir Albert saw great advantages in the new system, but only 'so long as the Official Side representatives with whom we were dealing . . . covered their own rear: that is to say, made sure that they were not putting a foot wrong from the point of view of any department.' He believed that great care was taken on this point. 'The Treasury officials with whom we negotiated so much during the early months of the war were always very careful – must have been very careful – before taking a critical step in any negotiations, to . . . make sure that their rear was covered by . . . going to a selection of heads of departments – say half a dozen – whose staff would have a particular interest, perhaps, in the projected agreement, to make sure if it was acceptable to them. If it wasn't, then the negotiators on the Official Side would have to decide whether they were going ahead or . . . whether they would bow to this expression of dissent, and try a fresh line.'

Respondents from the Official Side confirmed this view of the way things were done. Treasury autonomy did not mean that the departments were under the Treasury's thumb. 'The Treasury took immense pains to ensure that they weren't. If they were under the Treasury's thumb, it was because they had crept there themselves!' It 'wasn't a question of the Treasury doing all these things in its own arrogant self-satisfaction. We did in fact at various levels and in various ways keep in very close touch with the service as a whole on whose behalf we were doing this work.' One such way was through regular meetings of establishment officers. 'It is through these meetings . . . that Official Side policies get built up. . . . Departmental problems are thrown up, and your establishment officer is an absolutely key link between your department and the National Whitley.' Regular gatherings of this kind were supplemented by *ad hoc* arrangements to deal with particular issues. The wartime discussions on the future of the service provide a good example. 'We called it the Structure Committee, and the Staff Side produced a team of their own leaders to discuss it all with us. Now the Official Side team consisted of three [or] four people perhaps from the Treasury, who were working on this kind of topic in the Treasury, but also . . . perhaps half a dozen principal establishment officers or their immediate lieutenants from different departments. . . . Of course, . . . what we were talking about have very different implications for, let us say, the Ministry of Labour and the Inland Revenue from what they might have for the Home Office, and therefore we would select a team of half a dozen wise men from the departments, and form a team in that sort of way.'

While the war lasted, it was not always possible to proceed with such deliberation. Often, 'you just had to meet and decide that afternoon, and it was just what two or three people said to each other which really settled things for the whole service, though of course we did try to keep in touch with departments as far as possible.' Since 1945, however, there have normally been 'opportunities for consultation and taking a little time over a problem', and the implementation of the Priestley Report may be taken as an example. 'Of course, the Treasury had to be in the lead . . . but the Official Side team did consist not only of us chaps in the Treasury . . . but of selected establishment officers throughout the service . . . and of course we . . . discussed the line that was to be taken in our next round of negotiations with the Staff Side in committee, and nobody was ever shy of piping up and what was produced was quite genuinely a common line. Of course, as the conventions of these things require, when it came to the negotiations with the Staff Side, what normally happened was that the Official Side team sat pretty mum and left Tom Padmore to play the hand, but it was the rest of us, you see, who had dealt the hand. . . . You had to leave the chap in charge to . . . play his hand his own way but . . . what he was determined to try to get, what he was determined to resist, . . . had been settled in committee beforehand.'

THE STAFF SIDE

Towards the end of the war serious consideration was given by the Staff Side to the structure of Whitleyism when peace returned. Day pointed out that 'there would be no general predisposition to return to peacetime arrangements or to perpetuate wartime arrangements' and that 'the essence of the problem was how best to reconcile speed and efficiency on the one hand and the working of democratic machinery on the other'.[1] A committee set up to study the problem reported in 1945. It recommended that the associations should establish closer contacts with one another, and that relations between the associations and the Staff Side should be strengthened by means of annual or biennial conferences of executive committees. It was expected that these conferences would eventually become deliberative but they failed to develop in this direction and after a few had been held, the idea was dropped. The committee further recommended that the central structure of the Staff Side should be strengthened to cope with its enlarged role, for 'with all our display of union strength, tradition and prestige, not one of us can negotiate a war bonus, change our pension conditions or even alter the rules of travelling, subsistence, removals or billeting'.[2]

During the post-war period there has been a substantial increase in the number of central agreements covering the whole civil service. Naturally, central agreements are subject to central review, which makes more work for the National Staff Side. For example, the principle and methods of settling pay are covered in a national agreement and the work of the Civil Service Pay Research Unit has been controlled by a joint steering committee on which the National Staff Side provides the representatives of the employees. A wide range of joint committees are manned in a similar way. Some of them – for example, the Civil Service Efficiency Committee – have been set up as a result of Staff Side initiative. The Staff Side operates domestically, as it were, through a series

[1] NSS 377.02.   [2] NSS 377.01.

of sub-committees and its main policy committee includes the general secretaries of the six largest unions. It has met weekly, and Sir Albert Day remembered it as 'a very happy band of brothers for the most part. We had great fun, we did a great deal of business, we had a lot to worry us and we didn't let that upset us.' The full Staff Side meets monthly to receive reports from various committees and to make policy decisions. Negotiations with the Official Side are handled by the relevant committees on major matters. A great deal of the work is, however, handled by Staff Side Officers, headed by the Secretary-General.

The good offices of the Staff Side are often used in helping to resolve disputes which may arise between the Official Side and constituent organizations of the National Staff Side on grade issues. With a competent staff to support the full-time officers, well-equipped headquarters, and a national journal – the *Whitley Bulletin* – the National Staff Side has become a throughly efficient negotiating instrument.

There is general agreement that since 1939 there has been a remarkable growth in the unity of the Staff Side, as compared with the first two decades of Whitleyism. Of course, the potential had been there from the start. 'This was the first time when we'd had the need to get together to discuss matters of common interest. Previously, the unions were dealing with their own domestic affairs. But now they were faced with the need to determine a common policy on broad national issues, such as superannuation and subsistence. And this made it necessary for them to get together and to devise a common policy for all of them.' As shown above, very little of the potential had been realized prior to 1939. Yet unless the Staff Side amounted collectively to something more than the associations severally, what use was it? It had to become an entity in its own right, and 'the pressure of war . . . necessitated the Staff Side's accepting that role'.

Pay was the key factor. War brought 'the Staff Side together because they knew that that's where the money was'. In the circumstances, the only admissible argument for higher pay was the rising cost of living – a factor which affected everyone, and the lowest paid most. This helped to close the biggest gap, that between the postal workers and the rest. 'There was a continual reluctance, particularly on the part of the Union of Post Office Workers, to relinquish their sovereignty in some spheres of negotiation, particularly pay. But when it became apparent that the Staff Side acting as a whole could achieve, even on pay, things for the whole civil service that couldn't be achieved by the individual unions, there was an understandably greater willingness to work under the umbrella of the Staff Side. . . . The most important element in pay during the war . . . was the war bonus and it was only working through the Staff Side . . . that it was possible to do anything on the war bonus at all and Day's ability to marshal convincing arguments on war bonus matters . . . evoked from the constituent elements in the Staff Side a loyalty and an acceptance of the standing of the Staff Side.'

A leader of the Union of Post Office Workers, Lord Geddes, confirmed this analysis. In the growth of Staff Side unity 'the major point was [joint] pay negotiations. . . . Once you put the Union's pay negotiations into the hands of the Staff Side, that in itself was a unifying force. . . . You could use the argument of the lower-paid, you see. You were doing your [joint] pay negotiations very largely on cost of living and you could always argue that it affected the postman far more than it affected anybody else . . . and therefore . . . the most important factor in unifying the Staff Side was [joint] pay negotiations.'

As the sense of unity grew, it was fostered by the standing orders relating to the way in which decisions were made. They were based on a recognition that major issues should not be decided by bare majorities, either of members, or of the constituents whom they represented. There has never been a system of card votes. Each member's vote counts the same, irrespective of the size of his association. It has often been possible to decide issues without a vote at all. The chairman, in Sir Albert Day's recollection, simply says 'at an appropriate stage in the debate, "It looks to me pretty clear as though the Staff Side wants to do so and so and so and so", and there's a chorus of "Agreed". You don't have to ask for a formal vote.' When a vote is called for, the normal method is by simple majority on a show of hands. When, however, a major issue of policy arises, a special procedure is brought into play – set out in capital letters in the standing orders to emphasize its importance. It reads, 'on questions of policy, endeavour shall be made to reach agreement: in default of such agreement, for a decision to be effective at least two-thirds of those voting, and not less than ten in number, must have voted in favour'. This sets a limit to the power of the majority, by ensuring that they cannot overrule any substantial minority. A further possibility was contemplated, not in the standing orders, but in the Staff Side constitution itself. Article 3 states the objects of the National Staff Side, the last of which is 'to take such other action as may be agreed by all constituent groups'. This refers to a situation in which no progress can be made within the Whitley system, but where some members may wish to use the Staff Side machinery to concert other action, such as a political campaign. Again, Sir Albert Day explained. 'If someone raised . . . an issue which, like equal pay, was not negotiable . . . or to put it more accurately, if someone raised a motion . . . affecting something which was not really Staff Side business . . . then there had to be unanimity.' In other words, the representative of any one association, no matter how small, was given a power of veto over all the rest. Of course, rules of this kind do not in themselves produce united action. They could simply have led to stalemate. But they have made it unprofitable for any one group to propose courses of action which were likely to alienate any substantial section of staff opinion. They reflect at least a desire for unity.[1]

Staff Side unity has never meant, however, complete identity of view among its members. In spite of the convention that Staff Side policy is normally expounded by its leader, the Official Side have always been well aware of the variety of attitudes among those with whom they were negotiating. 'The individualists were on the Staff Side', to quote one member of the Official Side. 'One knew quite well that there would doubtless be differences of opinion on that Side – more so than on the Official Side – because members of the Staff Side quite legitimately have got contrary aims to each other, because the interests of one class are not the same as the interests of another, and of course they had hammered out a line and they left it to their spokesman to put it forward.'

There was general agreement that, apart from the officers, the individual who contributed most to the growth of Staff Side unity was Len White, who succeeded W. J. Brown as General Secretary of the Civil Service Clerical Association. He was instrumental in 'converting the National Staff Side from a battleground of conflicting organizations to a co-operative effort for each and all, and the contrast for anyone who has lived through both types of organization is amazing!' 'Len White, when he became General Secretary following W. J. Brown, made all the difference. I think there's no doubt that he consolidated the Staff Side, improved its unity and made a great contribution.' There was an amusing contract between the attitudes of two respondents towards White's politics. A member of the Official Side knew that he adhered to the extreme Left but found him nonetheless 'an immensely decent fellow with whom you could work and whom you could trust'. A Staff Side colleague, on the other hand, seemed a little shocked at the apparent contradiction between White's preaching and practice. 'He had his own left-wing views that he could cynically put aside whenever it was necessary to do so.'

LEADERSHIP IN NATIONAL WHITLEYISM

On the Staff Side the style of leadership has profoundly changed. The present holder of the office, Leslie Williams, believes that 'it is a very difficult role to play'. In the past, it was even more difficult because there were several roles to be played at the same time. First of all, the Staff Side leader is Vice-Chairman of the National Whitley Council. This

[1] Shortly after the close of the period covered in this book, the constitution and standing orders of the National Staff Side were revised. The text referred to here is that which was in force until 30 September 1969.

causes no complications. It is 'an honourable title, much valued . . . [but] with no effective role.' Even when the Council used to meet, the Vice-Chairman did not take the chair in the Chairman's absence.[1] Now, of course, the office is merely a historical vestige. Secondly, before 1947, the leader was a representative of one of the major associations which constitute the Staff Side. When Sir Albert Day took office, for example, he was General Secretary of the Society of Civil Servants. Thirdly, until the same date, the leader presided over meetings of the Staff Side, with the usual responsibilities of mediating between antagonistic persons and groups and resolving conflicts on policy. For the first two decades, successive leaders managed to combine these roles fairly satisfactorily.

But the new style of negotiations adopted on the outbreak of war added to them a fourth role – that of principal agent of the Staff Side in its dealings with the Treasury. As Sir Albert Day put it, it 'implied that . . . I went alone to do the business, or I went along with particular colleagues either because I wanted support or because they'd got an interest to watch.' The consequence was that, while the principal representatives of the main associations continued to be closely involved in negotiations, some members of the Staff Side felt themselves relegated to a secondary position. Day himself described the manner in which he used to report back to his colleagues. 'If one is imbued with this idea that unity matters more than anything else, this thought is bound to creep out in all that one does. One speaks to the Staff Side . . . as though it were unthinkable that anyone should vote against a motion, because obviously the general interest requires that it should go through.' Not unnaturally, some resentment was felt on occasion. As one slightly dis-gruntled respondent put it: 'not much was done by [joint] committee. It was done by direct contact, with . . . people . . . added to the officers on the Staff Side according to the subject matter for discussion. . . . Consequently my personal contacts with National Whitley Council Official Side members were small. . . . I disliked *diktats* from Treasury Chambers or, for that matter, from National Staff Side offices. And that is a psychological factor that the officers of the National Staff Side shouldn't overlook.'

They were, in fact, very much aware of it. 'The pitfall', Sir John Simpson explained, 'is that if you become the confidant of the Official Side, and you're continually having discussions with them, many of them off the record, quite a lot of them on the understanding that this is strictly between you and me, you then run the risk that the people on your side begin to suspect that you've gone over to the other side. . . . When we reported these discussions to the Staff Side . . . we were some-times belaboured by characters like W. J. Brown . . . for having sold the pass.'

[1] With one or two exceptions. See above, p. 33.

It is a great tribute to Day that he succeeded in retaining the confidence of the Staff Side, in spite of occasional doubts that he had momentarily lost sight of its best interest in the seductive atmosphere of the Treasury. 'Where Albert was so able . . . is that, although there were occasions . . . when there was a suspicion of that, he was always able to rebut it. . . . He never became really suspect.' The wartime period was marked, as T. R. Jones recalled, by a 'growth in the confidence of people on the Staff Side in the integrity and capacity of their leaders. So that the main policy committee of the Staff Side, which met . . . every other day more or less in the beginning of the war, and regularly met at least once a week, comprised Day, the chairman, myself, the secretary, [and] only five other people, the leaders of major associations, and they were quite happy to let Day and myself discharge any tasks which had been decided upon by the committee and to report back, and that situation developed to the point where . . . [he] went over as an individual and saw one individual on the other side.'

Day's achievement was in part the result of remarkable personal gifts. A member of the Official Side who saw a lot of him during the war, recorded this verdict. 'He had immense patience, and immense capacity to keep his temper in circumstances of extreme difficulty – mainly with his own side – he had some very difficult chaps on his side – and he really did have . . . the gifts and the qualities of a negotiator and of a really good trade union representative. He stuck to his guns, he went patiently on, but he kept a very, very difficult team together.' T. R. Jones, his close colleague for many years, contributed the following sketch. 'Day's manner, so deliberate and so quiet, achieved effectiveness of a kind which was quite outstanding. And indeed, after one deputation, the Chancellor of the Exchequer . . . murmur[ed] to Day as the meeting ended, "You would have made a fortune at the Privy Council bar!" . . . That's an indication of the quality of his advocacy. And he never indulged in fireworks. . . . He always kept his passion under control. Even when he felt fairly deeply about something, there was always that restraint. So you never got fireworks from any meeting that Day attended, but the business achieved was the important thing.'

Not less important was the way in which Day ensured that he had the constant support of his colleagues. He would only carry on negotiating 'so long as I could say . . . that I'm not putting my foot an inch further forward than I think the Staff Side will allow me to go. If I am in doubt, I go back and ask them. . . . There have been a number of occasions when I reported to the Staff Side of Committee A . . . [that] I'd reached a certain position in negotiation. I thought that was the end but I wouldn't mind having another try for something a little more. The Staff Side would then say, "You try, and if you don't succeed, close immediately. Don't come back to us." One of his fellow members confirmed this account. 'Of course, the chairman was very seldom empowered to reach a conclusion. He had to get what he could from the Official Side and then report back to the full Staff Side who were finally responsible for either agreeing or not agreeing. And there were occasions when the chairman would reach a semi-final settlement with the Official Side and came back, and was told that this [was] not good enough, and he had to go back to the Official Side and say, "Well, I'm very sorry. Although I thought this was all right, the Staff Side are not prepared to accept, and we want this, that or the other", and attempt to get an improvement in the offer. And sometimes of course this did happen.'

Day's simultaneous playing of several roles was something of a *tour de force*, justified by the emergency of wartime. When it became clear after the war that Whitleyism was not going to revert to its pre-war pattern, thought had to be given to the permanent status of his office. Douglas Houghton took the lead in this. The first task was to separate the role of association representative from that of Staff Side leader. 'The chairman of the Staff Side laboured under the disability of being the leader of another big organization . . . and the responsibilities which arose during the war of doubling that job with the Staff Side job – . . . the Staff Side were meeting on emergency matters almost daily at one stage' – were very great. With the return of peace, moreover, it once more became legitimate for the associations openly to pursue their own goals. There was therefore a risk that Day, as General Secretary of the Society of Civil Servants, might receive directives which would clash with those he was getting from the Staff Side. 'People like Houghton saw that this really wasn't satisfactory. So when the war was over, [he] set himself to bring an end to this arrangement and to go all out for a full-time paid chairman of the Staff Side, because until the change took place, the chairman of the Staff Side's salary was derived from the job he really wasn't able to do but had to devolve on his deputy.' 'The fact that for the first time, the Staff Side had an officer who was not an official of another union created . . . a different style. It also created a new situation for the Official Side, in that they were able to have a continuous dialogue with a person on the Staff Side who really hasn't got a divided loyalty of any kind.'

Secondly, Day's role as chief negotiator had to be separated from that of presiding officer at Staff Side meetings. T. R. Jones explained: 'The reason why this was done was because it had been felt that . . . the chairman occupied a dual function. Sitting on a small policy committee which met every week, he sat in the chair, and participated in the discussion. . . . He was not merely presiding at the meeting, but he was contributing as an active participant in the meeting. . . . It was felt that that ought to be changed, and it was changed by the device of [electing a President] . . . who sat at the end of the table and kept order. Whereas [previously] the chairman not only did that but took part in all the discussions.' His colleagues felt that Day sometimes came to such meetings with an emotional commitment to a particular course of action. The Treasury 'knew that if they came to an informal agreement with him, he would fight to try and achieve that agreement on the Staff Side. He didn't always succeed but they knew he would try.' This was not objectionable in itself, but it did call for a separation of roles. In the words of Douglas Houghton, 'I took the view, and so did others, that when he became a full-time chairman, he ought not to be everything, and therefore we adopted the system of . . . an elected [President] who should preside over meetings and generally be the elected officer of the Staff Side. This spared the Staff Side any feeling that their full-time officer was not only their servant but their master as well, and this has worked very well.'

Day's intention was to retire in 1955, but the succession problem proved unexpectedly complicated. His 'contribution as chairman of the National Staff Side . . . was of quite outstanding importance and quality. For the first time, the Staff Side had a leader whose ability and integrity combined made him a really outstanding personality – someone who was accepted by the Official Side as well as the Staff Side . . . as a person of very great ability and outstanding integrity.' Fortunately, there was available, in the person of L. C. White, a man who seemed fully equal to the task. In the words of his precedessor, he 'had a very clear idea of what Staff Side unity required'. Opportunity was taken to tidy up the terminology of Staff Side offices. It was obviously confusing to have both a president and a chairman, and so the title of Secretary-General was adopted for the leader-elect. In future, the presiding officer was to to be known as the Chairman, and he was to have enhanced authority. He was to be Chairman of Committee A and a member of all committees, and was to be closely involved in the work of the Staff Side, including negotiations with the Treasury. 'In general, the Chairman will be the guide and counsellor to the secretariat, and will carry weight and responsibility as the elected head of the organization.'[1] But these plans were frustrated for, on the eve of taking up his new post, White suddenly died. In Leslie Williams's words, 'we all had a sort of sense of doubt as to how we were going to fill the gap'.

To get over the immediate difficulty, Day agreed to stay on for a further year. The choice eventually fell on Richard (now Sir Richard) Hayward, of the Union of Post Office Workers. It was something of a handicap to him that he came from a union which had all its members in a single department. This meant that he lacked 'the background of experience that Day had . . . in running a large, general service organization.' When Day eventually departed, Douglas Houghton took on the

[1] NSS 337.05.

76

job of Chairman of the Staff Side. The intention was, of course, that, with his long experience of Whitleyism, he would be able to help the relatively inexperienced Hayward. Contrary to everyone's expectation, however, the arrangement proved somewhat cramping to the latter. It was the period when the Priestley Report was being implemented. In joint meetings, particularly, it was difficult for Houghton, merely because he was better known, not to overshadow Hayward. Not until 1958 or thereabouts did the new Secretary-General succeed in fully establishing himself. When he did so, however, it was a perfectly natural development. As a Staff Side Committee had pointed out 'the concentration of power in the hands of the . . . [Secretary-General] is a reflection of the similar concentration of power in the hands of the Establishment Officers of the Treasury'.

Hayward soon displayed 'great verve and enthusiasm . . . and great fertility of imagination. . . . In some ways he could seize much more quickly [than Day] on possibilities of achieving movement in a difficult negotiating situation. His capacity for advocacy wouldn't match up to Day's initially but . . . in a relatively short time he developed into a first-class leader of the Staff Side. A different personality from Day altogether, a very lively sense of humour – bubbled over in a way that Day could never do – and, altogether, a well-rounded person who made his mark rapidly with the Staff Side, and equally rapidly with the Official Side. . . . Perhaps the greatest tribute that one can pay to Hayward is that he had no difficulty in establishing himself as firmly in the esteem and regard and respect of the Official Side as Day, which was a really quite striking achievement, because Day had achieved an eminence in this field which was quite unique until his time.'

In 1966, when Hayward was appointed Chairman of the Supplementary Benefits Commission, his place was taken by Leslie Williams, who had until then been General-Secretary of the Society of Civil Servants. By that time Williams had gained a wide experience of staff association activities and of Whitleyism at the national, departmental and local levels. He had himself been a civil servant, first in the Post Office as a sorting clerk and telegraphist, and later in the Inland Revenue. Here he was active in the Inland Revenue Staff Federation, and served for a time as Staff Side Secretary to the Inland Revenue Departmental Whitley Council. In 1947, he was appointed Assistant Secretary in the Society of Civil Servants, and became the Society's General Secretary in 1956. He was a member of the Staff Side of the National Whitley Council in this period and served as its Chairman from 1960 to 1962.

Thus, when Leslie Williams became the civil staff associations' chief representative, he brought a notable background to his new tasks. He had long personal experience of the National Whitley Council and of some of the major departmental councils. He had worked closely with his two immediate predecessors and both men had become his close personal friends. Although handling the Staff Side's business in his own distinctive way, as must all holders of his office, he acknowledges the strong and valuable traditions he inherited. Soon after he became leader of the Staff Side, the Fulton Committee presented its report. He has led the Staff Side in the wide ranging negotiations on the future organization of the civil service. The Official Side know him to be as effective a protagonist of staff interests as were his predecessors, and at the same time, no less conscientious a trustee of the fabric of Whitleyism.

IMPLEMENTATION OF FULTON

The implementation of the Fulton recommendations provides a good illustration of how Whitleyism was working in its fiftieth anniversary year. The recommendations affected many important aspects of the civil service, such as structure, recruitment, management, training and organization. The ensuing programme of work has been very largely a joint enterprise between the two Sides of the National Whitley Council.

On the Official Side, the Civil Service Department has naturally taken the lead. But the developments required are a matter for the service as a whole. The main burden of implementing change falls on the individual departments. It has, therefore, been essential to consult them fully at every stage. To achieve this end, a framework of interdepartmental committees was set up to guide the work on Fulton. The main forum has been a Steering Committee, consisting of permanent secretaries and top professionals from a number of departments, under the chairmanship of Sir William Armstrong. Four sub-committees were set up, reporting to the Steering Committee, and consisting of Deputy Secretaries, Principal Establishment Officers, and senior professionals. The topics referred to them were: grading structure, recruitment, management and training, and the organization of work.

National Staff Side machinery makes possible a parallel process, whereby the views of the various associations can be harmonized. The two Sides have met in a special Joint Committee of the National Council, which has been set up as the main forum for consultation and negotiation. Particular topics have been discussed in other joint committees, e.g. the National Whitley committees on training and superannuation.

From the point of view of management, the advantage of this procedure is that, once agreement has been reached, there is every likelihood that it will be accepted and put into effect throughout the service. Given the size, geographical scatter and diversity of work, this is a very great gain. Changes worked out in this way are introduced more slowly than if they were unilaterally promulgated. But the expenditure in time and effort is held to be justified. From the viewpoint of the staff, there are possible drawbacks. The rank and file may grow restive, feeling that their leaders are neglecting urgent bread-and-butter questions – above all, pay – and giving too much attention to issues which may seem rather remote to the man at the desk. The difficulty here is one of perspective. The associations have a duty to their members in the long term, as well as in the immediate future. Simply by giving more time to a current pay claim, there is no certainty that a staff association leader will get more money for his members. But by giving some thought now to changes which will come to maturity in ten or fifteen years, he has a very good chance of being able to enhance his members' prospects throughout their whole careers. To put it in the crudest terms, the total pay received by a civil servant from the day he joins until the day he retires depends in only a small degree on the salary scale applicable at any one point of his career. More important in the long run are such things as the structure of the service, with its greater or lesser opportunities for individual members; wastage and recruitment, affecting as they do the promotion prospects of existing members; and the training provided to fit civil servants for more responsible posts. There is another difficulty for staff leaders. If they go too far in influencing management with regard to issues such as those just referred to, they may seem to their members to have become part of management itself.

Part of the explanation of such fears is that members of the two Sides are now on excellent personal terms. Their meetings are generally conducted in a cordial atmosphere, with considerable freedom of speech on both sides. In many cases, members of one Side feel considerable respect, and even friendship, for individuals on the other side. It is not surprising that some members of the rank and file may fear that their leaders will be less vigilant for their interests in such an atmosphere than were their fore-runners in more bracing times. A hypothetical tax-payer could feel, too, that the guardians of the public purse might relax their grip on its strings a little too easily by comparison with their predecessors. Such apprehensions, however, spring from a misunderstanding of the roles the parties play. A large part of a higher civil servant's professional work consists in negotiation – with other departments, with interest groups, and with government contractors, for example. In the process, he often has to say no, and has to learn how to do so without breaking off all relations with the other side. This skill is what members of the Official Side exercise, and is quite consistent with their responsibility for defending the public interest in negotiations. They can turn down one request, and still go on to discuss another claim in a calm and friendly way. A staff representative reaches a similar point by a rather different route. At any one time, he has a great many claims in various stages of negotiation. If he flies off the handle when one is rejected, he knows the success of others will be imperilled. He realizes, therefore, that it is ultimately in the interests of his members to maintain good relations with those on the Official Side, even though his activists might applaud strong words spoken in hot blood.

All this is true even in a negotiation on a subject, such as pay, where the interests of the Sides clearly diverge. In many Whitley fields, however, such divergence is much less clear. Training is an example. Here the two Sides tend to work in quite a different way, not as if they were engaged in a negotiation, but as if seeking a common solution to a common problem. Both Sides have their reasons for wishing to expand the amount of training, and especially central as distinct from departmental training. There remains, of course, a difference of emphasis, since each Side still has its own objectives to pursue as well. The Official Side's primary concern is to provide enough, but no more than enough, training to improve efficiency, especially in the use of certain modern techniques, and as a secondary aim, to demonstrate to outside critics that this is being done. The Staff Side's aim, quite properly, is to ensure that there is enough training to enable each individual member of the service to make the best of himself and improve his chances of promotion. In particular, they are concerned that those who have entered the service at the lowest levels should have the best chance to compete with those who come in, for example, direct from universities. Hence a training programme large enough to satisfy the Staff Side may be larger than the Official Side think necessary. Differences of approach, and sometimes even of substance, result. But it seems fair to say that these differences are argued out just as thoroughly in the round-table atmosphere of a joint working party as they would be in a polarized negotiating situation.

CHAPTER 4

PAY AND CONDITIONS
OVER FIFTY YEARS

Pay and conditions are inseparably bound up with one another. To meet a demand for improved conditions almost always costs money, whether it is for longer paid holidays, a more generous allowance of sick leave, or a more frequent change of towels in the washrooms. From another point of view, the conditions of service have to be taken into account in fixing the rates of pay. The security of tenure of civil servants, and the fact that they can look forward to superannuation on retirement, have for generations been held to justify rather lower salaries than prevail in other branches of employment. The point was clearly made by Sir Russell Scott, then chairman of the National Whitley Council, giving evidence before the Tomlin Commission in 1929. 'Remuneration is only one of a number of factors in the conditions of service of civil servants, and . . . in fixing remuneration due regard must be had to those other factors in the conditions of employment of civil servants, notably security of tenure, prospects of promotion, leave and sick-leave privileges, and pensionability.'[1]

There are three basic philosophies about pay in the public service. It can be argued that salaries should be as low as possible, that they should be sufficiently in advance of those in the private sector to set a good example to other employers, or that they should be comparable with those in the private sector. The first policy – that of screwing down the pay of public servants to the lowest possible level – is not quite so hard-hearted as it may appear. The wages bill must be paid from the tax-payer's pocket. Since many tax-payers are normally worse off than the general run of public servants, the whole operation may involve taking from the poor in order to give to the moderately well-to-do. Whether justified or not, this way of looking at the question was at one time quite common among those who occupied themselves with the problem. It comes through, for example, in the remarks of the Playfair Commission (1875) on boy clerks. These boys were taken on at fourteen and sacked at nineteen. The Commission approved, because 'a very

---

[1] L. D. White, *Whitley Councils in the British Civil Service: a study in conciliation and arbitration,* Chicago, 1933, p. 158.

ordinary boy, early in his career, will do more than half a man's work, while he can be got for less than half a man's wages, and . . . the best boys will do more than an average man's work'.[1] The Commission took a similar view of the employment of women in the Post Office. 'Women are well qualified for clerical work of a less important character, and are satisfied with a lower rate of pay than is expected by men similarly employed. We, therefore, see no reason why the employment of female clerks should not be extended to other departments where the circumstances will admit of it.'[2]

The second policy was endorsed by the House of Commons as early as 1893, in a resolution relating to workers in naval establishments. The House resolved 'that the conditions of labour as regards hours, wages, insurance against accidents, provision for old age, sickness, etc., should be such as to afford an example to private employers throughout the country'.[3] It did not become the guiding principle in negotiations between the government and its employees, however. In 1929, a member of the Tomlin Commission asked Sir Russell Scott whether the Treasury would agree 'that government departments are supposed to lead the country on the question of salaries and wages, and that therefore the government is in a sense bound to set a standard' in these matters. Scott replied: 'the view which the government has taken cannot, I think, be described quite in the terms you have used'. In reply to an earlier question, he had already laid down the official line. 'It would not be right to prescribe for civil servants rates of remuneration which were out of scale with the standards normally obtaining amongst good employers outside the public service. . . . They must not be . . . unduly high, because any such disparity . . . would have the effect of elevating civil servants into a privileged class, and so of doing an injustice to the community, which *ex hypothesi* would be worse off, and has always to foot the bill.'[4]

Philosophies one and two having been eliminated, only number three remains: the pay of civil servants should be comparable to the level that prevails in the private sector. This is an extension of the 'fair wages' principle which was enforced on government contractors in the days before Whitleyism. It was expressed, for example, in a resolution of the House of Commons in 1909: 'the contractor shall . . . pay rates of wages and observe hours of labour not less favourable than those commonly recognized by employers and trade societies (or, in the absence of such recognized wages and hours, those which in practice prevail among good employers) in the trade or district where the work is carried out.'[5] As applied to the civil service, it means (to quote once more Sir Russell Scott's evidence of 1929) 'that the rates of remuneration and other

[1] B. V. Humphreys, *Clerical Unions in the Civil Service*, Oxford, 1958, p. 31.
[2] Ibid. p. 32.   [3] White, p. 156.   [4] Ibid. p. 159.   [5] Ibid. p. 157.

conditions of employment in the public service must be such as to compare well with the rates of remuneration and other conditions of service normally available outside the public service in competing occupations.'[1] In the absence of reliable figures, it was for many years difficult in practice to apply this principle. But the Priestley Report (1955) not only endorsed the principle once more, but also recommended the setting up of a Pay Research Unit to provide the necessary data. A member of the Official Side, who was largely concerned in the implementation of Priestley, formulated the policy that has operated since that date. 'The fundamental consideration that must . . . govern the pay of public servants is that . . . [they] must neither be a privileged class nor an oppressed class. Public employment ought to be broadly in line, in all its conditions, with private employment.'

THE FIRST JOINT COMMITTEES

When the National Whitley Council was set up in 1919, the associations expected that it would provide them with the opportunity to solve the problems which had troubled them for so many years. This would be achieved through joint consultation with the Official Side.

At the second meeting of the Council, on 14 October 1919, two committees were set up: one was to undertake the reorganization of the civil service, the other was 'to consider the increase in the cost of living and its effect upon the salaries of the civil service, whether permanent or temporary, and to report to the Council'.[2] An instruction to 'report to the Council what changes in the scales and rates of payment should be made'[3] was deleted before the resolution was agreed. Two committees were set up at the third meeting of the Council on 20 February 1920, both of them on the suggestion of the Staff Side. The first was to 'consider and report upon the principles and methods of promotion',[4] it being understood that the question of promotion boards could be considered under these terms of reference. The second resulted from a memo. on the higher education of civil servants drawn up by Sir William Beveridge which the Staff Side wished to see used as the basis for an experiment. The Official Side were unable to accept the memo. but proposed that a committee should consider 'the encouragement of the further education of civil servants and their training in higher administration and organization.'[5] The Staff Side intimated to the Official Side in June 1920, that they planned to raise the question of superannuation, and the Official Side set up a committee to discuss the questions that might arise. It had held only two meetings prior to the Council meeting of 26 October 1920, when a joint committee was established to consider

[1] Ibid. pp. 158–9.   [2] NWC Minutes, Vol. i, p. 24.   [3] Ibid.
[4] Ibid. p. 28.   [5] Ibid.

the general conditions of superannuation in the administrative and legal departments of the civil service. The Chairman of the Council had doubts however whether the committee would be able to begin effective work in the near future because every member of the Council was so busy. In fact all the committees started meeting shortly after their appointment and all had produced at least one report by March 1922; the Reorganization and Further Education Committees had each produced two.

The Reorganization Committee was concerned with the classification of the service into the three classes recommended by the MacDonnell Commission in 1914, and with the assimilation into these of the numerous existing grades. It held over forty meetings and produced two reports which were discussed by the National Council. The first report, of 20 February 1920, was considered by the Cabinet on 22 March 1920, at which Sir Warren Fisher, Permanent Secretary to the Treasury, was present. Ministers were impressed with the desirability of accepting without change the first and unanimous Report of the National Whitley Council which, it was hoped, 'would enjoy the confidence of, and exercise valuable influence throughout, the civil service'.[1] The report was approved by the Council and put into effect by Treasury Circular. Before the second report could be presented the problem of starting pay on assimilation had to be taken to arbitration, and the effective date for reorganization, after long arguments, had to be fixed by the Treasury by executive action. The final report was produced on 28 January 1921.

Reorganization brought new salary scales to many civil servants, but the Staff Side wanted also to hedge against the increase in the cost of living which had continued since the war. At the second meeting of the National Staff Side on 29 August 1919, a committee was appointed to consider a general war bonus claim and the method of prosecuting it. Its report was placed before the next National Staff Side meeting on 15 September 1919. After considerable discussion it was decided to refer the matter to a joint committee of the National Whitley Council in such terms as allowed the individual associations to take their own immediate claims to arbitration while the joint committee sought a permanent solution. The Joint Cost of Living Committee was accordingly appointed. The Staff Side immediately began to prepare their case, seeking the help of outside organizations such as the Labour Research Department. The first meeting of the Joint Committee was held on 23 February 1920. Shortly afterwards the National Staff Side decided to press for an interim increase of 10 per cent. The Official Side resisted this but agreed that if negotiations went on for longer than two months they would consider an interim increase. The Committee's progress was reported regularly to the National Staff Side who took the

[1] Cab. 23/20 15/20 (6).

major decisions; for example, the decision to continue to press for an interim increase.

On the Official Side the major decision was taken by the Cabinet. A memo. prepared by the Treasury was placed before the Cabinet on 31 March 1920. The three alternatives open to the Cost of Living Committee were compared: (a) the existing bonus, awarded on 31 March 1919, by the Conciliation and Arbitration Board in the expectation of falling prices, (b) the Staff Side proposal which would give civil servants the purchasing capacity which they had had before the war, (c) the Treasury scheme which provided for a bonus to be revised every year or half year. The Cabinet approved scheme (c), on the condition that there should be a sliding scale arrangement in which the amount of the bonus would rise and fall with the rise or fall in the cost of living index. At the same time, the Cabinet ruled that the Whitley Council should deal, when discussing grading, salary and bonus, only with grades carrying salaries of £500 a year or less. Evidently the limitation on its sphere of reference was not made clear to the Staff Side of the Committee for when it complained to the National Staff Side that no proposals had yet been made for a bonus on salaries of more than £500 p.a., the latter agreed to raise the matter on the Council. However when it did so on 9 April 1920, the Chairman 'ruled that it would be better not to embarrass the procedure of committees by discussing in full Council matters on which the committees had not reported. He suggested that the more regular course would be for an informal consultation to take place between the Chairman and Vice-Chairman of the Cost of Living Committee.'[1]

The Committee's report was presented on 8 May 1920. It provided for a bonus to be paid to *all* permanent civil servants and to be revised every four months during the first year and every six months thereafter. It was to vary according to the changes in the official cost of living index on a base of 130 (representing the increase of 1 March 1920 over July 1914). The figures for the preceding period would be averaged and the bonus would rise or fall by 5/130 for every change of five points in the index above or below 130. The bonus awards were to be tapered – 130 per cent of ordinary remuneration where this was no higher than £91 5s, 60 per cent on the next £108 15s, (i.e. up to £200), and 45 per cent between £200 and £500.

THE 'SUPERCUT' DISPUTE

The importance of this dispute is that it brought into the open a basic ambiguity in the Whitley system. Should it cover all civil service salaries ? Or should it cover only those up to a certain limit ? Questioned

[1] NWC Minutes, Vol. i, p. 38.

on this point at a meeting of heads of departments in June 1919, Sir Malcolm Ramsay had stated that the Ramsay–Bunning report 'draws no limit at all'.[1] Yet as noted above, the cabinet, when considering the offer to be placed before the Cost of Living Bonus Committee on 13 March 1920, ruled that 'the Whitley Council should only deal as regards grading, salary and bonus, with salaries of £500 p.a. and below'. As a first step towards establishing salaries above that figure, the Chancellor of the Exchequer was to invite three prominent men to advise him on the proper salary of a Permanent Under-Secretary.[2] The discussions of the Reorganization Committee were similarly restricted by the Official Side on the grounds that departmental peculiarities made it impossible to standardize the highest posts. In fact, Treasury objections went further than that. In a memorandum to the cabinet, Sir Warren Fisher had earnestly deprecated 'discussion at a Whitley committee (which consists, as to one half, of the rank and file of the service) of the re-muneration of the controlling and of the higher grades of the civil service'.[3] On the other hand, the Cost of Living Committee had been told that 'if the . . . scheme becomes operative it will in any case be applied so as to include officers on rates of salary up to £1000 p.a., and on scales of salary with maxima not exceeding that amount'. When the report was discussed by the Council of 12 May 1920, the Vice-Chairman drew attention to this clause which was, he said, ambiguous, and it was agreed to add a footnote making clear the bonus payable on salaries between £500 and £1000. This encouraged the Staff Side in the belief that most salaries over £500 were within the purview of the Council, even if the very highest were reserved for unilateral decision by the government. The report was agreed and put into effect by Treasury Circular.

The cost of living rose quickly during 1920 and 1921, and bonuses rose in consequence. The Government had to ask parliament for more money and the National Whitley Council became the centre of contro-versy in the House of Commons. On 25 July 1921 the cabinet took note of the economies in bonuses which the Chancellor proposed to announce. 'The attention of the cabinet was invited to the strong feeling among men in the higher ranks of the civil service in regard to the attitude assumed towards them in parliament and press. It was pointed out that these devoted public servants, who had never spared themselves, and on whom the public administration depended so largely for its success, had been stigmatized as shirkers in war and as over-paid in peace. . . . These remarks were received by the cabinet with expressions of the fullest sympathy.'[4] So that the higher paid civil servants would once again be

[1] WC 1/1. [2] Cab. 17/20 (3).
[3] T1/12595/21284/1920.
[4] Cab. 23/264/61/21 (4).

able to look the taxpayer in the eye, the bonus on salaries over £500 was to be cut. When Sir Warren Fisher announced the decision to representatives of the higher grade associations, they all condemned it as a breach of understanding, if not of an explicit agreement.

On the following day, the Chancellor announced the 'supercut' in the House of Commons, and went on to say that the 'Whitley Council can only deal with salaries under £500 a year and people in higher grades than that are not subject to the ordinary operation of the Whitley Council'.[1] The Financial Secretary asserted that the area of salaries over £500 p.a. 'has never been submitted to the National Council – not only never has been but never can be, and for this reason: if you submit salaries of over £500 to the National Whitley Council, you are calling upon the Official Side of the Council to perform an impossible task – the task of themselves deliberating on and deciding their own salaries. That, it cannot be too clearly understood, has never been done.'[2] The debate was fully reported in *Whitley Bulletin* and the restriction to salaries less than £500 was raised by the Staff Side at a special meeting of the Council on 4 August 1921. The Official Side refused to discuss it because due notice had not been given of this constitutional point. It was raised again in the Council on 16 August, and the Official Side repeated that salaries of more than £500 could not be debated in the Council. The Staff Side continued without success to press for abolition of the supercut. In 1926, the Joint Consultative Committee of higher grade associations took the question to arbitration. The Court ruled that the agreement had been an honourable one but rejected the claim for restoration of the bonus because the country could not afford it. The abolition of the supercut was part of an all-service programme launched by the National Staff Side in 1928.

PROMOTION

When the Promotion Committee met in November 1920, there were a number of principles of promotion that the Staff Side wanted to introduce. At the request of the Official Side they produced a complete scheme. It included a proposal for Promotion Boards, which were already used in some departments, such as the Admiralty, but these must include staff participation. This was discussed at length after the Staff Side had assured the Official Side that they did not intend to interfere with the responsibility of the Permanent Secretary in a Department; his control would be exercised *through* the Board. The function of the Staff Side representatives would be to express the views of the staff who came into contact with the civil servant, and to satisfy themselves that justice was being done. There was detailed discussion of the

[1] H.C. Debs. ccccv, no. 106, p. 303.   [2] Ibid. cxlv, no. 106, p. 363.

scheme including the format of the report form. The committee reported in August 1921, recommending promotion boards in all departments which were too big for the permanent head to know all the members of his staff personally. The boards were to cover promotions up to ranks carrying a salary of £900 p.a. Evidence should be taken from one or more representatives of the Departmental Staff Sides. Adverse reports were to be communicated to the officer concerned. The Committee's report was approved by the National Whitley Council in March 1922.

The Promotion Committee resumed meetings in April 1925, when the Staff Side suggested a central authority to remove the inequalities between departments in the chances of promotion. The Staff Side were anxious to prevent outside recruitment while there were civil servants who could be promoted. After long discussions about how this could be achieved, the second report was produced in June 1928. It suggested that as an experiment as much notice as possible of a vacancy should be sent to all departments. They were then to circulate the information and applications for the post from civil servants should be forwarded through their Department.

FURTHER EDUCATION

The Further Education Committee produced a number of reports. The first was concerned with the provision for juveniles, and the aim of the second was to encourage Departmental Whitley Councils to stimulate a desire for further education throughout the Service. The Committee then went on to discuss the question of a Further Education Council and much controversy was aroused over whether this should be part of the Whitley machinery. 'Such an arrangement [Miss Lawrence] considered was open to objection and she regarded any suggestion that study at classes might constitute a claim to recognition in an official sense as very dangerous.'[1] The report advocated a voluntary Further Education Council whose constitution should be drawn up by a provisional Council of the representatives from each Departmental Further Education Committee in London, the managers of the Whitehall Institute and those members of the National Whitley Council who had shown a particular interest. The report was accepted and put into practice. Mr W. R. Fraser, the Official Side Secretary, commented 'I know that [Miss Lawrence's] view, with which I heartily concur, was that this Further Education movement is fraught with great danger to the peace of the civil service. Its more fanatical exponents (Sir Stanley Leathes on the Official Side and Mr Llewellyn on the Staff Side) will not be satisfied with anything short of a system of "compulsory voluntaryism" and although the proposal that the results of further education should

[1] WC 5/28/01.

be officially recognized has been withdrawn, it remains in the background. (I think Sir Stanley Leathes' ideal civil service would be one in which half the people do the work and the other half were qualifying for promotion over their heads by means of further education.)'[1] The provisional Council met in June 1924, and the constitution was approved and the ten representatives of the National Whitley Council appointed in March 1925. Although the Civil Service Council for Further Education was separate from the National Whitley Council, its courses were advertised in *Whitley Bulletin* and members of the Whitley Council continue to serve on its Executive Committee.

SUPERANNUATION

The Staff Side had a very large number of questions to raise on the Joint Superannuation Committee and at the first meeting agreed to divide them into those which could be dealt with without legislation and those which would require an amendment to the Acts. They started by claiming that all full-time unestablished service should count for pension. The Official Side rejected this on grounds of cost and the Chairman, Sir Malcolm Ramsay, asked them to draw up a list of other matters with which they wanted to deal. This list was submitted to the Council in November 1923, and referred to the Committee. It included the acceptance of the principle that pensions were deferred pay, compulsory retirement at sixty, voluntary retirement between fifty-five and sixty with accrued pension rights, as well as the claim for all service to be pensionable. At the next joint meeting of the committee, on 30 June 1924, the Chairman stated that discussion must be limited to those proposals which did not require any substantial increase in the total cost or any legislation. The National Staff Side authorized the Staff Side of the Committee to continue discussions but these became increasingly rare and little progress was made. No further report was issued.

THE ROYAL COMMISSION, 1929–31

In 1929 the Royal Commission (Tomlin) on the Civil Service was appointed and the associations prepared evidence for it. The National Staff Side gave evidence on most of the major issues of the day, taking the same stand as they had on committees. In its Report in 1931 the Commission approved promotion boards but asserted that merit should be the only consideration in filling the higher posts and in the middle ranges it should be the deciding factor. A major change was recommended in superannuation to allow women to provide for their dependants by opting to come under the 1909 Act. In future on establishment

[1] WC 5/28/02.

half of previous unestablished service should be allowed to count for pension. In the case of remuneration the Royal Commission rejected the Staff Side's claim that the state should be a model employer on the grounds that this was incompatible with the principle of comparison with outside pay. This latter was the principle which should be followed for 'broad general comparisons between classes in the service and outside occupations are possible and should be made. .... In effecting such comparisons the state should take a long view. Civil service remuneration should reflect what may be described as the long term trend, both in wage levels and in the economic condition of the country.'[1]

On these grounds the Commission condemned the cost of living bonus. As shown above, this bonus was a legacy of the First World War. After intermittent negotiations, it had been brought up again on the National Staff Side in July 1928. Following informal discussions with the Chairman of the Council and the Permanent Secretary to the Treasury, the Official Side offered to stabilize the bonus at $67\frac{1}{2}$ while the average cost of living figure remained between $62\frac{1}{2}$ and $72\frac{1}{2}$. However, at the Council meeting on 11 October 1928, this was rejected and a committee was appointed to inquire into the workings of the bonus system. The Staff Side attacked the cost of living index because it was not related to middle class incomes, and proposed changes in the system of tapering which the Official Side rejected as being too expensive. Disagreement was registered. In the following year the index fell to 60 and it was agreed to stabilize at a figure of 65. The bonus fell to 60 in 1931, while the index was 55. The Staff Side protested and a campaign to 'stop the drop' was launched.

It was against this background that the Royal Commission considered the question. 'At the present time it is not the practice for the remuneration of clerical and analogous workers outside the service to be varied automatically in accordance with changes in the cost of living figures. No reason is seen why the wages of civil servants should be fixed on a basis different from that generally adopted.'[2] Furthermore there were great difficulties in revising the remuneration of all civil servants on the basis of a single formula for 'while the figure may be appropriate to certain staffs it is inapplicable to others.'[3] Therefore the bonus should be consolidated with basic pay, and rates of consolidation were listed.

The Report was presented to parliament in July 1931, and at the National Whitley Council meeting in December the Vice-Chairman formally moved 'that before any action is taken to give effect to, or arising out of, the recommendations of the Tomlin Commission the

---

[1] *Report of the Royal Commission on the Civil Service, 1929–1931*. Cmd. 3909, para. 308.
[2] Ibid. para. 340. [3] Ibid. p. 342.

fullest opportunity shall be afforded on each specific issue for discus
sion with staff representatives through the appropriate channels with a
view to reaching agreed decisions.'[1] The Chairman welcomed this as
he had been going to make such a suggestion himself and a joint
negotiating committee on remuneration was set up. At the committee
meetings in February and March 1932, the Official Side fully accepted
the Commission's scheme for consolidation but because of recent
change in the economy and in the financial condition of the country
consolidation was offered at 3 per cent less than the Commission's
terms. The Staff Side, on the other hand, declared themselves
emphatically in favour of the principle of the automatic sliding scale
in accordance with the cost of living. Comparison with outside pay was,
said the Vice-Chairman 'statistically impracticable and economically
inequitable'.[2] The sliding scale, however rough and ready, did provide
immediate and easy figures and therefore redress in times of rising
prices. Consolidation was rejected at present when the cost of living
was at its lowest. Informal discussions took place between Staff Side
and Official Side representatives but no consolidation scheme was
agreed. However a report was produced in July 1932, stabilizing the
bonus at the same level as long as the cost of living figure was between
55 and 60. Informal negotiations continued on consolidation and
eventually, despite resistance from the Staff Side, consolidation on the
lines proposed by the Commission was imposed by the Treasury.

This committee was one of four suggested by the Joint General
Purposes Committee and accepted by the National Whitley Council in
July 1932. The Remuneration Committee became Committee A,
Committee B dealt with the recruitment etc., of the reorganization
classes, Committee C with a range of topics including promotion,
Committee D with superannuation. Some of the committees' work was
the routine discussion and approval of the Commission's recommendations; for example the first report of Committee C in November 1932
agreed to the removal of the Members of Parliament from the Official
Side of the Council, the continuation and development of the Departmental Whitley Councils, and the acceptance of paragraph 504 of the
Commission's Report which recommended that the Chairman, Vice-
Chairman and Secretaries of the Whitley Councils should be serving
civil servants. Its third report in April 1935, however, was concerned
with interdepartmental promotions. Where a department did not
employ administrative class staff they should bring to the notice of the
Treasury any officer under 30 who qualified for promotion to Assistant
Principal. The nominees would be considered by an informal committee
including representatives of the Treasury and Establishment Officers
from the principal departments, but the department in which the

[1] NWC Minutes, Vol. v, 11 Dec. 1931.   [2] 5/55/01.

vacancy occurred should still have freedom of choice. Committee D reported on superannuation in 1934 and in 1935 an Act was passed which allowed women to opt for the terms of the 1909 Act, and which provided for the counting of half of unestablished service on establishment.

THE IMPACT OF THE SECOND WORLD WAR

When war broke out in 1939, the National Staff Side set up a committee to consider a war bonus scheme and it recommended in December 1939, a sliding scale based on the cost of living index. This was refused by the Official Side who sought a flat rate bonus, and so a publicity campaign was launched with meetings all over the country. Discussions with the Official Side continued and in May 1940, because of the grave war situation, a flat rate bonus was agreed but without prejudice to the Staff Side's view that it ought to be a percentage bonus. In July 1940, the Staff Side claimed an increase, and this was refused by the Official Side because there had not been a big enough change. After further negotiations and an interview with the Chancellor of the Exchequer in November, an increased flat rate bonus was imposed by the Treasury. Negotiations continued on this pattern throughout the war. Consolidation was agreed at the end of the war.

THE PAY OF HIGHER CIVIL SERVANTS

An *ad hoc* advisory committee on the pay of the higher civil service was set up in 1948 under the chairmanship of Lord Chorley. Its appointment was not agreed between the two sides although it 'had been clear . . . to both sides that the appointment of an advisory body of this kind was the right way of dealing with the issue.'[1] It took evidence and presented its report in February 1949. It did not concern itself with the effect of the government's policy on prices and incomes but 'we have interpreted our terms of reference as requiring us to consider civil servants' salaries in their long term relationship to the general salary and wage structure of the country'.[2] The salaries should be improved because they had been allowed to fall behind in the inter-war years although the work had increased, they were low in comparison with salaries in government sponsored employments, and they should take account of the increase in the cost of living. The Chancellor accepted the recommendations.

A Chorley co-ordinating committee was set up on the Staff Side

[1] NSS 130.14.
[2] *Report of the Committee on Higher Civil Service Remuneration, 1949.* Cmd. 7633, para. 4.

consisting of the higher grade associations – the First Division Association, Civil Service Legal Society, Association of Officers of the Ministry of Labour, Customs and Excise Controlling Grades Association, Association of Inspectors of Taxes, Society of Civil Servants, and Institution of Professional Civil Servants. It kept the Staff Side informed of the negotiations which took place but was not responsible to them. The Treasury proposed to spread the award over three years, starting on 1 October 1949. The associations were very concerned at this and particularly at the effect on pensions which were based on the average of the last three years' salary. They were concerned also with the relationship between the salaries of more than £2000 p.a., which were dealt with by the Chorley Committee and those below this which were dealt with under the ordinary procedure of the National Whitley Council. In September 1949, the co-ordinating committee was called to meet the Chancellor to hear him explain that because of devaluation the increase due to be awarded on 1 October would have to be deferred. However he gave way on the pensions issue so as to allow pensions to be calculated on the full amount of the Chorley awards. The Staff Side was very dissatisfied with this, and, when in April 1950, the Civil Service Arbitration Tribunal ruled that, although there was merit in the claim of the Principals and Assistant Principals, they would not make any award because it was necessary to ensure stability of wages, the National Staff Side began to complain that the civil service was being unfairly penalized by the government's policy. They wrote to the Prime Minister who replied on 2 May 1950 that the 'government is, of course, bound to observe towards it own employees the policy it hopes and expects that other employers will observe towards theirs'.[1] The Prime Minister received a deputation from the Staff Side but reiterated that he was unable to accept their claim that the government's policy involved harsher treatment for the civil service. The increases were fully implemented in October 1951, and the Co-ordinating Committee then concerned itself with the professional and technical salaries which were dependent on the Administrative Class awards.

JOINT PAY NEGOTIATIONS

The implementation of the Chorley Report encouraged the Civil Service Clerical Association, Society of Civil Servants and the Institution of Professional Civil Servants to make claims. In June 1951, the National Staff Side agreed that they should set up a sub-committee to consider whether negotiations based on the cost of living should be undertaken by the National Staff Side. It produced its first report

[1] NSS 130.01 A.

in July which concluded that in adjusting wages reliance should be placed on a single criterion, the index of wage and salary rates. Such joint pay claims should be lodged *ad hoc*, the Pay Committee deciding when to lodge them. 'The Committee assumes that it does not need to argue the case for central co-ordinated action on pay, the events of the last nine months having brought a general realization of the disadvantages of piecemeal pay settlements over the whole Service.'[1] The report was amended by the Union of Post Office Workers at the meeting of the National Staff Side in August 1951, so that claims were to be made on the basis of the Ministry of Labour wages index while a salary index was being negotiated with the Treasury. Also any agreement should last for a maximum of three years. On 14 August, the Staff Side Chairman met Treasury officials to explain this and to assure them that the associations would wish to retain their rights to negotiate separately. He was told that the scheme would require the Minister's approval. Informal discussions continued between Sir Albert Day and the Treasury while the Staff Side debated the advantage of central negotiations. It was eventually decided to press for automatic increases when the Index of Wage Rates moved by five points. Joint meetings of the Pay Committee were held in December 1951, and January 1952. When it became clear that the Official Side stood firm on its offer of 10 per cent for salaries under £500 p.a., tapering to 2.5 per cent on those of £1500 p.a., without automatic adjustments during the next three years, the Staff Side accepted it. Attempts to revise the agreement on the basis of the index failed in November 1951, and in 1953.

In 1954 a leader in *The Times* led Day to probe the possibility of further central negotiations. All the associations on the National Staff Side except the Union of Post Office Workers and the Post Office Engineering Union (the Civil Service Union participated in respect of part of its membership) formed a committee. It was agreed to negotiate centrally and a letter was sent to the Official Side. 'There is a common thread running through all of these claims submitted recently by the constituent associations of the necessity for an increase in civil service salaries pending the Report of the Royal Commission and in relation to the movements that have taken place in outside remuneration. The Treasury will obviously be looking at these claims comprehensively and I am to request that the Treasury will now reply collectively to the Central Pay Negotiations Committee.'[2] An interim settlement was agreed in November 1954, but it did not provide for comprehensive increases. Its two defects from the Staff Side point of view were the small increases given to juveniles and the tapering in the higher grades. A further claim was made in 1955 but the Treasury held that no

[1] NSS 130.06 A.   [2] NSS 130.11.

economic change had taken place since the 1954 settlement and therefore the claim was not justified. It was taken to arbitration and 5 per cent was awarded. A further central agreement was made in March 1956.

THE ROYAL COMMISSION, 1953-5

The Priestley Commission pointed out the need for 'explicit principles that will commend themselves as fair both to the staff concerned and to the community as a whole; and that can be applied by successive governments without impairing the non-political nature of the service'.[1] The main principle should be 'fair comparison with the current remuneration of outside staffs employed on broadly comparable work taking into account the differences in other conditions of service'.[2] A second consideration should be the maintenance of internal relativities; this would not override fair comparisons but would have to be used where comparison was not possible. The present methods of collecting evidence for fair comparisons should be broken down into two, (a) collecting facts and (b) the application of these to obtain figures on which to negotiate rates of pay. The first task should be given to an independent unit which should for each grade investigate an agreed list of good outside employers in order to find jobs undertaken by their employees which are equivalent to those undertaken by the grade in the civil service. The second part of the process should be to allow for other conditions of service, for example non-contributory superannuation and luncheon vouchers, in order to produce the true money rates for the jobs. The civil service should be a good employer in that it should pay somewhat above the average rates in the country as a whole. But since the field of outside organizations chosen should consist of good employers the right range within which to make comparisons should be around the median. When there were exceptional increases in outside wages this process should be supplemented by central pay claims. This process of pay research was not to apply to the higher grades whose pay was to be settled by a standing advisory committee appointed by the Prime Minister.

The Royal Commission's major recommendation on superannuation was that the question of counting unestablished service in full and retrospectively should in future be regarded as one of cost rather than of principle. In the case of hours, the Royal Commission noted that they had risen to a 91-hour fortnight in London and in three-quarters of the provincial offices. The Staff Side sought a 77-hour fortnight, inclusive of lunch breaks, while the Treasury suggested 88 hours in

[1] *Report of the Royal Commission on the Civil Service, 1953-55.* Cmd. 9613, para. 75.
[2] Ibid. para. 96.

the provinces and 84 in London, inclusive of lunch breaks. The Commission recommended 78 hours net in the provinces and 74 in London.

A large joint committee was set up to negotiate on the report. It was led on the Official Side by Sir Thomas Padmore, Second Secretary at the Treasury, and on the Staff Side by the Secretary-General. The committee studied the proposals and in many cases accepted them. On some issues they made slight changes. For example, while the five-day week was to be put into practice without delay, provision was made in certain departments, such as the Post Office, for a longer period of opening, although individual civil servants would only work five days. The formal meetings were accompanied by informal discussions and the report was published at Easter 1956. It was ratified by the National Staff Side and embodied in a formal agreement. The Establishment Circulars were issued in July. The Commission's proposals on superannuation were dealt with by a separate joint committee. Agreement was reached on the minor issues such as increased gratuities for temporary staff and these were embodied in the Superannuation Act, 1957. Since by that time, the Pay Research Unit had been set up, and the new Standing Advisory Committee on the pay of higher civil servants had begun its work, it can be said that the implementation of the Priestley Report took only two years.

There remained, however, certain problems still outstanding. No agreement had been reached on the reckoning of unestablished service prior to 1949. The Staff Side claimed that it should be counted in full, but despite two interviews, and correspondence with the Chancellor of the Exchequer, they failed to change the Official Side's view that this could not be accepted on cost grounds. The Staff Side were extremely disappointed, particularly as they had reduced the overall cost by dropping their claim for retrospective adjustment of the lump sums already paid to pensioners. In his letter to the Secretary-General of the Staff Side on 26 March 1957, the Chancellor, Mr Peter Thorneycroft, made it clear that the Treasury would not even consider retrospection in the future because of the cost. The editorial in the May *Whitley Bulletin* noted that the hopes of a more sympathetic reception from Mr Thorneycroft, on account of the interest he took in the Staff Side's policy towards the 1949 Act, was unfounded. Questions continued to be asked in the House of Commons. The movement revived when Mr Heathcoat Amory was appointed Chancellor of the Exchequer. The Staff Side met him but again the policy was rejected on grounds of cost. During the general election of 1959 the National Staff Side wrote to every candidate asking if, should he be elected, he would be willing to receive a deputation of his civil service constituents to discuss the case for counting unestablished service in full. In 1960 the Staff Side launched a publicity campaign with mass meetings in London and the provinces. The campaign has continued: in 1965, for example, it was discussed with James Callaghan, as Chancellor of the Exchequer. But the Treasury has remained adamant.

The Standing Advisory Committee on the pay of the higher grades, under the Chairmanship of Lord Coleraine, held its first meeting in February 1957 and decided to take as its first task the effect of the general pay settlement of 1956 on the higher grades. They took evidence from a number of sources including the National Staff Side. They were anxious to relate the pay scales of Assistant Secretaries to those of Principals. In May they recommended an increase relative to the $5\frac{1}{2}$ per cent central pay increase, on the grounds that the Commission had said that such increases should not apply automatically to the higher civil service but that the Advisory Committee should decide whether anything should be done in consequence of them. They then informed the Prime Minister that they would be undertaking a general review of the pay of the higher grades in the autumn. They collected data and in 1959 made recommendations for new pay levels for the Treasury grades.

The Committee may carry out surveys on its own initiative, or as in December 1962, they may do so as the result of joint submissions by the Official and Staff Sides. The margin between the higher grades and the pay research grades has to be maintained and therefore the pay of Under Secretaries has to be reviewed regularly. The Staff Side are involved in submitting evidence to the Committee and in negotiating with the Treasury the salaries which follow on from those of higher grades. Despite protests from the Staff Side that it was unnecessary, the Committee's Seventh Report, of August 1965, was referred to the National Board for Prices and Incomes. The Report was passed without change.[1]

PAY RESEARCH AND INCOMES POLICIES

The Director of the Pay Research Unit was appointed on 1 August 1956, and the Unit began work in October 1956, on a survey of postal and telegraph officers. The Unit soon discovered that there were some grades, for example postmen, for which there were no outside analogues,

[1] In 1971 the Standing Advisory Committee on the Pay of the Higher Civil Service was disbanded. Its functions were taken over by the Top Salaries Review Body which was asked to advise the government about the salaries of senior civil servants who are at and above Under Secretary level, and also on the pay of the judiciary, board members of the nationalized industries and MPs and ministers. The Review Body has been invited to review the pay of senior civil servants every two years.

and these jobs had to be broken down into factors, e.g. sorting, which could be compared with factors in outside jobs. The main problems however were the length of time it took to survey all the grades in the service, resulting in long intervals between the operative dates of reviews and therefore large increases when they eventually came. Governments, which were during this period trying to impose incomes restraint on the country, were continually embarrassed by the amount of backdating which accompanied every pay increase in the civil service. Starting in 1961, in an attempt to reduce this, surveys were undertaken in a sequence lasting five years. In 1966, the Chancellor of the Exchequer decided that the period of backdating for civil service pay settlements should be limited to six months from the date on which agreement was reached. The Official and Staff Sides then concluded the 1967 Agreement on Pay Research and Pay Negotiations in the Non-Industrial Civil Service which provided for the stream-lining of pay research procedures with the object of ensuring that settlements could be reached within six months of the operative date from which the pay increases were due.

So much for the machinery. In order to see what it produced, it is necessary to revert to 1957, when a central pay settlement was negotiated pending the operation of the Unit. Priestley had expected that once the Unit began work, such increases would no longer be necessary but even when it began to undertake surveys in sequence, central pay increases were necessary for the grades not currently in pay research. A further increase was obtained in 1959. Following prolonged negotiations in 1960, a 4 per cent increase was agreed, to be paid immediately. For the future, the necessity for a further central pay settlement should be considered when the wages index moved by five points. This agreement was not, however, ratified at association conferences, the major associations feeling that they could achieve more outside central pay agreements.

On 25 July 1961, the Chancellor of the Exchequer announced in the House of Commons a pause in wages and salaries, although all existing agreements would be honoured. On 1 August, the National Staff Side wrote to the Chairman of the National Whitley Council, Sir Norman Brook, about the necessity of maintaining Priestley principles in the face of the Chancellor's statement that the pause must apply in the public sector. They met the Chancellor on 10 August, and were informed of the government's policy. 'The existing negotiating machinery would continue to function as would the Pay Research Unit but, in this latter regard, any offer made by the Official Side would be for future implementation and there would be no subsequent question of retrospection. With regard to the Arbitration Tribunal, the government must withdraw, for the time being, from its scope, the timing and stages of putting an award into effect. This would mean that the operative date would not be arbitrable, neither on pay nor on cases involving other conditions of service.'[1]

At a special meeting of the National Staff Side the Pay Committee was authorized to organize meetings of protest at the interference with the arbitration machinery and the principles laid down by Priestley. Meetings were held up and down the country including a huge mass meeting at the Central Hall, Westminster. Confidential meetings continued with the Official Side for the general discussion of pay issues in the hope that authority to negotiate would be given at a later stage. There were continuing protests at the interference with the Arbitration Board and the National Staff Side had a meeting with the Minister of Labour, with no success. The Staff Side then put in a central pay claim for $5\frac{1}{2}$ per cent because of the 5.5 points movement in the wages index. On 1 January 1962, the Union of Post Office Workers started a work-to-rule and the Civil Service Clerical Association announced that similar action would begin on 17 January. The Chief Secretary to the Treasury, Henry Brooke, saw representatives of the Staff Side on 16 January and told them that it was hoped that the wages pause would end on 31 March 1962, and that salary increases agreed since 31 July 1961, and the awards of the Arbitration Tribunal held in abeyance, would come into operation. The Civil Service Clerical Association called off their campaign, but because there was no provision for retrospective payments, the Union of Post Office Workers continued their work-to-rule, and the Post Office Engineering Union announced that they would start similar action on 20 January 1962. As a result of further negotiations, the Official Side offered 2 per cent increase in March which was immediately rejected by the Staff Side and the claim was taken to arbitration.

The Staff Side based its case on the principle of fair comparison, as laid down by the Priestly Commission, and reiterated that there should be clear principles by which to settle the pay of the civil service. Permanent damage could be done to the confidence of the service in these principles if it was felt that the government was abusing its position as an employer. $5\frac{1}{2}$ per cent was claimed. The Official Side objected, arguing that the cost of meeting such a claim would be excessive, and referring to the norm for increases which was $2-2\frac{1}{2}$ per cent. The White Paper had conceded that comparability would still have a part to play but that in the immediate future more regard should be paid to general economic considerations. The Tribunal awarded 4 per cent as from 1 April 1962.[2]

A further claim was made six months later. But in the second half of 1963 discussions started on revising the pay research structure.

[1] NSS 130.36 B. [2] Cf. p. 117 ff.

The agreement was signed on 6 February 1964, to reduce the pay research cycle to four years, the main classes and grades being investigated and the minor ones maintaining the existing internal relativities. For the civil servants not in pay research in each of the years there were to be central pay increases of 3 per cent on 1 January 1964 and 3½ per cent in the following two years. The Secretary-General of the Staff Side made it clear to the Official Side that any deterioration in the economic situation should not mean a review of the agreement before 1966. However by mid-1965 the associations began to be concerned that they were slipping behind outside pay. In October 1965, a joint meeting of the Staff Side's Committee A and Central Pay Steering Committee resolved to recommend the National Staff Side not to jeopardize the agreement by refusing to accept the 3½ per cent increase. However an attempt should be made to underpin the next agreement.

The National Staff Side had begun to discuss the advisability of a new three year agreement when in July 1966, the six month standstill on wage increases was announced. The Secretary-General of the Staff Side immediately made it clear to the Treasury that there would be strong resistance if the public service was singled out. Throughout the following period Committee A and the Official Side kept in close touch, and the Staff Side were assured that there was no intention of singling the civil service out. However a number of claims were outstanding, their proposed date of operation being 1 January 1965. Negotiations on these continued but the date was deferred to July 1965, and the increases were phased so that the total increase was not received until 1 January 1967.[1]

Under the terms of the incomes policy the National Staff Side were able to negotiate an increase for the lower paid civil servants. In March 1968, the Staff Side formed a deputation to the Chancellor following the statement of the Secretary of State for Economic Affairs in the budget debate that large pay increases might have to be achieved in stages. They emphasized that pay research was only a catching-up operation. Nevertheless of the increases awarded in 1968, only 7 per cent was granted immediately, the balance being held until 1 January 1969, with no backdating. Two central pay increases were negotiated, 5 per cent for those who had had no increase since January 1966, and 3 per cent for those who had had an increase in 1967. Staging has caused a good deal of discontent among the associations particularly

[1] After discussions with the National Staff Side the Official Side agreed in February 1968 to reduce the pay research cycle to three years: in May 1970, following a report by a joint working party set up by the Official and Staff Sides of the National Whitley Council, the Official Side agreed to a further shortening of the cycle to two years.

with regard to pensions which are calculated on the average of the last three years' salary.

THE STAFF SIDE IN PAY NEGOTIATIONS

In retrospect, it may seem odd that the Staff Side did not go all out for consolidation of the bonus obtained during the First World War with basic salaries. This would have made it easier to defend pay levels if the cost of living continued to fall without precluding the possibility of demanding more pay if conditions improved. But all the factors making for disunity on the Staff Side in the inter-war period were at their most intense whenever pay was under discussion. Members tended to view one another's claims with suspicion, as if all civil service pay had to come out of a fixed fund, so that more for someone else would mean less for one's own constituents. The representatives of the lower-paid looked with jealousy on the claims of the higher-paid, thinking always how much better off the latter already were. The spokesmen of the higher grades listened with equal distaste to the demands of the lower ranks because they feared the erosion of the differentials they valued on social as well as on economic grounds.

Lord Geddes expressed the frustration the postal workers felt under this regime. Their delegates 'really couldn't sufficiently sway the Staff Side in the direction in which the Union wanted to go, which was clearly to lift up the lower paid worker. Whereas the view of the Staff Side was not only to hold what they'd got but to improve, and this is where you got the main antagonism. . . . We were only allowed to advance as far as the others were willing to let us advance. . . . They did not appreciate at that time the use that could be made of the lower-paid worker, and therefore they were not prepared to let the lower-paid worker . . . dominate policy. . . . Before the war, we weren't of use to the Staff Side and therefore you had this antagonism, this feeling of frustration, as it were, on the part of the Union that Whitley was no damned good anyway!'

The failure to settle the bonus question was largely because the two biggest associations, the Union of Post Office Workers and the Civil Service Clerical Association, were 'diametrically opposed in their views'. The postal workers thought it too great a risk to give it up, lest the cost of living should rise. W. J. Brown, the leader of the clerks, judged that it would not rise, and was therefore willing to take the risk. The smaller groups divided, some one way, some the other. For example, the Institution of Professional Civil Servants tended to side with the postal workers on this issue. The result was a deadlock, broken in the end by the Tomlin Commission, as shown above. The staff had no alternative but to accept, and the policy was implemented in the depths of the world slump, when the cost of living was of course extremely low. Had the Staff Side been able to agree earlier, when the cost of living was higher, 'they could have got a much better bargain'.

In pay, as elsewhere, the turning point in the history of the National Whitley Council was the Second World War. The war bonus had the result of centralizing pay negotiations in the National Staff Side, since very few grounds remained for associations to negotiate bilaterally on behalf of their members. Lord Geddes recalled his Staff Side colleagues beginning to realize that, the more the postal workers came up, the more the remainder of the service would come up too. 'Whenever we got a rise, we became as it were the spearhead of the attack, and once we achieved anything, you automatically carried on to the others. So that the thing changed because they appreciated our power, our strength, in our own field, which they . . . could use. Particularly during the war, where you had central pay negotiations, and the period which lasted after the war, we were able to influence the situation, because very often the arguments for central pay were based on the lower paid worker. And therefore we became of use to the Staff Side.'

Analogous developments took place in the Staff Side's attitude towards the most highly paid civil servants. These had been excluded from the purview of the Council on the grounds that, otherwise, the Official Side would be determining their own pay. Many Staff Side leaders in the early days would have liked to bring all salaries within the Whitley orbit. But this was not because they had any desire to push up the remuneration of permanent secretaries and the like. Since the war, however, the Staff Side as a whole has become very much aware of the link between the salaries of the most highly paid civil servants and all the others. Staff leaders generally pressed for the establishment of the Advisory Committee, and support its work, because they see that more pay at the top provides them with an excellent argument in favour of more pay all the way down. The new development has 'helped a lot in getting the ceiling lifted on civil service pay, and this, of course, affected all the people below. It was an important, [even] revolutionary . . . development in negotiations in the public service'. The old habit of imagining all pay as coming from a fixed fund has died. Now, in an inflationary age, the staff regards the fund from which pay comes as flexible. A successful claim by another group may actually help one's case, instead of militating against it. Consequently, the Staff Side has found it much easier to work together on pay than they did between the wars. 'A very great departure from all precedent is the way in which, in recent years, the National Staff Side have found it possible, first of all in their own ranks, and secondly, in negotiation with the Official Side, to deal directly with the general problem of pay for the civil service as a whole.'

The new situation has extended the work of the National Staff Side. It has become directly responsible for the management of the Pay Research Unit, set up in consequence of a recommendation from the Priestley Commission. The Commission had suggested that the new machinery should be answerable to the Minister of Labour. But this was changed during the course of Joint Committee negotiations on the implementation of the report. It was agreed instead that the Unit should be 'under the general control and direction of the Civil Service National Whitley Council. Control shall be exercised through a Committee composed of six members from each side. Day-to-day control of the Unit shall be vested in a director, who shall . . . be responsible to the Committee for carrying out the programme of inquiry and observing the priorities laid down by it.[1] 'The Unit was to undertake inquiries "in relation to grades or classes referred to it by the Committee".' Fields of relevant comparison could be suggested only by either side of the Committee or by the director of the Unit. The director was required to submit to the Committee such periodical reports (including an annual report on the Unit's work) as the Committee might direct. In addition, either Side could call for reports, either in relation to a particular grade or class, or in relation to pay movements generally. The staff of the Unit would normally be drawn from the civil service, but complementing, grading and appointment would be on lines approved by the Committee. The director would have to consult the Committee before appointing additional officers for particular projects, and assessors who would advise when necessary on the duties and responsibilities with which comparisons were being sought. Participation in these activities enhanced the standing of the National Staff Side. The use staff associations, acting on their own, could make of the Unit was restricted to requesting the director 'to supply ascertained facts relating to the grades they cover'.

There is no doubt that pay research brought substantial benefits to civil servants. Nevertheless, it did not solve all the problems, and the search for solutions to those which remained has enlarged the scope of the National Staff Side still further. In particular, pay research was not sufficient in itself to settle all pay issues in an age of inflation. It took time, and it gradually became clear that, to cover even the main grades and classes, it would be necessary to programme the surveys over a period of years. If civil servants were forced to wait for pay increases until their turn for pay research came round, they would tend to drop far behind their analogues in the private sector. Pay increases to enable them to catch up would need to be large, and would give the public the false impression that civil servants were getting lavish treatment. Similarly, if settlements were back-dated far enough

[1] *Whitley Bulletin*, Vol. xxxvi, 1956, p. 68.

to be fair, the sums involved would be so large that the public would tend to regard them as over-generous. In order to avoid these difficulties as far as possible, the pattern grew up of *ad hoc* central pay settlements, based upon general trends in pay outside the civil service, to bridge the gap between pay research exercises. This development culminated in the pay agreement of 1964.[1] It was there laid down that the main classes and grades should be surveyed by the Pay Research Unit on the basis of a four-year cycle. Central pay increases for grades not in pay research in the year in question were agreed, to take effect from 1 January 1964, and each of the two succeeding years. Central pay negotiations had become, and were to remain, an essential part of Whitleyism. As the name implies, they can be conducted only by the National Staff Side.

None of this should be taken to mean, however, that the National Staff had become an entity independent of the staff associations which constitute it. The Staff Side of the Joint Committee set up to manage the Pay Research Unit consisted of the General Secretaries of the principal staff associations, together with the Secretary-General of the National Staff Side.[2] The same key figures were closely involved in central pay negotiations. The rise of the collective entity has not been at the expense of the constituent parts. What had happened was that the leaders of the staff in all grades had learnt the lesson inherent in Whitleyism from the beginning: that there were many things staff associations could achieve by working together which none of them could achieve on its own.

[1] Ibid. Vol. xliv, 1964, pp. 42–3.   [2] Ibid. Vol. xxxvi, 1956, p. 142.

CHAPTER 5

ARBITRATION

THE CONCILIATION AND ARBITRATION BOARD 1916-22

The Conciliation and Arbitration Board for Government Employees was set up on cabinet authority in 1916 as the result of pressure from the Post Office for a war bonus. The Board consisted of three people – a Chairman appointed by the government, one member of an employers' panel appointed by the Treasury and the department concerned, and one member of an employees' panel appointed by agreement between the Ministry of Labour and the Parliamentary Committee of the Trades Union Congress. The civil service associations objected because they had not been consulted about the composition of the employees' panel, and because they felt that the Chairman was not impartial. Secondly they were dissatisfied with the terms of reference which provided only for claims for increased remuneration; they wanted their conditions of service to be considered also. Most of the Board's problems arose however from lack of experience of arbitration procedure on both sides. In its record of proceedings for 1917 the Board stated: 'divergence of view between the Treasury representative and the departmental representatives has been frequent and marked. Many cases were frankly differences between the Treasury on the one hand and the claimants and their departments on the other, rather than between employees and employer.'[1]

However both the Heath Report and the Ramsay–Bunning Report in providing for the establishment of Whitley Councils in the civil service assumed that the Board would continue in operation. Sir Malcolm Ramsay stated in discussion: 'The Committee feel however that every effort should be made to avoid recourse to arbitration, a solution very undesirable in itself and one which in the long run must necessarily impair the influence and authority of the National Council.'[2] After the introduction of the Whitley Councils the number of claims submitted to arbitration was greatly reduced. Between

[1] L. D. White, *Whitley Councils in the British Civil Service: a study in conciliation and arbitration*, Chicago, 1933, pp. 101, 108.
[2] WC 1/22.

1 May 1917 and 1 August 1919, the Board heard ninety-nine claims; between August 1919 and July 1921, the number fell to nineteen. The Board had the duty to conciliate before allowing a claim to come before them for arbitration. Staff leaders sometimes had 'their first meetings with the Treasury and with departmental heads . . . in the Arbitration Tribunal. There'd been no discussion of *any* kind. And this is why the . . . arbitration machinery of those days was used so much as a conciliation body, because it was [a way of] getting the parties to meet.' The normal procedure was to send the two sides away to see how far they could get by talking things over. The development of bilateral negotiation procedures, and of Whitleyism, reduced the need for this conciliation function. It is notable, however, that the first reference to arbitration by the National Whitley Council, that of starting pay on assimilation which had been the subject of disagreement on the Reorganization Committee, was referred by the Board back to the parties who eventually reached agreement.

This claim was heard on 1 August 1920 but in June the secretary of the Board had written to the Treasury seeking guidance on the Board's function in relation to the Whitley Councils. He feared that appellants would play the Board and the Councils off against one another. 'It is inevitable, for instance, that claims involving the determination of identical principles will be brought by one class direct to the Board and by another class to the Whitley Councils with results equally embarrassing to both bodies: in fact the Whitley Councils may find themselves in such a case faced with the alternative of regarding their hands as tied by some decision of the Board or of treating the matter as tantamount to an appeal to them against a decision of their own appellate tribunal.'[1] A memo. on this letter, written by F. P. Robinson, the Official Side Secretary, asserted: 'The essence of Whitleyism is agreement; the essence of the Arbitration Board is disagreement. Whitley Councils supersede nothing and are merely a piece of machinery for arriving at agreement. When it is clear that agreement cannot be reached, the question passes from the realm of Whitleyism and we are where we were before the establishment of Whitley Councils. If the disagreement is in regard to wages, the normal course is for the staff to apply to the Arbitration Board. The establishment of Whitley Councils, therefore, has not affected con-stitutionally the position of the Arbitration Board, but it is hoped that it will have the effect of lessening the number of disagreements with which the Board has to deal. It is still possible for the Arbitration Board to bring about agreements by conciliation, although the frequency of this will presumably be lessened by the probability that all possible channels of agreement will have been exhausted on a Whitley Council

[1] WC 7/53.

before the matter reaches the Arbitration Board.'[1] The question was discussed with the Ministry of Labour and it was agreed that 'neither the civil service authorities nor the Whitley Councils can take away the right of the civil service associations to have matters referred to the Arbitration Board, even if Whitley machinery is available and may not have been used'.[2] This decision was communicated to the secretary of the Board.

However by 20 June 1921, the Chancellor of the Exchequer was arguing in a memo. to the Cabinet that 'the main justification for setting up the Arbitration Board has disappeared with the institution of Whitley Councils in the civil service'. Furthermore it was 'impossible to secure that discussion on Whitley Councils is without prejudice to the course of arbitration, seeing that the Arbitration Board would not normally be able to award less than the Official Side is prepared to offer, and that therefore the Staff Side stand to lose nothing by proceeding to arbitration'.[3] The Chancellor must not lose control of expenditure. Therefore the Board should be abolished and where arbitration is necessary this should be undertaken by agreed arbitrators with the consent of both parties. Members of Parliament should be added to the Official Side and this addition 'could quite fairly be presented to the Staff Side as a means to secure impartiality in the deliberations of the Council'.[4]

The memo. was discussed by the Cabinet on 30 January 1922. They agreed to the abolition of the Board but rejected the idea of *ad hoc* arbitration arguing that 'if at any stage there is disagreement it will be open to either side, in the ordinary way, to suggest arbitration by consent as a method of making further progress'.[5] The addition of Members of Parliament was referred to the Chancellor of the Exchequer and the Minister of Labour for further consideration and decision.

On 21 February 1922, the Third Report of the Geddes Committee on National Expenditure was published advocating the abolition of the Board because the Whitley Councils had rendered it unnecessary. On 21 February, the Chancellor (Sir Robert Horne) asked the Chairman, Vice-Chairman and Secretaries of the National Whitley Council to call on him, and he told them of the Government's decision to abolish the Board and the reasons for doing so. A Treasury memo. set out the arguments which the Chancellor was to use. Firstly it was more than ever necessary for the Chancellor of the Exchequer to have full control over the public finances 'and the Geddes Committee recommended the abolition of the Arbitration Board on this ground alone'.[6] Secondly the main justification for the Board had gone with the introduction of the Whitley Councils, and 'the combination of free

[1] E 153. [2] Ibid. [3] Cab. 24/125, CP 3061.
[4] Ibid. [5] Cab. 23/29, 6/22, (12). [6] F 8732/2.

and frank discussion on these with the right of the staff to appeal to an outside body in the cases of difference places the civil servant at an unjustifiable advantage in questions of remuneration'.[1] However the addition of MPs would secure impartiality.

THE CAMPAIGN FOR RESTORATION OF ARBITRATION 1922–25

The Staff Side members were entirely unprepared for this decision and protested strongly against it, but the Chancellor announced the abolition of the Board in the House of Commons on the following afternoon, 22 February, by means of a private notice question. A special meeting of the National Staff Side was held on 25 February, at which W. J. Brown of the Civil Service Clerical Association and J. W. Bowen of the Union of Post Office Workers proposed a motion protesting against the abolition, affirming the Staff Side's conviction that the existence of the Board was essential to the effective working of the Whitley scheme, and calling upon the government to replace. the Board by another independent body with power to settle disputes Opinion was very diverse even among members of the same group. Some members welcomed the abolition of the old Board and sought more suitable machinery. Others thought that this was not necessary since they could appeal to the House of Commons. W. E. Llewellyn, Vice-President of the Confederation, supported the first part of the resolution but found the remainder unwise. 'The Chancellor had indicated that the government desired that the Whitley Councils should operate effectively, and the scheme should be given a further trial under the new conditions.'[2] The Chairman, G. H. Stuart-Bunning, said that he was not very fond of the Board, and revealed that the Ramsay–Bunning Committee had considered its abolition. 'The question of making use of it had been very fully discussed on the National Provisional Joint Committee, and they came to the conclusion that until the Whitley Councils were working effectively the Board should be continued.'[3] He had told the Chancellor on 22 February that it was not yet time to abolish the board. Nevertheless he was not in favour of the resolution as it stood. It was carried nineteen to two. The subsequent actions of the Staff Side were taken against the wishes of the Chairman and these were among the reasons for his resignation in May. He had been prevailed upon to withdraw it by August.

[1] F 8732/2.   [2] NSS minutes, Vol. i, 25 February 1922, p. 1.
[3] Ibid. p. 2.

At a further National Staff Side meeting on 28 March a motion was passed calling for a Court of Appeal consisting of three people, one nominated by the government, one by the Staff Side, and a Chairman whose nomination was agreed between the two sides. Action for restoration of the Board was delegated to the General Purposes Committee. The abolition was noted at the National Whitley Council meeting on 31 March, but the campaign for restoration took place outside the Whitley network. The Staff Side wrote to the Prime Minister and to the Chancellor of the Exchequer asserting that an independent Court of Appeal was essential. At the General Purposes Committee meeting on 11 April, a parliamentary campaign was decided upon. A letter was sent to all MPs appealing to them to support the claim for restoration of the Board. On 15 May, a deputation was sent to the Chancellor of the Exchequer at which the Staff Side argued that 'with all the good intentions in the world, with all the desire that they may have for coming to an amicable agreement with the Official Side, there must be times when both sides will feel so strongly upon points of principle that reference to an impartial body ought to be made'.[1] The Staff Side did not want to deprive the government of the overriding power of control but did think that when they functioned as employers they should provide, as they expected other employers to provide, a legitimate outlet for grievances and a means by which in the event of disagreement both sides could be examined by a third party. Without this the Official Side would have a veto. The Chancellor reiterated his argument about lack of control over expenditure, but conceded that in any really suitable case the government would be willing to go to arbitration.

The Staff Side produced publicity leaflets; for instance, one giving the government's arguments for abolishing the Board and the Staff Side's replies to them. These were distributed to the associations who were asked to send them to MPs. The issue was debated in the House of Commons on 27 July 1922, and a list was compiled showing the position of each MP on the issue. Staff Side leaders however considered that the turning point of the campaign came on 10 April 1923 when, after much pressure from the Staff Side, the government was defeated in the House of Commons on the starting pay issue.[2] They believed that the government then realized the value of an Arbitration Board.

On 4 May 1923, when the Staff Side formed a deputation to the new Chancellor, Stanley Baldwin, the principle of arbitration for the civil service was conceded. A joint committee was set up to formulate a constitution for the Board and its terms of reference. There was a good deal of friction over the latter; the Staff Side objected to the exclusion of all grades with salaries of more than £700 per annum, and

[1] NSS 265.03 A.   [2] Cf. White, pp. 173–5.

they saw the Chancellor, Philip Snowden, about it on 27 June 1924. Two further interviews were sought with the Chancellor in July and November without success and, despite the continued discontent of the Staff Side with regard to the proposals excluding daily hours and grading, the report was accepted at a joint meeting on 23 January 1925. Before signing it however the Chairman of the Staff Side sought and received confirmation that 'neither the Treasury nor the departments concerned would raise any obstacles to going before the Court' and that 'the carrying out of the awards would be an honourable obligation, subject only to such limitations as might conceivably be imposed by the overriding power of parliament'.[1] The report was submitted to the Chancellor and then signed by both sides. The Treasury Circular was issued on 14 March 1925.

THE CIVIL SERVICE ARBITRATION TRIBUNAL

The machinery for arbitration was to be the Industrial Court. The Civil Service Arbitration Tribunal was to consist of such members of the Court as the President of the Court may direct, but it was understood that Chairman would be the Present or the Chairman of a division of the Court, one member would come from a panel appointed by the Minister of Labour as representing the Chancellor of the Exchequer for the time being, the other member would come from a panel appointed by the Minister of Labour as representing the National Staff Side. Civil servants and officials of civil service associations were not to be eligible. By convention, this restriction has since been extended to ex-officers of the associations. Emoluments, weekly hours of work and leave were arbitrable; cases of individual officers were specifically excluded. Terms of remit were as far as possible to be agreed.

On 25 February 1929, the cabinet approved a memo. by the Chancellor of the Exchequer and a draft circular to departments concerning the procedure to be followed in dealing with claims for their staff because there had been 'cases in the past in which departmental authorities in discussing questions of remuneration affecting their own staffs, have openly declared their willingness to make larger concessions than the Treasury were prepared to sanction'. The departments were to be informed that '(a) No statement will be made by departmental representatives during the course of negotiations or at arbitration, which might be held to commit their department to agreeing with or recommending a proposal requiring Treasury sanction, unless that proposal had been discussed and agreed with the Treasury. (b) Should a department desire to accept, or to advance

[1] NSS 265.03 C.

to its staff representatives, proposals which the Treasury is not prepared to sanction, the question at issue between the department and the Treasury will be settled officially before any statement is made to the staff representatives.'[1]

The first members of the Staff Side panel were elected from among a number nominated by the associations. The Institution of Professional Civil Servants wanted the members to be selected on a group basis, one appointed by the Confederation, one by the Post Office group, one by the Joint Consultative Committee and one by the Institution of Professional Civil Servants. This was refused, as was a demand by the Joint Consultative Committee that a particular nominee be selected. 'Should this request not be complied with the Joint Consultative Committee and the Council of the Institution of Professional Civil Servants have decided to take the instructions of their constituent bodies as to their future relations with the National Whitley Council.'[2] This was one of the factors leading to the withdrawal of the Joint Consultative Committee from the Council in 1926. The first four members of the panel were Madeleine Symons of the National Union of General Workers, Frank Hodges, formerly Secretary of the Miners' Federation and lately Civil Lord of the Admiralty, A. G. Walkden, General Secretary of the Railway Clerks' Association, and J. J. Mallon, Warden of Toynbee Hall and a signatory of the Whitley Report. The Staff Side panel has included many distinguished people such as H. J. Laski, L. S. Woolf, Barbara Wootton, Margaret Cole, Ernest Green, and H. A. Clegg. Since 1938 there has been a preponderance of academics. The appointments are for three-year periods and are renewable; H. J. Laski served for twenty-four years from 1926 to 1950, and Margaret Cole for twenty-one years from 1943 to 1964. Members of the panel have resigned when they were appointed to government bodies; for instance Allan Flanders resigned in 1965 when he became a part-time Industrial Relations Adviser to the National Board for Prices and Incomes. The Minister of Labour refused on one occasion to approve the Staff Side's choice. Both the Staff Side and the Official Side nominees are now appointed by the Secretary of State for Employment.

STAFF SIDE DISSATISFACTION

As early as the National Whitley Council meeting of 6 October 1925, W. J. Brown of the Civil Service Clerical Association was complaining that departments were refusing to allow cases to go forward to arbitration. This was discussed by the Chairman, Vice-Chairman and the Secretaries on 5 November, but the Staff Side were not satisfied,

[1] Cab. 24/171, CP 75(25).   [2] NSS 265.12.

and early in the New Year they wrote to the Prime Minister asking for an interview. This was refused but a lengthy interview with the Financial Secretary, R. McNeill, took place on 18 February 1926, at which the particular cases were discussed. The Staff Side remained unplacated. 'We accept the statement that the Arbitration Agreement confers in theory equal rights upon government departments and staff organizations. In practice, however, the latter are heavily handicapped by the fact that a government department can hinder, or even prevent, arbitration proceedings and still impose its will on the service, whereas a staff organization, having exercised its right of veto, has no remedy if the department chooses to enforce its proposals by executive action.'[1] In April they wrote again to the Prime Minister assuring him that they were loath to trouble the House of Commons with the issue, but again he refused to accept a deputation. In a memo. for the Prime Minister, Chancellor of the Exchequer, Financial Secretary and Permanent Secretary to the Treasury, Sir Russell Scott wrote: 'The plain fact about the arbitration scheme is that in the event of differences arising within the scope of the Arbitration Court either side is entitled to take the other side before the Court. The government may frequently find it expedient to submit a disputed case to arbitration before it takes executive action, but there is all the difference in the world between saying this and saying that the government must go first of all to arbitration in such cases. It is a serious matter for the government to accept the judgment of an outside authority responsible to no one but itself in matters affecting national finance. It would be the negation of all government to submit to the view that the executive has no right to take action in the public interest before this outside authority has first of all prescribed what action it should take.'[2]

The Staff Side continued to be restive, and in 1927 set up a sub-committee of the General Purposes Committee to draw up a memo. on arbitration. It collected information about difficulties in arbitration procedure. Its first report was produced in March 1928, complaining of delays in the departments in putting decisions into effect. It suggested that departments should have greater latitude in matters of domestic concern. During the debate on the report, the Confederation argued that the Tribunal should have the power to conciliate as well as arbitrate, and that it should be separated from the Industrial Court. The latter was not advocated by the sub-committee for fear that the government would take the opportunity of withdrawing the agreement again.

The Staff Side expressed their grievances to the Royal Commission on the civil service, 1929–31. It supported the principle of arbitration in the civil service. 'Before dealing with these grounds of complaint we should observe that the state has adopted a liberal policy in agreeing

[1] NSS 265.03 B.   [2] E 16622.

to admit the principle of compulsory arbitration over so wide an area. The acceptance of this principle involves some surrender of control on the part of the state over the remuneration and conditions of service of the majority of non-industrial civil servants. This course, however, has some practical advantages in so far as it avoids parliamentary agitation in connection with the claims of numerous small classes of civil servants.'[1] The Commission accepted the need to re-define a 'class' and agreed that the arbitrable limit should be raised to £1000 a year. But it argued that there was no need to give the Tribunal powers to conciliate because the power was inherent in every tribunal. It also saw no reason to separate the Tribunal from the Industrial Court. The questions of the arbitrable limit, grading, class and conciliation were discussed on Joint Committee C in 1934, and all were remitted to the Joint General Purposes Committee. In June 1935 this Committee appointed a sub-committee and eventually disagreement was registered on the first three and it was agreed not to pursue the fourth.

In 1936, however, the Tribunal was separated from the Industrial Court. Since 1927, when the Industrial Court had issued revised Rules of Procedure for the Tribunal without their consent, the Staff Side had argued that the Court should not have the right to change the Tribunal, which had been set up by a Whitley agreement. By 1936 both Sides were objecting to the President of the Court's insistence on his right to choose for the Tribunal a member of any of the Industrial Court panels rather than from those specifically appointed to deal with civil service claims. Paragraph 2 of the constitution was changed by agreement between the two sides and the Civil Service Arbitration Tribunal was separated from the Industrial Court. The Chairman of the Court, Sir Harold Morris, remained Chairman of the Tribunal until 1942, when the position was taken by Sir David Ross, Vice-Chancellor of Oxford University. Between 1952 and 1968 the Chairman was a barrister, Sir George Honeyman. He was succeeded by an academic, Professor H. A. Clegg, a former member of the Staff Side panel.

Another source of dissatisfaction for the Staff Side has been the arbitrable limit, the level above which grades are not able to go to arbitration to settle their salaries without the consent of both parties concerned in the claim. The first limit was £500, the maximum of the Assistant Principal grade. When the new Tribunal was introduced in 1925, the limit was raised to £700, except for those grades where the minimum of the pay scale was less than £700; this was above the Assistant Principal maximum but ruled out the Principals. In 1939, Principals were included for the first time, when their scale minimum was £800 and the arbitrable limit was raised from £700 to £850. When

[1] *Report of the Royal Commission on the Civil Service, 1929–31*, Cmd. 3909, para. 510.

in 1947 the limits were raised to cover salaries above £1300 a year, or scales with a minimum of £1150 or more and a maximum above £1300 (the Principal scale then being £900 to £1220), the three higher grade associations in the departments (Association of Inspectors of Taxes, Association of Officers of the Ministry of Labour and Customs and Excise Group) objected that these limits did not bring within the scope of arbitration officers whom they regarded as being on a similar level to Principals. After some discussion, the new levels were accepted by the Staff Side along with a written assurance from the Treasury that they would agree to voluntary arbitration about the limit wherever they could, and especially where arbitration for a lower grade would be hampered unless the higher one were also within arbitration. The Staff Side maintained in evidence to The Royal Commission (1953–5) that hopes based on these understandings had not been realized, there having been a number of cases where the Official Side's attitude had seemed to them unreasonable. For this and other reasons the Staff Side felt that permanent and authoritative machinery was needed to provide a readily available form of arbitration on the salaries of the higher grades. The Official Side did not consider that it was appropriate for senior civil servants, who occupied a delicate position as policy advisers to ministers, to have the right to take the government to compulsory arbitration but were in favour of the government having at its disposal in these matters a body of advisers of the highest standing. The Commission recommended the establishment of the Standing Advisory Committee on the Pay of the Higher Civil Service, which was set up in February 1957. It has exercised a general oversight of major questions affecting the remuneration of the higher civil service and advises the government, either on request or on its own initiative, as to what changes are desirable.

PROCEDURE[1]

The agreed procedure of the Tribunal has not greatly changed over the years. When negotiations have broken down, the request for arbitration is made jointly through the Industrial Relations Branch of the Department of Employment. The terms of reference are normally agreed beforehand by the parties but they may, in the event of disagreement, send in separate statements. All cases are treated urgently: the agreement on arbitration provides that under normal conditions a claim should be heard not later than six weeks from the date on which it is remitted to the Tribunal. Each side has a main spokesman and a team of advisers. Where the Official Side is a department the team includes a member of the Treasury. The Staff Side is normally

[1] For a vivid, though self-centred, view of arbitration procedure, see W. J. Brown, 'So Far . . .', 1943, pp. 190–6.

a single association. The National Staff Side has gone to arbitration only twice since the war, over central pay in 1962 and over hours in 1964.

Meetings of the Tribunal are held in public. Each side produces a statement which for many years was read out but is now taken as read. Offers during negotiations which are marked 'without prejudice' must be excluded from the argument unless both parties consent. The spokesman for the claimants (i.e. usually the staff association) draws attention to the main points in their case. The Tribunal, and the other side through the Chairman, may put questions. Then the other side present their case, answer questions and rebut the claimants' case. Either Side may call witnesses, though only the Staff exercises this right in practice. It is customary to inform the other side who is to be called. Witnesses may be questioned by either side, and by the Tribunal itself. The claimants have the right of reply. Proceedings are normally completed in one day. The Tribunal then consider the case in private and the decision is sent to the parties and published by the Stationery Office. No reasons need be given for the award. If the members of the Tribunal disagree the Chairman may make an umpire's award but this is very unusual. Of 590 cases in which awards were handed down between 1925 and 1959, only twenty-five were not unanimous.[1] Although conciliation is not within its terms of reference the Tribunal has very occasionally referred cases back to the parties for further negotiation.

PRIESTLEY AND AFTER

One result of the implementation of the Priestley recommendations, notably the setting up of the Pay Research Unit, was a fall in the number of arbitration cases. During the seven years, 1949–55 inclusive, there were 205 cases: or on average, 29 a year. During the seven years, 1956–62, by contrast, there were only 123 cases, averaging 18 a year. Some arbitration cases cover only a handful of civil servants, whereas others involve numbers running into six figures. To get a true picture, therefore, it is necessary to take into account also the numbers of staff whose pay and conditions came under review during the periods in question.

Nos. Involved	1949–55 (a)	1956–62 (b)	(b) as percentage of (a)
1–1000	125	71	56·8
1001–100,000	72	40	55·5
+100,000	6	4	66·7

It is noteworthy that there was least decline in the 100,000-plus category. To put it another way, the number of civil servants affected

[1] S. J. Frankel, 'Arbitration in the British Civil Service', *Public Administration*, Vol. xxxviii, 1960, p. 199.

by decisions of the Tribunal fell to a lesser extent than did the number of cases.[1] The decline continued in the period, 1963–9 inclusive, when there were 62 cases, or nine a year. But it is difficult to say how far this was due to pay research, and how far it should be attributed to the disenchantment of the staff associations with arbitration as a result of the incomes policies operated by successive governments.

Although the post-Priestley approach to pay settlements has, in the great majority of cases, assisted the two sides to reach agreement, it seems to have had the incidental result, when disagreements do occur, of making them more complicated. Prior to 1956, the written statements of case were on the whole fairly short. Since that date, however, most cases have been associated with pay research, which rarely gives results so clear-cut that they can be applied automatically. Where the two Sides have drawn different inferences from them, and arbitration has ensued, the statements of case and supporting documentation have in some instances been very bulky. The 1967 agreement on pay research and related topics sought to remedy this defect. 'In the event of a disputed claim being referred to arbitration, the period of retrospection from the date of the award which will attach to any increases in pay awarded by the Civil Service Arbitration Tribunal will not exceed six months (as in paragraph 1 of this Agreement) plus six weeks.' This placed the onus on the Side wishing to go to arbitration to streamline the proceedings so far as possible in order to enable the Tribunal to complete its work within the extra six weeks allowed. If the evidence submitted in support of the claim were so bulky and complex that the proceedings dragged on beyond the six weeks limit, the staff affected would lose part of the award retrospectively. An exchange of letters between the two Sides emphasized the importance of speedy arbitration. J. J. S. Shaw (for the Official Side) wrote that 'it should be our joint aim to . . . complete the processes of arbitration within the limits of retrospection laid down in the Agreement'. Leslie Williams confirmed that 'the Staff Side wish to underline the importance of the declaration. . . . The new Agreement will not secure the support of civil servants unless both Sides prove that the intention of the arrangements can be fulfilled.'[2]

THE IMPACT OF INCOMES POLICY

The adoption by the government of an incomes policy in 1961 introduced new difficulties so far as arbitration was concerned. Since the

[1] The number of cases analysed in the table is less than the totals given in the earlier part of the paragraph. This is because the published reports do not in all cases give the numbers of staff covered by the claim.

[2] These quotations are taken from *Whitley Bulletin*, Vol. xlvii, 1967, pp. 22, 37 & 39.

Priestley Report, the government had accepted the principle of fair comparison for settling civil service salaries. Now it enunciated a norm to be observed in the determination of everyone's pay. If the increase indicated by the former principle exceeded that suggested by the latter, what was the government to do? To yield would bring the incomes policy into disrepute. To resist would almost certainly lead to arbitration. And if the Tribunal's award turned out to exceed the government's norm, further problems would arise. Should the government refuse to implement such an award altogether? Or should it stagger the increase to make it accord with the norm? For example, if the norm were 3 per cent per year, an award of 6 per cent, implemented as an increase paid over two years, could be defended on the grounds that it did not infringe the incomes policy.

A Treasury memorandum of 1957 stated official policy on implementing the awards of the Tribunal. 'At the time of the institution of the Board an undertaking to honour the awards was given by the Chancellor of the Exchequer in the following form: "the Treasury were authorized by the Chancellor to sanction without question the awards of the Board, and the Chancellor of the Exchequer agreed to present to the House of Commons, and to be responsible to the House for, estimates based on the awards of the Board." This pledge was renewed by subsequent Chancellors of the Exchequer. It is clear that under it the government was bound to accept the decision of the Board and that it was not open to the Chancellor thereafter to dispute its correctness or to ask the House to reject it. . . . Thus there is no doubt that the 1925 circular means that the government is bound to accept the awards of the Court, subject only to the overriding authority of parliament, as distinct from the government, that it will not itself propose to parliament the rejection of an award once made, and will be responsible to parliament for estimates based on an award.' But was the government bound to do all these things immediately? When the Chancellor informed the Staff Side in 1961 that the operative date of awards would not be arbitrable, mass meetings were organized to protest at this interference with the arbitration machinery. The possibility of holding back an award touched a very sensitive Staff Side nerve. Delay in implementation obviously reduces the amount of cash which eventually finds it ways into workers' pockets. In the extreme case of those close to retirement, it may even mean that they never get the benefit at all.

A test case was not long in coming. In December 1961, the National Staff Side decided to make a claim for a central pay increase for the civil service based on the 5.5 per cent increase in the wages index since the last central pay increase. A few associations, including notably the Union of Post Office Workers, and the Post Office Engineering Union, exempted themselves from this. A joint meeting with the Treasury took place at which the National Staff Side made their claim. On 26 March 1962, the Treasury replied offering 2 per cent if acceptable also by the two postal unions for certain grades of their members, and if the effective date for Pay Research Unit awards in 1961–2 were postponed until 1 January 1963. This decision was taken by the Chancellor of the Exchequer. At their meeting on the same day Committee A rejected this and decided to go to arbitration. The terms of reference were agreed between the two sides: 'That the national rates of pay of all grades of non-industrial civil servants, save those listed at (b) below, should be increased by $5\frac{1}{2}$ per cent with effect from 1 April 1962.'[1] Certain specified grades in the Union of Post Office Workers and one other association were excluded, as were those whose maximum was more than £2418 (i.e. the higher grades), and those who had had settlements since 1 January 1961.

The case was heard on 21 May 1962 before Sir George Honeyman, Chairman, Alderman S. M. Caffyn, Official Side panel, and H. D. Hughes, Staff Side panel. The Official Side team consisted of Treasury officials led by J. J. S. Shaw, and the Staff Side team consisted of the General Secretaries of the major unions led by R. A. Hayward, Secretary-General of the National Staff Side. The Staff Side case was based firmly on fair comparisons as set out by the Priestley Commission, and argued that 'the Official Side are committed to the need for principles of pay that can be applied consistently and to the principle of fair comparison to serve that need'.[2] Evidence was produced to show that since 1955 salaries had been increasing faster than wages and that civil service salaries were lagging behind. The 5.5 per cent claimed was however based on the Ministry of Labour wages index. 'It is the view of the Staff Side that the application of the doctrine of comparability ensures that civil service pay will not move markedly out of line with that outside the service. If as a result of the government incomes policy, the upward movement of wages and salaries is slowed down, it is bound to be reflected in civil service pay by the operation of "fair comparison".'[3]

The Official Side's case was based squarely upon the incomes policy and cost. 'The cost of the claim is £22m. In reply to the claim the Official Side has made an offer of a 2 per cent increase covering the same categories of staff with effect from the same operative date at a cost of £8m. a year. The issue before the Tribunal is therefore solely one of quantum.'[4] What the Tribunal had to consider was the bearing of the incomes policy on civil service pay. The problem in the economy was one of disporportionate increases in money incomes. Negotiated

[1] NSS 130.39.   [2] Ibid.   [3] Ibid.   [4] Ibid.

wage and salary agreements had contributed to this. The Chancellor had said that 2–2½ per cent would be the norm for increases from 1 April 1962, and the Staff Side claim did not qualify as an exception. 'The issue before the Tribunal is therefore quite simply this. Should the Staff Side's claim be settled, as they suggest, on a basis which ignores completely recent events and the need, now generally accepted, for an incomes policy? Or should it be settled, as the Official Side argues, by reference to the interim incomes policy which is essential to the achievement of the government's objective of settling the economy on a firm foundation and of providing for its sound and steady growth?'[1] In the end, the Tribunal split the difference, by deciding 'that the national rates of pay of all grades of non-industrial civil servants covered by the terms of reference shall be increased by 4 per cent with effect from 1 April 1962.'[2]

Basically, the struggle was between the traditional method of settling civil service pay, and the government's incomes policy. As *The Times* put it: 'The Treasury said last night that the government would honour their obligation to pay the increase in full, but they greatly regretted the size of the award, which, they considered, was not consistent with the need to relate pay increases to the rate of increase of total national production. They recognized that the size of the award had been influenced by pay increases in private industry between October 1960, and February 1962, the dates used by the civil servants' unions in their arguments in support of a claim for a 5½ per cent increase. But the government were bound, the Treasury said, to make known their view that the award appeared to have been made with insufficient regard to the requirements of national policy on incomes, in spite of the comprehensive evidence on the economic situation and the national interest which their spokesmen had put before the Tribunal.'[3] In such a situation, what is the duty of an independent Tribunal? H. D. Hughes, the Staff Side panellist who heard the case, has discussed the issue and concluded that 'principles of incomes policy accepted by both parties – the public service associations and the government as employer – can legitimately be taken into account as relevant criteria in determining an award.'[4] But, whatever the Tribunal may decide, 'the government in its "sovereign" capacity, if not as employer, must in the last resort be able to enforce its policies. . . . If a major arbitration award conflicted with government

[1] Ibid.
[2] Civil Service Arbitration Tribunal, case 415, *Certain Grades of Non-Industrial Civil Servants*, 5 June 1962.
[3] *The Times*, 7 June 1962.
[4] H. D. Hughes, 'The Settlement of Disputes in the Public Service', *Public Administration*, Vol. xlvi, 1968, p. 52.

policy, the onus would be on the government to decide whether or not to refer it to the National Board for Prices and Incomes and whether or not to delay or implement it.'[1] In the event, all the Tribunal's awards have in fact been honoured, although the full effect of some of them has been delayed. Some awards, notably that of 1962, have been implemented only at the cost of important government policies.

CONCLUSION

Is it possible to discern any general tendency in arbitration awards? Has the process been, on the whole, favourable to one side or the other? Or have the arbitrators tended to split the difference between claim and offer? S. J. Frankel has analysed 607 cases, covering the period 1925–59, in order to answer such questions as the above. His conclusion was that the Tribunal did not usually split the difference. Sixty-seven per cent of its decisions were 'quite clearly in favour of one side or the other – 43 per cent for the Official Side and 23 per cent for the Staff Side.'[2] Only 33 per cent fell into what Frankel called the 'zone of compromise'. Reflecting on 'the human propensity to be rather more decisive in dealing with small issues than with large ones', Frankel went on to look at the major cases only, i.e. those involving more than 15,000 civil servants each. There were 55 awards in this category, of which 53 per cent were in the 'zone of compromise', as compared with 29 per cent which came down on the Official Side, and 18 per cent on the Staff Side. Frankel sums up by saying: 'all in all, taking both the bare statistics and the qualifying factors in account, a fair generalization would seem to be that the gains and losses on both sides are nearly in balance, with the Official Side enjoying the edge'.[3]

[1] Hughes, pp. 52–3.   [2] Frankel, *loc. cit.*, p. 206.   [3] Ibid. p. 207.

CHAPTER 6

INDUSTRIAL AND POLITICAL ACTION

One of the basic paradoxes of Whitleyism is that, while it was devised for private industry, it has achieved its greatest success in the civil service. Douglas Houghton commented on this point. 'It has proved far more successful in the public sector than in the private sector. And the reason for it is, of course, that if people have in any case almost jettisoned industrial action, strike action, and so forth, as a means of settling their disputes, . . . because of being in the public service, . . . [they] fully utilize all the opportunities of negotiation, of persuasion, of argument, that the Whitley Council system gives. . . . There has been true negotiation in the framework of the Whitley Council in the public sector to a greater extent than outside because neither side . . . has been able to use the big stick.'

The one occasion when the National Staff Side came near to industrial action was the General Strike of 1926. A number of civil service associations, including the Union of Post Office Workers, Post Office Engineering Union and Civil Service Clerical Association, were affiliated to the Trades Union Congress. This had led during the summer of 1923 to correspondence between the civil service correspondent of the *Daily Telegraph* and the Treasury in which the former alleged that the civil service associations were being used by socialists to further the cause of the Third International. The Treasury took this somewhat less seriously but Sir Russell Scott sent a memo. to the Financial Secretary and the Chancellor of the Exchequer warning them that 'several civil service associations are affiliated to the Trades Union Congress and in effect if not formally to the Labour Party' and that 'lobbying in the House of Commons and the badgering of parliamentary candidates have come to be regarded as recognized methods for ventilating and securing the redress of civil service grievances'.[1] In December 1923, the Union of Post Office Workers through its journal *The Post* exhorted its members to vote Labour.

On the first day of the General Strike in May 1926, the Staff Side General Purposes Committee met to consider the steps to be taken. There was evidently no question of calling their members out on strike and virtually all of the 12,640 civil servants who went on strike were

[1] E 11532.

industrials. The following resolutions were adopted, (a) being agreed *nem. con.* with one abstention and (b) being passed by 4 to 2 with one abstaining and one absent on urgent business. This vote reflected a direct clash between the representatives of higher civil servants and the rest of the Staff Side.[1]

(a) That an assurance be sought from the Treasury that during the crisis civil servants would not be called upon to perform any work other than the normal duties of their class or grade; a copy of the letter to be sent to constituent groups and Staff Side secretaries of Departmental Whitley Councils.

(b) That advice be given to all civil servants not to volunteer to perform during the crisis any work other than their normal duties, and to report to the headquarters of their organizations (through the local branches) any attempt to cause them to perform any work outside the normal duties of their class or grade. Pending a further communication however, all civil servants should obey the orders of the competent authority, making protest in the proper form if such orders conflict with the principles stated above.[2]

The Chairman of the National Staff Side, George Middleton, accordingly wrote to the Chairman of the National Whitley Council and to the Departmental Staff Sides. He immediately began to receive critical letters from the latter. The Joint Consultative Committee publicized their opinion that it was the duty of every civil servant to undertake any work during the national emergency. They were invited to attend a meeting of the General Purposes Committee on 10 May where the issue was discussed but no attempt was made to come to a decision. At the end of the year the Joint Consultative Committee left the National Staff Side, because the latter's action over the General Strike made them feel that the Staff Side was dominated by a small number of militant unions who did not pay enough regard to the wishes of the higher grade associations.

Douglas Houghton's recollections confirmed this view. 'What nearly broke up the Staff Side was the General Strike of 1926. That was the most critical period because the General Purposes Committee of the Staff Side met when the General Strike had been declared, and issued a statement regarding the behaviour of civil servants in those circumstances, and said something to the effect that civil servants should do their own job and nobody else's. . . . This was undoubtedly under the influence of the more industrial, particularly Post Office, unions.' One

[1] For previous manifestations of this feeling, see L. D. White, *Whitley Councils in the British Civil Service: a study in concilliation and arbitration*, Chicago, 1933, pp. 42–8 and 113.
[2] NSS GPC, Vol. ii, 3 May 1926.

group which represented the higher grades did not secede however. This was the Institution of Professional Civil Servants, and it remained largely as a result of the personal efforts of its Honorary Secretary, F. A. A. Menzler. Following the departure of the Joint Consultative Committee, the Treasury maintained that on higher grade matters 'effective negotiation with the Staff Side of the National Whitley Council or a Committee of the Staff Side is not practicable for the reason that the Staff Side as now constituted cannot be regarded as sufficiently representative for the purpose'.[1] Nevertheless, the continued adherence of the Institution meant that the Staff Side could still make out a good case to represent the non-industrial civil service generally, and not merely the lower grades thereof.

This was shown when the Joint Consultative Committee sought direct negotiations with the Treasury. It failed to achieve recognition as a body capable of acting on behalf of its constituent associations, although Sir Russell Scott noted that there was no reason why discussions of a general character should not take place, since he regarded the Committee as 'a body which is exceptionally well qualified to take part in such communications'.[2] Subsequently, the Committee applied to the Treasury for a separate Whitley Council for higher grades, but neither that, nor a higher grades committee in conjunction with the Staff Side, was approved, and each association had to negotiate separately. But the Treasury was sympathetic to the higher grades; a memo. by the Official Side secretary ended with the suggestion that 'we might add words to the effect that my Lords would be surprised to learn that civil servants holding high and responsible positions find any real difficulty in securing a sympathetic consideration of any reasonable claims they may have for improvement in the conditions of their employment'.[3]

The Joint Consultative Committee presented the National Staff Side with the greatest challenge to its authority as sole spokesman for the staff on general matters. But all the associations retained the right to negotiate directly with the Treasury or with their department on behalf of the grades they represented as they had been able to do before Whitleyism. In the early years such large groups as the Confederation were thus almost as effective as the Staff Side. But the Confederation broke up in 1939, and the higher grade associations gradually returned to the Staff Side, mainly through amalgamations. The First Division Association, in response to an invitation from the Staff Side, came back in 1947.

THE TRADES DISPUTES ACTS

One of the main results of the General Strike was the Trades Disputes

[1] EG 83/116/01.　　　　　　[2] E 6590.　　　　　　[3] Ibid.

Act of 1927, which sought to cut off the civil service staff associations from the labour movement as a whole. On 14 July 1926, the Cabinet agreed that the Chancellor of the Exchequer should announce such a measure in the House of Commons. The Trades Disputes and Trade Unions Bill required every civil service association to be approved by the Registrar of Friendly Societies before it could be recognized by the Treasury. Membership of associations had to be confined to persons employed by or under the crown. Associations had to be independent of any outside trade union or federation of trade unions. They must not have any political objectives or be associated directly or indirectly with any political organization. The civil service unions immediately set up the Civil Rights Defence Committee to organize opposition to the Bill. It approached MPs and asked them to resist the measure which would 'reduce civil servants to the level of civil serfs'. It passed into law, nonetheless, in 1927.

The Act did not prevent civil servants from striking. 'There is no law which imposes penalties on civil servants who strike.... But... striking, even if not illegal, is a disciplinary offence on the part of a civil servant.'[1] A small number of unofficial strikes have occurred from time to time, but official strikes have been very rare. A few associations, including notably the Union of Post Office Workers, have maintained strike funds.[2] In spite of the Act, a number of associations continued to feel the need for links with organized labour. A retired member of the Staff Side recalled the means that were found to achieve this. 'We were able to retain unofficial contact with the Trades Union Congress and so had the benefit of their advice and assistance informally. . . . We had the best of both worlds really, and we saved our affiliation fees!'

The Act prevented the associations from collecting a political levy, the main purpose of which was to sponsor parliamentary candidates. The Civil Service Clerical Association made a voluntary collection to support their General Secretary, W. J. Brown, when he stood for the House of Commons. The Union of Post Office Workers launched the Direct Parliamentary Representation Society as a means of getting round the ban. It lasted until the repeal of the Trades Disputes Act in 1946. There were civil service MPs before Whitleyism and they have proved very useful over the years in rallying support in the House of Commons for civil service demands. Despite Whitleyism, the associations have found it necessary on a number of occasions to launch a parliamentary campaign. This has usually taken place after it became clear that the Official Side position could not be changed until there had been an alteration in government policy.

[1] H.M. Treasury, *Staff Relations in the Civil Service*, 43, 1965, pp. 19–20.
[2] See also below p. 197.

THE REPEAL OF THE ACT, 1946

Interest in civil rights among the associations remained dormant in the 1930s, although both the Trades Union Congress and the associations sought the repeal of the Act. Civil rights were not discussed by the Tomlin Commission. In 1939 the Prime Minister, Neville Chamberlain, received a deputation from the General Council of the Trades Union Congress, backed by a letter from the National Staff Side, to demand repeal. The Treasury considered the possibility of allowing industrial but not political affiliation but decided against this. They also rejected repeal since they asserted that many of the associations, and a large section of public opinion, approved of the Act. Representations continued to be made and in March 1941, the Prime Minister, now Winston Churchill, called a meeting of Conservative and Labour members of the government with a Liberal as Chairman to 'find out how the question of an alteration to the Trade Disputes Act, 1927, can best be handled so as not to prove a stumbling-block to national unity and the war effort'.[1] In May 1942, the war cabinet weighed up the advantages of an agreed settlement, which would ease the government's relationship with the trade unions in the many different questions that would arise after the war, with the disadvantages of annoying important sections in the House of Commons who felt that the issue had nothing to do with the war effort. It was agreed to ask Sir Walter Citrine, the General Secretary of the Trades Union Congress, to drop the matter for the time being.

In 1943 the Union of Post Office Workers applied for affiliation to the Trades Union Congress. The Treasury issued a warning, which was reproduced in the Post Office Circular, that 'members of the service should realize in advance the position in which they would be placed if an association of which they are members were affiliated to the Trades Union Congress. The effect of the law is as follows. If an association of which established civil servants are members becomes so affiliated, the result follows that the warning contemplated by the Act must be given to every established civil servant who is a member of the association. If, at the end of one month thereafter, that established civil servant has not resigned his membership of the association, he automatically becomes, in the words of the Act, "disqualified for being a member of the civil service". This has the effect that he loses his established position, and that all his accumulated pension rights are forfeited.'[2] It was pointed out to the cabinet that the problems of disqualifying 100,000 members of the Union would be immense. The Union did not, however, go ahead with its plan. The unions mentioned continued to press for industrial if not political affiliation. Ernest Bevin, Minister of Labour and National

[1] E 8641/029/1.
[2] *Post Office Circular*, 18 August 1943. See also *The Economist*, 3 July 1943.

Service, devised a form of amendment which prevented the associations from taking part in the political activities of the Trades Union Congress or from being under an obligation to strike in support of outside unions. This was discussed by the Treasury who felt that the initiative in the matter rested with the Prime Minister. In March 1945, Mr Churchill wrote to Sir Walter Citrine that there was no possibility of amending the Act because of the opposition to it of the majority of Conservative MPs. The Labour Party was pledged to repeal the Act and did so in 1946 immediately after they came to power.

Five associations immediately reaffiliated with the Trades Union Congress and in 1969 thirteen Civil Service associations formed Group 17 of the Trades Union Congress. Both the Society of Civil Servants and the Institution of Professional Civil Servants have considered affiliating to the Trades Union Congress, but decided against it. Only two associations have reaffiliated with the Labour Party, the Union of Post Office Workers in 1946 and the Post Office Engineering Union in 1964.

THE MASTERMAN REPORT

In 1943 a Select Committee of the House of Commons on Offices of Profit under the Crown reported that all civil servants should be disqualified by legislation from being members of the House of Commons. A Committee set up by the National Staff Side found that there was very little interest in civil rights among civil servants. But soon after the Labour Party came to power in 1945 the National Staff Side were given to understand that the question of civil rights was being discussed by a cabinet committee. The National Staff Side met the Treasury on 5 February 1947, and were received by Sir Thomas Padmore. They claimed that the problem was even more pressing now that there were to be more public boards and therefore more people would be affected by the prohibition on parliamentary candidature. They pressed for special leave without pay for a candidate during the election and after it if elected. Anyone wishing to stand for local government should notify their departments so that the latter could intervene if they wished. General reliance should be placed on the Official Secrets Acts and a proper reticence. The discussion was aimed mainly at informing the Official Side of the Staff Side's views.

On 27 March 1947, the Financial Secretary to the Treasury, Glenvil Hall, announced in the House of Commons that he would 'regard as improper any public criticism by a civil servant of policies for which a minister, whether of his own or of some other department, is responsible'. The National Staff Side discussed this and decided on an approach to the Prime Minister, and on 19 February 1948, the Chancellor replied that an independent committee was to be set up to consider the whole question. The *ad hoc* Staff Side Civil Rights Committee were angry at the delay and on their recommendation the National Staff Side wrote to the Chancellor of the Exchequer that they noted with concern that 'the government should deem it necessary, after months of consideration by a cabinet committee, to appoint an independent committee to advise them whether the Labour Party policy of long standing on the civil rights of civil servants should be implemented'.[1] The Committee was set up under the chairmanship of J. C. Masterman, Provost of Worcester College, Oxford. Evidence was duly submitted by the National Staff Side.

The Masterman Report was published in June 1949. It proclaimed the necessity of maintaining the impartiality of civil servants in the eyes of the public. This was 'so important as easily to outweigh any hardship felt by individuals who are deprived of the freedom to propagate political views among their fellow citizens'.[2] They had tried to divide the departments into those whose members could be fairly free politically and those who must be restricted, but had found this impossible. Therefore they drew a horizontal line, freeing completely the industrials and such grades as cleaners and doormen, or postmen and telephonists in the Post Office. They had considered drawing two groups above this line but decided not to because all these grades formed an entity in the public mind. On promotion a civil servant would have to renounce his political activities but these would not necessarily be forgotten, and large numbers of quite junior staff came into contact with the public and had a degree of discretionary power affecting the citizen. An example given at the time was that of the clerk in an employment exchange. If he were a known Conservative, a Labour man applying for a job might allege that he had been discriminated against if turned down. For those above the line the existing rules about parliamentary candidature and such activities as canvassing would be maintained. Before taking part in local politics they would still have to seek the permission of their head of department who should take into account the rank and duties of the applicant, the embarrassment that might be caused to the department and the possible demands on official time. The heads of departments should draw up a list of those departments whose staff must be excluded completely from these arrangements. The government accepted the Report. Its promptitude in doing so evoked comment from the opposition benches. John Boyd-Carpenter referred to the 'astonishing and most incomprehensible fact that the government could

[1] NSS 210.04 C.
[2] *Report of the Committee on the Political Activities of Civil Servants*, Cmd. 7718, para. 48.

commit themselves to acceptance and implementation of these proposals without consulting the Staff Side or the House of Commons'.

ACTION ON THE REPORT

A copy was sent to the National Staff Side who welcomed the liberation of the grades below the line but deplored 'the Committee's appallingly reactionary proposals not merely to maintain but to tighten and add to the existing restrictions on all other grades'.[1] On 2 July, the Staff Side decided to call for a meeting of the National Whitley Council and to ask the Chancellor to defer action on the Report in the meantime.

Before the meeting, Sir Edward Bridges, as Permanent Secretary to the Treasury and Chairman of the Council, circulated a memo. to the Official Side. He pointed out that the attitude to be taken by the Official Side at the meeting of the National Whitley Council on Friday, 22 July, must be governed by the fact that ministers had publicly announced their acceptance of the Masterman Report. In effect, therefore, the Official Side would be able to do little more than report to ministers the views held by the Staff Side, and they could not, and should not, hold out any hopes that the ministers would vary their decision. But it would be proper that, as part of the business of hearing what the Staff Side had to say, the Official Side should seek clarification of any points open to doubt. Some members of the Official Side attended a meeting on 19 July to discuss this, and others were invited to send their opinions to Sir Edward Bridges.

The Council met on 22 July 1949. 'Mr Day said that a vast amount of business had been done on an agreed basis through Whitley machinery since the National Whitley Council last met in 1941. Reciprocal consultation based upon frank co-operation and mutual confidence had produced greatly improved relations and a friendly spirit between the two sides. The informality of proceedings which had grown up during the war had lasted and worked admirably. This informality had, however, the inherent danger that the government and the Official Side might forget the existence of the National Whitley Council and overlook the rights of the Staff Side. The treatment of the problems of communists and fascists had first revealed this risk. Representations made by the Staff and taken away for consideration by the Official Side had received no answer through Whitley channels; instead, the matter had been disposed of by a parliamentary announcement. On the civil rights of civil servants, again, the Staff Side made representations which the Official Side took away in the ordinary Whitley manner for discussion. The peremptory fashion in which the Masterman Committee had been appointed, its terms of reference decided, and its report adopted without

[1] NSS 210.04 D.

consultation with the Staff Side showed that they had relied too much on informality and that the time had come to reassert the rights and responsibilities of the National Whitley Council and the rights of the Staff Side.'[1] The Staff Side resented the imposition of new restrictions on those civil servants above the line. In the past departments had allowed a good deal of freedom which would now be lost. The non-manipulative grades in the Post Office would be for the first time prevented from canvassing. Local government candidates would presumably be prevented from discussing national politics. The codification of conditions under which civil servants could stand for local government would mean new restrictions. Furthermore the line of demarcation was drawn too narrowly. The whole question should be brought back within the Whitley system and settled by negotiation 'not within the limits imposed by the Report, but on merits, more sensibly and more acceptably to the service'.[2]

The Official Side adjourned for a short interval and when they returned the Chairman outlined the circumstances which had led up to the appointment of the Masterman Committee. 'The political activities of civil servants constituted a very difficult and contentious problem and Whitley discussions which had been held had not seemed likely to promise hope of an agreement. Moreover, important issues of public policy were involved which went outside the normal ambit of the National Whitley Council. The government therefore decided to seek the advice of an independent Committee to which the Staff Side had been given full access. As the matter had been remitted to an outside Committee in this way, there would have been difficulty in bringing it back to the National Whitley Council, as this could only result in going over the same ground again, and the government therefore decided in favour of the course – which was not an unusual one – of publishing the Committee's report together with an announcement of their views on it.'[3] He did not intend to answer the Staff Side's detailed points but dealt only with the question of discussing the Report within the Whitley framework. He would however take the Staff Side's views back to ministers. After a short discussion the meeting was adjourned.

After the meeting the Official Side considered the possible action to be taken – either to open negotiations to discover a compromise, which would involve discussing the whole question of the line of demarcation publicly accepted by the government; or to discuss simply the details of promulgating the report. The view was taken that it was 'important to avoid referring to the National Whitley Council as the *appropriate* machinery in this connection. The Official Side do not consider that it is'. It was decided to get the Staff Side to put their case in writing for

[1] NSS 326.01 B 67th meeting p. 2.　　　　　　[2] Ibid. p. 4.
[3] Ibid. p. 5.

submission to ministers, and the government agreed to suspend action on the Report for the time being.

In their statement, the Staff Side were 'constrained to submit' to the inclusion in the area of restriction of grades down to Assistant Principal and its equivalents, but argued that it was not necessary for junior Executive Officer grades to be restricted. The purpose of joint discussions would be to agree on a line at which the two approaches (restricting and liberating) would meet. 'While willing to contemplate a compromise settlement on some such basis as is outlined above, the Staff Side desire to put on record the belief they still hold that in this matter of civil rights the only right principle is freedom exercised with discretion.'[1] Ministers eventually decided that it would be politic to agree to discussions, and this was accepted along with a suggestion originally made by Day that the grades below the line should be freed in time for the election. The government then decided to postpone any action on the Report until after the election.

The Staff Side lobbied every candidate during the election in February 1950, and in April pressed again for a joint committee. The Treasury thought that, as the general political situation was so difficult, the government would not want public discussion of such an issue. A meeting of the Official Side decided in May to reject the idea of a joint committee but to agree to a meeting of the National Whitley Council. This was held on 12 June 1950. The Staff Side reiterated their view that the essential question was how the line should be redrawn. After discussion of the advantages and otherwise of a joint committee, the meeting was adjourned. The Official Side decided at a meeting afterwards to recommend to ministers joint discussions which would not in any way commit the government. The Prime Minister and Chancellor agreed to this.

The first meeting of the joint committee was held on 4 October 1950, and was exploratory. Before the next meeting the Treasury considered the idea of a 'grey' class, a subdivision of the grades above the line, which would be able to be politically active subject to a modified code of reserve. Its members would be able to canvass, hold office in a party political organization, write political articles and speak in public. This was not however brought up at the next joint meeting on 15 November. Departmental views on it were not very favourable. However, it was discussed confidentially with Day and then raised in the committee on 18 January 1951. The Official Side produced a written statement of its proposals which the Staff Side discussed and then commented on at the meeting on 8 April. The Staff Side placed great emphasis on the necessity of maintaining existing rights if they were more liberal than those for the 'grey' class.

[1] NSS 210.04 E.

Very lengthy discussions ensued but by the beginning of 1952 the two Sides had come close enough for a joint report to be drafted. The report contained the Staff Side's proposals for inclusion of grades up to junior Executive Officers and possibly some higher grades within the area of complete freedom; the Official Side had rejected this. It also contained the agreed alternative that there should be three groups: those below the line as recommended by the Masterman Committee (about 650,000); a 'grey' class of typists, clericals, and grades parallel to the junior Executive Officers and Post Office manipulative supervising officers (about 290,000); and the remainder who would not be able to take part in national politics but might seek departmental permission to take part in local politics. Of the 'grey' class, about 185,000 would have an open general licence to take part in all national and local political activities, while the remainder would have to seek departmental permission to do so. About 45,000 would probably get it. The great majority of those who would not were in local offices of the Ministry of Labour, National Insurance, Inland Revenue, and National Assistance Board. The committee was unable to agree on two points: whether junior Executive Officers should be included in the intermediate class, and whether canvassing should be excluded from the activities for which permission was necessary. The Staff Side said yes and the Official Side, no.

The Financial Secretary, John Boyd-Carpenter, and the Chancellor, R. A. Butler, naturally approved the Official Side's stand on these points. But after receiving a deputation from the Staff Side, they were further considered by ministers. They endorsed the Official Side's position in February 1953, and, although there had been a change of government and although ministers were not committed by the discussions, they accepted the Report. It was presented to Parliament in March with an introductory statement by the government which ended: 'The Government are satisfied that the scheme set out in this Paper imposes restrictions on civil servants only where they are necessary if the confidence of the public in the political impartiality of the civil service is not to be impaired. To preserve this confidence political reserve must be maintained not only by those civil servants who work in the spheres where policy is determined: but also by those who work in local offices and deal directly with the individual citizen in relation to his personal circumstances. It is the latter who are "the civil service" to the individual citizen. Under the arrangements now to be introduced the government have no doubt that freedom will be given wherever it can be given without detriment to the interests of the state, and they are confident that these arrangements will commend themselves to public opinion generally as a fair and reasonable solution of a difficult question.'[1]

[1] *Political Activities of Civil Servants*, Cmd. 8783, para. 15.

The National Staff Side had accepted the joint committee report on a personal basis but certain members, notably L. C. White of the Civil Service Clerical Association, feared that when the executive Committees of the associations (who had not been consulted during any of the joint discussions because of their confidential nature) saw the report there might be widespread repudiation. The Staff Side had tried to change the Government's position on the two outstanding points but failed. This led to a number of quite heated discussions on the Staff Side although meanwhile the Establishments Circular putting the provisions of the White Paper into operation was accepted. Finally the Civil Rights Committee was asked to report on the White Paper. It did so at the beginning of 1954 supporting the traditional Staff Side position.

THE RULING ON COMMUNISTS AND FASCISTS, 1948

In 1947 the question of the victimization of a civil servant on political grounds was again brought up on the National Staff Side. Emergency Committee A discussed the details of cases in which there was *prima facie* evidence of victimization and recommended to the Staff Side that they should assert that if nothing more was attributed to a civil servant than membership of the Communist Party there were no grounds for dismissal. This was accepted by the Staff Side. At a joint meeting with the Treasury on 7 May 1947, Sir Albert Day mentioned three specific instances in which at the last moment permission for departmental action had been refused by the Treasury and in each case the person concerned was a member of the Communist Party. Sir Edward Bridges, Permanent Secretary to the Treasury (although not yet Chairman of the National Whitley Council), suggested that it might be possible to establish a central co-ordinating machinery to ensure that when security inquiries about a civil servant were likely to be adverse the lay point of view could be brought in. He realized that this did not answer the Staff Side's immediate question about grounds for dismissal.

Despite pressure from the Staff Side, no answer was sent for nine months, the Treasury giving the reason that the decision was being taken at the highest level. On 8 March 1948, Bridges informed Day that the government's decision was to be announced in the House of Commons at question time, and it was agreed that the reply would be sent simultaneously to the National Staff Side. On 15 March the Prime Minister made the government's policy clear: 'Experience both in this country, and elsewhere, has shown that membership of, and other forms of continuing association with, the Communist Party may involve the acceptance by the individual of a loyalty which in certain circumstances can be . . . inimical to the State. . . . It is not suggested that in matters affecting the security of the state all those who adhere to the Communist Party would allow themselves to forget their primary loyalty to the state. But there is no way of distinguishing such people from those who, if opportunity offered, would be prepared to endanger the security of the state in the interests of another power. The Government has, therefore, reached the conclusion that the only prudent course to adopt is to ensure that no one who is known to be a member of the Communist Party, or to be associated with it in such a way as to raise legitimate doubts about his or her reliability, is employed in connection with work, the nature of which is vital to the security of the state. The same rule will govern the employment of those who are known to be actively associated with Fascist organizations. I should emphasize that this action is being taken solely on security grounds. The state is not concerned with the political views, as such, of its servants, and as far as possible alternative employment on the wide range of non-secret government work will be found for those who are deemed for the reason indicated to be unsuitable for secret work. It may, however, happen that it is impossible to find suitable employment elsewhere in the civil service for individuals with specialist qualifications and in such cases there may be no alternative to refusal of employment or dismissal.'[1]

On 16 March, Committee A discussed this as a matter of urgency and referred it to the National Staff Side. On 25 March, the Staff Side met to discuss a resolution moved by the Institution of Professional Civil Servants: 'That this Staff Side, while supporting all appropriate measures against civil servants who are disloyal to the state, reaffirm its adherence to the principle that all civil servants should be free to join any lawful political party and to associate with persons freely chosen by themselves, regardless of the political views or attachments of such persons. This Staff Side further reaffirm its view that any attempt to penalize a civil servant (for example by transfer, dismissal or refusal to establishment) on account of his or her political views against whom there is neither evidence nor reasonable suspicion of actual or intended disloyalty, is inconsistent with this principle; and that where any charge of actual or intended disloyalty is made against a civil servant the grounds of the charge should be clearly stated to such civil servant and adequate machinery for appeal, with the aid of appropriate staff association representatives if desired, should be provided',[2] and an addendum moved by the Union of Post Office Workers: 'Nevertheless the Staff Side notes with satisfaction that the government intends to take appropriate action to safeguard state secrets, the unauthorized release of which might endanger the security of the state.'

[1] H.C. Debs. ccccxlviii, c. 1703–4.
[2] NSS minutes, Vol. xi, 28 March 1948, on which this paragraph and the next are based.

The Institution of Professional Civil Servants argued that there was no evidence that any civil servant who was a member of the Communist Party had ever betrayed or intended to betray state secrets. The Institution was particularly interested because scientists and technicians could not be transferred as easily as could members of the general classes. Furthermore if these people were dismissed from the service there was reason to believe that pressure would be brought upon firms undertaking government contracts not to employ them. Seconding the motion, the Civil Service Union felt that the government was inserting the thin end of the wedge into the liberty of the people. Soon the procedure would be directed against all kinds of working class organizations. The Alliance moved that the discussion should be deferred, but after objections this was withdrawn for the time being. The Union of Post Office Workers opposed the motion and argued that if it could be shown that membership of the Communist Party was *prima facie* evidence of possible disloyalty, then the government was acting properly. Quoting from a number of documents the General Secretary of the Union of Post Office Workers, Charles Geddes, asserted that loyalty to the Communist Party must mean disloyalty to the state. It was not a question of proved disloyalty because the government were taking preventative measures. L. C. White for the Civil Service Clerical Association opposed the Union of Post Office Workers' addendum and announced that even if the Staff Side agreed to it the Civil Service Clerical Association would carry on the battle with any other sympathetic organization. The Society of Civil Servants were impressed by the fact that the statement on Communists and Fascists had been made by a Labour Prime Minister, and supported the motion although they thought some of the wording was careless. Douglas Houghton for the Alliance again moved the adjournment on the grounds that: 'no one had spoken as a civil servant. . . . Parliament was discussing the subject and it was clear that the civil service must submit itself to the will of parliament, for the community through parliament was entitled to say what sort of a civil service it would employ. There was no question of supporting the government, the civil service must work willingly for any government and it was his belief that it would be better to say nothing than agree to the resolution and the addendum.' A vote was taken on the substantive motion (the motion and the addendum together) and it was carried; twenty for and none against. It was agreed to send it to the press without comment.

While this discussion was going on the issue was being debated in the House of Commons and towards the end of the debate the Prime Minister explained the new arrangements for challenging Communists and Fascists in the service. The case against the civil servant would be supplied to him and he would be given time to study it and to make his reply. This would go before the departmental head who would consider whether action should be taken. If he decided to act, the evidence would then go to the minister who would determine whether there was a *prima facie* case for transferring the man or even for dismissing him. To help the minister to make a final decision on the evidence an advisory board of three was set up. This initially comprised three retired civil servants, but by the end of 1948 a retired staff association official had been appointed to a vacancy, and the constitution of the advisory board has remained the same ever since. Their procedure is to study the whole of the evidence, to examine the civil servant in person and any friends he may call to speak about his character, and then to tender advice to the minister. However, whether he takes their advice or not, the minister is responsible for the decision taken. 'But it is our intention to do this with the greatest possible tenderness for the individual, consistent with the security of the community and . . . the security of the fellow members of the civil service.'[1] The advisory board was still in operation in 1969.

A meeting of Committee A was held on 6 April at which it was decided that Day should write to the Prime Minister about the way in which the National Staff Side had been by-passed in the decision-making on the issue. The Prime Minister should be asked to authorize the Official Side to meet the Staff Side in order to clarify obscurities in the procedure. The Committee then discussed the points that they wanted to raise with the Official Side such as the availability to the civil servant of the whole case against him and his freedom to discuss it with his legal or trade union adviser. The Prime Minister replied to the Staff Side's letter that, on the assumption that no time would be lost, no case would come before the advisory board until the Staff Side had had the opportunity of discussing the procedure with the Official Side.

A joint meeting was held on 22 April 1948 at which the discussions were led by Padmore and Day. The Official Side listened to all the Staff Side's questions and said that most of them would have to be taken away for discussion with ministers. On 5 May, the Treasury replied that the individual concerned should receive the whole case in writing although the sources of evidence should not be revealed, and he would have fourteen days in which to rebut the charges. Where the individual denied the charges or where he expressed such a desire the case would go before the advisory board. He might discuss the case with anyone he wished to, and any supplementary documents supplied to the individual could be shown to his adviser. The Treasury did not agree however that the individual's association should have the right to be consulted as to where he was transferred to although it could make representations. Nor did they agree that the individual could call upon

[1] H.C. Debs. ccccxlviii, c. 3423.

someone to accompany him before the three advisers and to act as his advocate; outsiders might speak for his character but not conduct his defence for him because justice would be best served by keeping the proceedings as informal as possible.[1]

On 7 May, Committee A discussed this letter in detail and decided that representation of the civil servant by his association was of fundamental importance. Day saw Padmore and Winnifrith about this and reported back to the Committee. 'The Official Side told me ... that they had already made the most faithful report to the Prime Minister of our representation on this subject, emphasizing very heavily the importance we attached to it and saying it was their impression that we would be content if trade union representatives alone were conceded without any right, for example, to take a legal adviser. The Prime Minister himself, after consultation with other ministers, had taken the decision conveyed to us in Padmore's letter.'[2] The National Staff Side accordingly wrote to the Prime Minister but he refused to accept their arguments and announced that the three advisers would start hearing cases the following week.

The Staff Side scrutinized the 'purge' closely. In July 1948, they wrote to the Prime Minister about the agreement between the Secretary of State for Air and representatives of his staff which implied that the whole of the headquarters of the Air Ministry was to be secure. This meant that outstations were also in this category and the Staff Side complained that therefore the security operation was no longer limited in its scope. The Prime Minister replied that each minister had the responsibility of deciding how far his department's work should be secure. In October they wrote again to the Prime Minister about cases in which the supporting evidence was not being made available to the individual concerned, and he agreed to receive a deputation. On the morning of the deputation, 3 November, the Staff Side met to agree the line to be taken. They decided not to press the points about trade union representation or the scope of the purge, but simply to criticize the way the purge was being carried out. The Prime Minister's reply was received on 1 December; out of the twenty-two cases which had so far come under the purge procedure there were only four in which supporting evidence could have been supplied but was not; in five other cases it would also have revealed the sources of the evidence. The Secretary-General took up personally the cases of two civil servants who were purged, but while he was working for them one disappeared to Rumania. By May 1949, fifty people had been given notice that they were to be examined, none had been dismissed, three had resigned, twelve were awaiting transfer and nine had not yet replied to the charges.

[1] NSS 210.06 A.
[2] Ibid.

THE RULINGS ON CHARACTER DEFECTS

On 7 January 1952, members of Committee A were invited to meet A. J. D. Winnifrith to receive advance notice of the government's intention to institute further security measures in the whole field of atomic research and in key posts in the rest of the civil service. These were announced in the press the same day. The new procedure was intended to identify those who were temperamentally unfit for secure work because, for instance, they were garrulous or were occasionally the worse for drink and then talked too freely. The questionnaire to be given to such people was released to the National Staff Side under a highly confidential classification so that they could prepare comments on it for a meeting with the Official Side. It was discussed by Committee A and then at two joint meetings with the Treasury and the Ministry of Supply. The questionnaire and the Establishment Circular were agreed.

In November 1955, as a result of the disclosures about Burgess and MacLean a Conference of Privy Councillors was set up by the government to consider security precautions in the public services. The Staff Side in their evidence to the Conference said that their concern was 'to see that the procedure, as it develops from stage to stage, is scrupulously fair to the individual and that his treatment at the end neither is, nor has any appearance of being 'punitive'.[1] They objected to the increasing scope of security operations both in terms of the definition of security risks and in the number of offices declared secret, to the delays in the procedure, to the failure to find transfers for displaced officers, and to the loss of all superannuation rights by those under fifty who were compelled to leave. They again brought up the question of representation by a trade union official.

The Conference reported in March 1956, approving the existing security arrangements but making recommendations to strengthen them. It was important for departments, through the supervising officers, to be aware of the character defects which tended to make a man unreliable or expose him to influence by foreign agents. Communist sympathizers and those living with a Communist spouse might also have to be regarded as security risks. 'The Conference is of the opinion that in deciding these difficult and often borderline cases, it is right to continue the practice of tilting the balance in favour of offering greater protection to the security of the state rather than in the direction of safeguarding the rights of the individual.'[2]

The government accepted the recommendations of the Conference although in the House of Commons' debate on March 21, the Home

[1] NSS 210.06 C.
[2] *Report of the Findings of the Conference of Privy Councillors*, Cmd. 9715, para. 15.

Secretary promised to inform the House when consultations with the Staff Side had taken place. Such consultations had been allowed for in the Report itself; the alterations in procedure 'will be notified to the staff associations concerned and an opportunity given for representations to be made before the alterations are promulgated in full'.[1] Joint meetings were held with the Treasury and the Staff Side obtained some important concessions: it would be exceptional to declare secret a whole department or staff of all grades in a department, departments would be reminded that the individual concerned must be given the evidence against him although not its sources, the limit of promotion for those suspected of being security risks would be Under Secretary although the Official Side made it clear that many of these posts would be excluded. The Staff Side protested at the extension of the new purge to include those sympathetic to communism, arguing that this would give scope to mischief makers. They again pressed for a friend to accompany the civil servant. The Chairman of the National Staff Side, Douglas Houghton, MP, wrote to the Prime Minister about this and received the reply: 'In this examination it is the constant care of the advisers to ensure that no allegation is allowed to pass unchallenged. Equally in their examination of the civil servant, the advisers frame their questions in their knowledge of the evidence, with the aim of giving him every chance to convince them that their suspicions are unfounded. The effect of all this is to make the advisers in a very real sense the "friend" of the individual appearing before them.'[2] Furthermore the friend would increase the security risk involved in the proceedings of the Advisory Board itself.

THE RADCLIFFE REPORT, 1962

In 1962 after the Blake and other spy cases a new Committee was set up under Lord Radcliffe to inquire into the security procedures in the civil service. It approved the advisory board system but pointed out that spies might be recruited for many other reasons than simply because they were Communists. Therefore more care should be taken over office security which they found was in many cases very lax. Access to documents and premises should be regulated. The positive vetting system was generally satisfactory, and they suggested that, where p.v. clearance was refused on a character defect alone and the civil servant's career would be adversely affected, he should be so informed and allowed to raise the matter with the head of his department.

The greatest change which the Committee suggested however was in relation to civil service trade union officials. 'We inquired into the

[1] *Report of the Findings of the Conference of Privy Councillors*, Cmd. 9715, para. 17.　　　　　　　　　　　　　　　　　　　　　[2] NSS 210.06 D.

penetration by Communists of the civil service staff associations and trade unions and were disturbed at the number of Communists and Communist sympathizers who were holding posts in those bodies either as permanent full-time paid officials or as unpaid officers or members of executive committees. We understand that there is no evidence that the Communists have made any exceptional effort to gain control of these unions, but they appear in fact to have achieved a higher degree of penetration here than in almost any other section of the trade union movement. No evidence has been brought to our knowledge that Communist trade union officers, whether serving on a paid or unpaid basis, have been detected in any form of espionage. Nevertheless we regard this presumably deliberate massing of Communist effort in the civil service unions as most dangerous to security, however one defines it.'[1] Therefore any department should have the right, in respect of establishments or staff employed on secret work, to refuse access and to refuse to negotiate with named trade union officials who were suspected of being Communists. Such officials would be challenged under the advisory board procedure.

National Staff Side comments on this were limited to the procedure to be used because the matter was judged to be one for the individual unions rather than the Staff Side as a whole. At the joint meeting with the Treasury on 18 April the implications of this recommendation were discussed. R. A. Hayward, the Secretary-General of the Staff Side, said that very careful handling of the issue was required or else great damage would be done to the Whitley machinery. The Staff Side's view was that trade union officials could not expect different treatment from civil servants in security matters, but a clear line should be drawn between secure and non-secure matters and adequate negotiating facilities must be maintained. They then commented on other points in the report and raised again the questions of superannuation for those who were compelled to leave the service before they were fifty, and the presence of a trade union official during only the early stages of the proceedings before the three advisers. Following consultations with ministers the Treasury wrote to the National Staff Side accepting many of their points but again refusing to change their policy on the last two. The National Staff Side then wrote to the Prime Minister about the presence of a trade union official and sent a copy of their letter to the Leader of the Opposition. At the same time, R. A. Hayward suggested to Sir Norman Brook that this concession would help the negotiations, over which it was amazing that a major dispute had been avoided. On 19 September 1962, the Prime Minister agreed to the presence of a friend during the civil servant's opening statement when there could be no chance of a security leak.

[1] *Security Procedures in the Public Service*, Cmd. 1691, para. 33.

POLITICAL ACTION BY STAFF ASSOCIATIONS

Quite apart from the rights of civil servants to take part in political life as individuals, circumstances may still arise in which their associations wish to exert political pressure. As shown above, this technique was well developed even in the nineteenth century, and one of the main aims of the Whitley scheme was to take civil service staff relations out of politics. 'The Whitley Council scheme was largely acceptable to the government that introduced it because it appeared to offer some hope of removing these controversial civil service issues from the field of political controversy.' According to Sir John Simpson, this aim has been achieved in relation to the great majority of questions: 'where there are matters which can be negotiated and agreed with the Official Side . . . then you don't get demonstrations and protest meetings'. Lord Geddes agreed. 'Meetings . . . you indulge in when you've got to. When you wanted to air a particular grievance, you'd have a mass meeting. Very often you had a mass meeting because it was demanded of you, not because you wanted it, but because the troops insist[ed] upon having it. . . . When I was General Secretary . . . once or twice I decided to erupt. But speaking now, I would say that mass meetings do little or nothing – and Members of Parliament even less!' A member of the Official Side confirmed these views. 'The joint effect of Whitleyism and compulsory arbitration has meant that, by and large, on the general run of civil service affairs, there has been no need, and it isn't . . . as effective to agitate in the House, as to agitate through Whitley channels which can lead to arbitration.'

Two of the respondents quoted in the paragraph above made the same exception to their general rule. This was superannuation. Since this field is regulated by Acts of Parliament, in marked contrast to other conditions under which civil servants work, political action may be justified. 'If it's something that even the Treasury has no complete authority [over, e.g.] . . . if there was a need to press for some big change in pensions, you'd have to do that by some form of demonstration, because the . . . final authority is parliament itself.' 'The exception here may be superannuation, which is of course always done by legislation and not by arbitration.' The legislation of 1948 and its aftermath illustrates this point. In 1947 a Joint Superannuation Committee was set up to deal mainly with pensions for widows and orphans. Negotiations were carried on in the committee and also in discussions between Treasury officials and Staff Side leaders, among whom Sir Albert Day was particularly involved. These informal discussions were supervised by the Staff Side of the Superannuation Committee and all developments were reported to the full National Staff Side. The resulting Widows, Orphans and Dependents Scheme was embodied in an Act of Parliament in 1948. The new benefits were provided through a reduction in the lump sum payable on retirement or through special contributions. Years of pensionable service were increased to forty-five for those who had reached the minimum retirement age of sixty and who had completed forty years of service. The *Whitley Bulletin* hailed the measure as 'a truly joint effort. . . . On no other major issue have the two sides collaborated so closely and so effectively in the true Whitley spirit.'[1] But, as in most negotiations, the Staff Side had had to give up some of its claims, and certain of the associations were disgruntled. They favoured political action, but Day deprecated their attitude. 'When you get into this immensely favourable negotiating situation . . . and if that elaborate system of machinery, behind which there's so much goodwill on both sides, doesn't in the end give you the right answer, never mind, keep it in the family. . . . When . . . we reached a major superannuation reform agreement and the report, which contained an immense amount of value to the . . . staff, . . . contained [also] a number of refusals of claims for which, in my view, there was not quite adequate justification, . . . some of the constitutents of the Staff Side . . . went political campaigning. I couldn't do anything to stop them. . . . But I deplored it all the same. They'd had their run, and they ought to have called it a drawn battle.'

The incomes policy raised much the same problem for the Staff Side 'We do get this problem occasionally of the extra-Whitley affair, where . . . the problem arises of whether we go campaigning or not, and of course, the incomes policy raised this . . . to some extent. It's a moot question whether when you've had a rejection on incomes policy grounds you've had the sort of fair refusal you were talking about. . . . Maybe one accepts it because one accepts the general background situation. But at the moment we are facing, or have been facing anyway, demands for campaigning, because the Chancellor has insisted on staging some of the pay increases. And although we've taken three deputations to him – which is . . . exhausting ourselves as well as all the normal channels – we haven't been able to make progress. So the question now arises . . . as with equal pay . . . do we campaign? I don't think we will actually. I think we'll probably let it rest.'

Since, however, campaigning may still become necessary, the need for political allies remains. This is accepted by the Official Side. 'Political lobbying is surely inherent in a democratic system. . . . The civil service unions were quite good on that. . . . They didn't try and exercise political pressure on matters like promotions and things like that.' Links between the Council and Parliament may take several forms. Firstly, there have from time to time been members of the Staff Side who also sat in the House of Commons: for example, W. J. Brown and Douglas Houghton. 'I think it was probably a great help in some ways to have on

[1] *Whitley Bulletin*, Vol. xxviii, 1948, p. 188.

the Staff Side people who, if the need arose, could raise their voices in the House of Commons. For example, I think it must have been in the minds of the Official Side when they were discussing things with the Staff Side that, if they were unreasonable, or unwilling to give serious consideration to proposals, there was always the danger that these ... chaps would raise the matter in the House. ... I think there's everything to be said in favour of one or two people who are on the Staff Side also being Members of the House.'

Secondly, it has long been the practice for staff associations, like other trade unions, to sponsor candidates at parliamentary elections. In the great majority of cases, they have sat as members of the Labour Party. This practice has gradually lost favour in the eyes of trade unionists generally, and the proportion of sponsored MPs in the parliamentary party has declined greatly since Labour's early days. Staff Side respondents pointed out some of the limitations of civil service MPs. In the first place, there was an inevitable conflict of loyalties between their constituencies and the sponsoring associations. 'When you become an MP, you've got to represent your constituency. ... In the Commons you can't get up when you like, you've got to catch the Speaker's eye. And you do that normally by going along to the Speaker's secretary, and saying, "Well, look, the debate next Wednesday week is one that absolutely vitally affects my constituency of Little Slocumbe. Could you see if the Speaker would call me?" ... Now the week after that, a debate on civil service pay comes up. Your members expect you to speak on it and you go along to the Speaker's secretary, and he says, "Now come on, make up your mind whether it's Little Slocumbe or the civil service. You can't have it all ways. Only nine of you could get up when you wanted to get up for Little Slocumbe and you were one of them. Now there are forty-one who want to get up on the civil service. You want to be one of them again." '

Moreover, sponsored Members are difficult to control. 'I suppose they were useful in putting questions, but if you ask me whether they had much more use than other MPs, the answer was no. They couldn't be relied upon except to put their own personal point of view. ... If I went to [W. J.] Brown to put a question my way round, there was no hope of it being put. ... It would be put Bill Brown's round, and when I wanted a question put in parliament, I didn't go to a civil service MP. I went to some other MP.'[1] Similarly, it was possible to approach ministers through MPs. But some staff association leaders preferred the direct approach. 'Members of Parliament can write letters to the Postmaster General. They can go and see the Postmaster General and put things to

---

[1] Brown's assessment of his own character is consistent with this account. 'Anyone who has ever tried to amend a document or resolution of mine will testify that I never surrender anything but the trimmings!', he wrote: see Brown, p. 53.

him. [But] I doubt very much whether they have anything like as much standing as the General Secretary of the Union going and saying the same things and putting the same things.'

The third way in which the Staff Side found parliamentary allies was by building up a panel of sympathetic MPs in ways similar to those used by interest groups in general. 'I would have thought it was still desirable to encourage some Members of the House to take an interest in the civil service, so that you always had a spokesman there whenever the occasion arose. This, I think, is true of almost every collective activity. My final job, before I retired completely, was chairman of [a trade] federation. You see, . . . I've gone from one side to the other! And even there we felt it necessary to have a dozen MPs who knew something about [our product], not because . . . anything was going to happen, but it was [desirable] . . . to have informed people there, and people to whom we could communicate and say, "Look, here's a brief on this thing that's coming up." ' There was safety in numbers; such a panel could be bigger than the number of sponsored MPs any association could afford. Hence if it was impossible for any one Member to act, another could always be approached. Moreover, while sponsored MPs have almost always adhered to the Labour Party, a panel of the type suggested could be drawn from all parties. 'I would have thought that, without asking them to be very active, it would be a good thing to cultivate a few Members of the House, on both sides if possible.'

Such a strategy was not only desirable, but also practicable. The National Staff Side has found it easier in recent years to gain the ear of MPs than associations could in former times. When asked whether Whitleyism had done away with the need for parliamentary allies, one respondent replied, 'Not a bit! Quite the contrary, I would have thought. The strength of Whitley lies in the fact that it can speak with a unanimous voice. . . . If the Civil Service Association of the old days wanted a meeting in the House, everybody said, "oh yes, we'll go and listen to them, but this is a rabble group". . . . But if you say, "The National Whitley Council Staff Side wants to meet Members of the House in a committee room", you get a sympathetic hearing.' This indicates the approach that has become standard. 'If approaches have to be made to Members of Parliament, there is everything to be said for going quite impartially to representatives of the various parties and indeed, during the Hayward regime, I can say positively that that was done. . . . Hayward went to the so-called civil service MPs and took them into his confidence, and sought their guidance and help, but he didn't restrict himself to those individuals. He took the view, which I share very strongly, that if one goes to the House, one shouldn't be dependent on the help and viewpoint of people with a specific civil service background. It can be helpful in some contexts, but on the whole it's better to cast your net wider.'

CHAPTER 7

WOMEN: THE FIGHT FOR EQUALITY

The MacDonnell Commission reported in 1914 that the Post Office was the largest employer of female labour in the civil service with about three thousand women in its clerical departments. They were recruited by open competitive examination but worked in separate divisions from the men and were paid on different scales. A few women clerks were employed in other government departments, 'particularly in the new labour exchanges and in the National Health Insurance Commission, but in many departments there was no definite system for recruiting the women. This was true also of the women typists who were employed in about half the public departments. About one thousand women were employed by the state to care for sick persons and prisoners; they served under the same conditions as men, apart from their salary and the marriage bar. A further one thousand were involved in domestic service. There were only a very limited number of higher grade posts open to women. There were about two hundred women inspectors employed in a number of departments including the Education Department and the National Health Insurance Commissioners and working under the same conditions as men, apart from their salary and the marriage bar. Finally there were a number of special positions for women, for instance those at the Board of Trade who investigated conditions of female industrial workers.

The Commission argued that the recruitment of women, like that of men, should be governed solely by the needs of the state. They could not accept that the difference of sex should be ignored because 'evidence shows that in the power of sustained work, in the continuity of service, and in adaptability to varying service conditions, the advantage lies with men'. The marriage bar should continue for, although the service thus 'loses the value of a woman's prior training, the majority of us regard it as essential to maintain the existing rule intact, and apart from considerations as to the welfare of the family (and these must not be ignored), believe that the responsibilities of married life are normally incompatible with the devotion of a woman's whole-time and unimpaired energy to the public service'. However, on equal pay the majority of the Commission believed that 'in so far as the character and conditions of work performed by women in the civil service approximate to industry with the character and conditions of work performed by men, the pay of women should approximate to equality with men'.[1] But the evidence was that women were not as efficient as men; for instance, many married and left the service before they were fully effective. Therefore men should be paid more.

Having established this principle, they found that actual differences in salary did not conform to it; for example highly qualified women inspectors received only half of the equivalent man's salary. The Treasury was recommended to institute a general inquiry to remove those inequalities not based on differences in efficiency. This was the majority report; a minority of the Commissioners felt that because of their lower output and their lack of family responsibilities women should always be paid less than men. Because of the war no action was taken on the Report.

EQUAL PAY AND THE MARRIAGE BAR

During the First World War, there was a great influx of women into the service, and during the first two decades of Whitleyism, it was one of the most important careers open to women. To be more precise, it was one of the most important careers open to single women. Female civil servants still had to resign their posts on marriage. Their main demand was for equal pay. 'It was, of course, a spinster's world,' as Douglas Houghton pointed out, 'emerging . . . from the war with wholesale slaughter of men. Indeed . . . the women's movement in the civil service was . . . a movement of those women who had to find their own way in life because all the men had gone. . . . That's why equal pay, equal opportunity, and things of that kind, were fought probably earlier and more effectively in the civil service than anywhere else.' Women civil servants showed relatively little interest in the removal of the marriage bar. For many of them, the bar to marriage lay not in Treasury regulations but in War Office records. The husbands they might have married had died in battle. It could even be argued that the exclusion of married women improved the career chances of spinsters. This helps to explain 'where . . . there was considerable opposition to the removal of the marriage bar' among women civil servants themselves.

One married woman member of the Official Side argued with some force that the removal of the marriage bar was a more important step towards equality than the achievement of equal pay. But there was little support for this view. The general feeling was that 'the marriage bar . . .

[1] *Royal Commission on the Civil Service, Fourth Report*, Cmd. 7338, paras. 19, 20 and 21.

was crumbling of its own volition'. One of the first women to enter the administrative class was told by a colleague: 'An attractive young girl like you shouldn't be in this. You'll be getting married and then what will happen to you?' She replied, 'Well, I just shan't bother with the ceremony, as I should prefer to go on with the job'. That was in the twenties: by the period of the Second World War, the process of crumbling had gone even further. 'When I was in the Treasury, I knew that somebody, who obviously should remain nameless, a very competent . . . girl, was in fact living with somebody to whom I knew she would like to be married. I can remember then going to her, and having her out to lunch and saying to her, "You know it's your business, but you can get married if you like, and we'll of course say O.K." . . . It was crumbling, and it was bound to crumble, and women would do what they wanted to do, because . . . no one could force you to get married if you chose to get along without [the ceremony], although I know, of course, it has its social inconveniences and difficulties!'

THE REORGANIZATION REPORT AND EXTRA-WHITLEY ACTIVITY

Pressure continued during the war for a recognition of women's rights throughout society. In 1918 women over thirty were granted the vote. In 1919 the Sex Disqualification (Removal) Act provided that a person could not be disqualified by sex or marriage from exercising any public function or from being appointed to any public office. But regulations were to be made, under the Act, for the method of admission of women to the civil service, and for the reservation for men of any posts in the civil service overseas. An Order in Council was made on 22 July 1920, to give effect to this, and regulations were issued by the Treasury in August 1921, stating categorically that all women civil servants should be unmarried or widows unless an exception was allowed in the interests of the service.

On 20 February 1920, the Joint Reorganization Committee of the National Whitley Council produced their first report. Before going on to the main body of their recommendations they discussed specifically the recruitment and status of women in the civil service proclaiming that 'it has been our earnest endeavour, while realizing that we are working in a field of strictly limited experience, to ensure that the opportunities afforded to women of proving their fitness to discharge the higher administrative duties of the civil service shall be full and liberal'.[1] They agreed that within the parallel classes of the civil service women should have a status and authority identical with that of men.

[1] *Report of the Joint Committee on the Organisation etc., of the Civil Service, 1920*, para. 8.

During the experimental period there should be separate establishment lists but departments should ensure that women were available for the same work as men and that they were given opportunities of proving their administrative capacity. The Staff Side of the Committee accepted the Official Side's suggestion that women candidates should be selected by Boards rather than by competitive examination but only on the condition that the question should be reviewed by the National Whitley Council within five years. In the case of the Clerical Class the Committee agreed that they were 'no longer in the experimental sphere. Experience has established that women are fully capable of discharging the clerical work of the civil service.'[1] They should be recruited by a written examination of the same standard as, but separate from, the one for men because of the higher age limit for girls and the separate seniority list. Women's pay in each class should be the same as men's at the minimum with the same increments up to a point; the women's maximum was lower than the men's.

The Report was considered by the Cabinet on 22 March 1920. Attention was drawn to the fact that it did not go very far in the question of equal pay for equal work. It was pointed out however that this would cost £6m and would have repercussions outside the civil service. The Cabinet also noted that the women's colleges were disappointed that women were to be recruited by Boards, not examination.[2] Nevertheless, the Report was approved. When it was discussed on the National Staff Side however the women's organizations objected violently to the section on the employment of women, and the Federation of Women Civil Servants withdrew from the Alliance, thus losing its seat on the Staff Side.[3]

On 19 May 1920, the House of Commons passed a resolution 'that it is expedient that women should have equal opportunity of employment with men in all branches of the civil service within the United Kingdom and under all local authorities, providing that the claims of ex-servicemen are first of all considered, and should also receive equal pay.' The only person to speak against the motion was the Financial Secretary to the Treasury (Stanley Baldwin) and it was carried without a division. The government refused to accept it on the grounds that the Reorganization Committee's Report was changing the situation already they would however be prepared to review the situation within the next five years.

On 5 August 1921, a second resolution was passed approving the temporary regulations for women's employment in the civil service provided that, after three years, women should be subject to the same

---

[1] Ibid. para. 11.   [2] Cab. 23/20 15/20 (6).
[3] B. V. Humphreys, *Clerical Unions in the Civil Service*, Oxford, 1958, p. 154.

conditions of entry and of service as men. However 'having regard to the present financial position of the country, this House cannot commit itself to the increase in civil service salaries involved in the payment of women in all cases at the same rate as men; but . . . the question of remuneration of women as compared with men shall be reviewed within a period not exceeding three years.'

Dame Maude Lawrence, Director of Women's Establishments at the Treasury and a member of the National Whitley Council, remarked in a memo. that it was 'curious that the women's organizations do not see that their so-called "victory" was a defeat all along the line for the extremists for there was no real interchangeability of posts with men, the problem of equal pay was shelved and the marriage bar retained'.[1]

Despite pressure from the National Staff Side the promised review of women's employment was never allowed to take place on the grounds that the poor financial state of the country did not allow the expenditure involved in implementing equal pay. In 1923, the Anderson Committee, set up to inquire into the cost of the public services, recommended that the pay of state servants should be governed by the laws of the market. There should be equal pay for equal value. As her chances of marriage decreased, a women's value to her employer increased. In the long term, as women became better at their work the demand for them would increase, and so therefore would their pay until equality of pay was achieved. The Committee even went so far as to envisage a time when it would be cheaper to employ men.

At the National Whitley Council meeting on 28 March 1924, the Vice-chairman moved that a joint committee should be set up to re-consider the position of women in the civil service with reference to the provisions in the Reorganization Report and in the resolutions in the House of Commons that there should be a review in three to five years. The Official Side replied that they could only convey the proposal to the right quarter. The motion was raised again at the next Council meeting on 21 November 1924, but amended so that there was no reference to the Reorganization Committee or to the House of Commons resolutions, and equal pay was excluded. W. J. Brown of the Civil Service Clerical Association argued that this still left some important issues such as segregation and aggregation to be discussed, but again the Official Side took the matter back for further consideration. Discussion continued at the following meeting on 27 March 1925, when the Official Side said that they were strongly of the view that no advantage would be gained by appointing a committee. The right course was to let the matter be dealt with by the Departmental Whitley Councils. The Staff Side were not satisfied and said that they would bring the matter up again, which they did but without success.

[1] E 3754/01/1.

After the Council meeting of 21 November 1925, it was however clear to the associations that no progress could be made on the issue through the Whitley system. On 27 November 1924, an informal conference of two representatives from each interested association decided that the matter could not be left in its present indefinite and unsatisfactory state, and set up a committee to consider the best method of securing equal pay in the civil service. On the basis of a memo. produced by W. J. Brown, it was agreed that pressure should be exerted on Members of Parliament to secure a select committee. The committee contacted MPs and encouraged individual members of the associations to do so, but very little was achieved. By January 1926, the Civil Service Clerical Association were dissatisfied with the organization of the campaign which they claimed was solely in the hands of the Executive Officers' Association and the Women's Federation. The campaign continued for a number of years but with less vigour. Equal pay became part of the National Staff Side's All-Service Programme in 1926 but action was then suspended pending the report of the Royal Commission.

THE ROYAL COMMISSION, 1929–31

The Tomlin Commission reported in 1931, recommending the policy towards the employment of women of 'a fair field and no favour'. As far as possible all posts should be open to both men and women although it was agreed that in some fields it was not practicable or desirable to do this. In their evidence to the Commission the National Staff Side favoured the retention of the marriage bar. Its abolition was advocated only by the Institution of Professional Civil Servants, Board of Education Inspectors Association (Women), the Council of Women Civil Servants (Higher Grades), the Association of Officers of Taxes and the Federation of Women Civil Servants – all higher grade associations with relatively small memberships. No Official Side witnesses favoured the removal of the bar. The Commission considered the arguments for and against the bar, and the practice of outside employers, and decided that the 1921 Regulations should be changed so that exceptions to the bar were allowable where a woman had special qualifications or special experience. The National Staff Side's evidence in favour of equal pay was based mainly on its approval by the House of Commons, and the innate justice of the claim; the Official Side opposition was based on the cost, now estimated at £3m. per annum. The members of the Commission were divided on the issue and only able to present the arguments for and against it.

In 1934 a Joint Committee on Women's Questions was set up to discuss the Commission's recommendations. The Committee agreed with the principle of a fair field and no favour, which, they said, should involve the opening up of all posts in the service to members of both sexes except where adequate and publicly announced reasons existed to the contrary. Aggregation of posts should begin immediately. It wanted the exceptions to the marriage bar principle to be more specific, including for instance the possibility of retention when the husband was physically incapacitated. No agreement was reached over equal pay, the Staff Side recording their opinion that 'equal pay as between men and women employed in the same class or grade is the logical accompaniment of "a fair field and no favour" and of aggregation'.[1]

THE 1935 CAMPAIGN

During 1933 and 1934 several groups interested in women's rights, including the National Association of Women Civil Servants and the Council of Women Civil Servants, were organizing a campaign for the right of the married women to work and for equal pay. The National Staff Side wanted to be part of it but insisted that they should be recognized as the sole representatives of the civil service. A long correspondence ensued with the National Association of Women Civil Servants, to get them to call off their action in favour of pressure for negotiation on a joint committee. In November 1934, a Staff Side committee discussed the issue and reported to the National Staff Side that 'in view of the known attitude of the government no useful purpose would be served by trying to reopen negotiations on this question with the Official Side and the matter should, therefore, be pursued through other channels'.[2]

The campaign, which was directed by a National Staff Side committee, was concerned with obtaining the maximum press and parliamentary publicity. Much material was supplied to MPs and they were frequently asked to take up the issue of equal pay if they were successful in the ballot for private Members' motions. Early in 1935, Ellen Wilkinson, MP for Jarrow, informed the committee that she had been successful in the ballot for a debate on the Estimates and that she would propose their motion. The debate would take place on 1 April. A mass meeting was held in London in March and letters were sent to MPs asking them to support the motion. Speeches in the debate were largely favourable and, although the government put the Whips on, the motion was carried by 156 to 148. But on the substantive motion immediately afterwards this decision was reversed. On 6 April, the Prime Minister, Stanley Baldwin, made a statement on the government's policy on equal pay. 'What we have to consider today is whether or not this is the time to make another very considerable advance, placing the civil service still further ahead of the current practice in the country as a

[1] WC 5/79.　　　　　[2] NSS Equal Pay, 1935, Campaign Box 1, File 1.

whole. Probably every Member of the House, certainly anyone who knows anything about it, is justifiably proud of our civil service, but I do not feel that we should be acting wisely in the long run if we were to attempt to establish for the service as a whole, or for any parts of it, whether divided by sex or otherwise, conditions much more favourable than those obtaining in the country as a whole, so as to call for criticism on the part of the general public.'[1] The National Staff Side passed a resolution regretting the government's refusal to implement the House of Commons' decision and sent it to the Prime Minister and to MPs.

In October 1936, the Treasury refused to allow the Institution of Professional Civil Servants to take to arbitration a claim for equal pay for women in the Scientific Departments of the National Physical Laboratory, the Admiralty and the Air Ministry, who had previously received the same as men. In 1937, a joint committee was set up to review the application of the Committee on Women's Questions. The Staff Side consisted of nine representatives from the National Staff Side and two from both the National Association of Women Civil Servants and from the Council of Women Civil Servants. The Committee agreed that where men and women were recruited together and where they had common conditions of service the maximum of the women's scale should be not less than 80 per cent of the men's, and the differential in any case should not exceed £175. This was explicitly without prejudice to the National Staff Side's belief in the principle of equal pay. The campaign continued but it was clear that its object could no longer be parliamentary action alone.

END OF THE MARRIAGE BAR

The widespread employment of women, and particularly of married women, during the Second World War, increased public interest in the marriage bar issue. The Treasury obtained the views of the departments in April 1945, and, having sounded the National Staff Side, formally proposed that a joint committee be set up to 'examine the working of the marriage bar in the civil service, and the arguments for and against its retention; and to consider and report upon the implications of the removal of the bar'.[2] Only three formal meetings were held; the last one in February 1936, to discuss and approve the draft report. This simply presented the history of the marriage bar and the arguments for and against it. It revealed that between 1934 and 1945 only 28 women had been retained on marriage. The committee could make no recommendations because the Staff Side was unable to agree to the abolition of the bar. The National Staff Side itself was divided on the issue as its evidence to the Committee shows (see Table 1).[3] The decision to

[1] H.C. Debs. cccx, c. 2448.   [2] WC 5/79/01.   [3] WC 5/79/02,

abolish the marriage bar was taken by the Cabinet in 1946. A meeting of the Official Side decided that there should be no retrospection.

TABLE I

In favour of retention	Decision taken	Total member-ship	Women members
Union of Post Office Workers	May 1944	147,000	51,000
Federation of P.O. Supervising Officers	May 1944	12,680	3,670
Inland Revenue Staff Federation	June 1945	27,000	14,800
Ministry of Labour Staff Association	April 1945	18,000	unknown
Association of Officers of the Ministry of Labour	June 1945	3,360	770
County Court Officers' Association	Nov. 1944	1,200	250
Abolition in toto			
C.S. Clerical Association	March 1944	142,400	94,400
Society of Civil Servants	May 1942	20,000	6,000
Abolition wholly or in part			
Institution of Professional Civil Servants	1919	31,000	unknown
Association of Inspectors of Taxes	May 1940	1,680	24
Undeclared			
P.O. Engineering Union		45,900	3,800
Federation of C.S. Professional and Technical Staffs		12,900	1,020
C.S. Union		10,500	3,500
Customs and Excise Group		5,000	none

THE ACHIEVEMENT OF EQUAL PAY

Equal pay, like the marriage bar, took on a new importance, as a result of the increased proportion of women in the labour force during the Second World War. In 1944, W. J. Brown, now once more in the House of Commons, introduced a motion in favour of equal pay which was signed by a large number of Members. In October 1944, the government announced a Royal Commission on Equal Pay.

In June 1946, the National Staff Side joined a committee on interested associations including the British Medical Association, the National Association of Local Government Officers, the National Federation of Professional Workers, the Medical Women's Federation, the National Union of Teachers, and the Educational Institute of Scotland to get the Royal Commission on equal pay to speed up their report and then to co-ordinate action on it. The Report was published in October 1946. It was extremely non-committal but did contain the admission that over a wide field within the civil service men and women were doing equal jobs and therefore the conditions existed for the application of equal pay. In February 1947, Sir Albert Day led a National Staff Side deputation to the Chancellor of the Exchequer, Hugh Dalton, and heard him condemn the report as 'a very poor report from the point of view of anybody who is deeply interested in the subject. I think it is long-winded, niggling, and partly no doubt handicapped by its terms of reference.'[1] In June, Dalton accepted the principle of equal pay on behalf of the government but said that it could not be applied at the moment because of the cost at a time when the government was expanding the social services.

The Joint Equal Pay Committee (the committee formed by the BMA etc.) and the Staff Side met to decide what action to take. In December 1947 the Staff Side wrote to the new Chancellor, Sir Stafford Cripps, suggesting that equal pay should be introduced over a twelve- to eighteen-year period through the entry of women at the women's minimum but their progression by men's increments to the men's maximum. This was followed by a deputation to the Chancellor in February 1948, when he praised the scheme but said that it was impossible to implement it because of the White Paper which was aimed at holding back expenditure. Some leaders of the campaign objected to the idea of equal pay by instalments. If the claim was just, they felt, it should be conceded immediately. Sir Albert Day disagreed. 'In many quarters there was an unqualified demand for equal pay at once. I took the view that that was just madness. To incur the immediate full cost of equal pay would be unthinkable for any government. And the best thing was to go for the first sixpence. In other words, get an instalment plan. . . . Many members of the Staff Side agreed with me, but we had some difficulty in maintaining that position against women's organizations, in particular, who were out-and-outers. I wouldn't have minded being an out-and-outer, if I'd thought it would do any good.' He was, however, very worried that the National Staff Side would be hampered in the future by having offered such an accommodating scheme, and he was not greatly reassured by Sir Stafford Cripps's assertion that he was anxious to see equal pay introduced, if possible in the life of that parliament.

Committee A, which had since the war been responsible for action on equal pay, determined to keep the issue before the government. In parliament the issue was discussed during the debate on the Address in November 1950. In January 1951, Day led a deputation to the new Chancellor, Hugh Gaitskell, to be told that although the economic situation had improved, rearmament left no spare resources for equal pay. The Chancellor's reasoned reply to this deputation was not received until 20 June, and coincided with his statement in the House of Commons. He said that the introduction of equal pay in the civil service would be the signal to the rest of the community to press for

[1] NSS Equal Pay, 1935, Campaign Box 4, File 7.

equal pay even where women were employed on purely women's work. The result would be inflation. On 18 July, a mass meeting of civil servants protested against the government's refusal to meet the women's claim, rejected the government's arguments and pledged support for the National Staff Side. Many of those at the meeting went on to the House of Commons to lobby their MPs. In August an Equal Pay Co-ordinating Committee was set up to initiate and co-ordinate propaganda activity. It organized a series of mass meetings in the major provincial centres which were designed to create and retain support for equal pay, and to obtain publicity. In the House of Commons a motion put down by Douglas Houghton MP, was signed by fifty Labour MPs, seventeen Conservatives and eight Liberals. When the new parliament opened in the autumn of 1951, he put down a new motion.

The Conservative Government, like the Labour one, was committed to the principle of equal pay and the National Staff Side speedily secured a meeting with the Chancellor, R. A. Butler. He assured them that he would introduce equal pay as soon as the economic situation improved, but in a letter in January 1952, he explained that the economy was in a worse state than he had expected and that equal pay was out of the question at present because of its inflationary impact. Furthermore he intimated that it probably could not be introduced in the life of that parliament. In May, equal pay was discussed in the House of Commons and approved without a division; this was supported by a mass meeting organized by the National Staff Side in conjunction with the National Federation of Professional Workers, National Association of Local Government Officers, National Union of Teachers, and the London County Council Staffs Association. As from 1 July 1952, London County Council staff were granted equal pay. In September the National Staff Side saw the Chancellor again; he rejected the introduction of equal pay at the moment but agreed that there could be joint discussions on the possible schemes. The first joint meeting took place a fortnight later at which Sir Thomas Padmore said that the Chancellor 'had conceived the talks rather as providing an opportunity for "experts" on both sides of the National Council to get together and to submit to him privately a scheme or schemes for consideration'.[1] A long discussion ensued on the extent to which the talks could be publicized since the Treasury were not keen that even the full Staff Side should know what suggestions had been put forward. The meeting was adjourned so that the Staff Side could consider this. The value of such talks was discussed by Committee A who then remitted the question to the executives of the associations. In November the National Staff Side informed the Chancellor that the discussions could serve no useful purpose.

A full scale publicity campaign was then launched, which included

[1] NSS Equal Pay, 1935, Campaign Box 6, File 10.

a Valentine greeting sent by the women of the civil service to the Chancellor on 14 February 1953. Signatures were collected on a petition which was to be presented to Parliament. In February 1954, the National Staff Side employed a public relations firm to organize the final stages of the campaign which was to culminate in the presentation of the petition and a mass meeting on 9 March. A number of mass meetings were held in provincial centres and a 'Miss Equal Pay' selected at each one to obtain the maximum publicity. On 9 March, business in the House of Commons was dominated by the equal pay issue, but the Staff Side were disturbed to hear the Chancellor say at Question Time that he had offered talks to the National Staff Side and these had been rejected; they immediately held a press conference to clarify the position.

In his Budget speech on 6 April 1954, however, the Chancellor announced that he would like to meet representatives of the National Staff Side himself to 'discuss with them the manner in which we are most likely to make progress and the basis on which further Whitley talks should rest'.[1] The meeting took place on 19 May, and the Chancellor informed the Staff Side that the change must be made over a period of time, but that if agreement was reached it was hoped to implement it within the present financial year.

THE JOINT NEGOTIATIONS

The first joint meeting was held on 28 May, when Sir John Winnifrith for the Treasury explained that a satisfactory scheme must not cost too much initially and must be administratively tolerable. Sir Albert Day replied that the Staff Side accepted the problem of cost 'but they would be bound to press for it to cost as much as could possibly be justified in the present financial and economic circumstances, otherwise they would be in serious difficulties and with their women constituents who disliked the idea of gradualism, wanted as little of it as possible and could not forget that several years had passed since the Staff Side had put forward their own gradual scheme in 1947'.[2] It was agreed that the 1947 scheme was no longer satisfactory.

In the period between the first meeting and the next one on 9 July, the National Staff Side had to choose between the two methods of applying equal pay – the intermediate scales scheme proposed by the Treasury in which every woman's pay would rise every year until it reached the appropriate point on the man's scale, or a scheme whereby women of fifty-seven and over would receive full equal pay immediately so that they would obtain the new scale of pension. Committee A agreed, on 22 June, that the best scheme would be a combination of the

[1] H.C. Debs. 526, c. 211.   [2] NSS 130.19/1.

two. The Joint Committee made slow progress at first; only four meetings had been held by 15 October 1954. Committee A suggested in September that, in the interim, pensions should be based on notional equal pay, but this was rejected by the Official Side after they had been advised by the Treasury Solicitor that this would create a dangerous precedent by breaking the principle that pension should be based on the salary actually received, and secondly that it might well result in pressure for increases in the pensions of women who had already retired.

Another problem was the pay of those grades which were staffed predominantly by women. Early in the negotiations the Civil Service Union agreed not to press that cleaners did equal work. In December 1954, the cases of typists and telephonists were considered. Following separate negotiations between the Treasury and the Civil Service Clerical Association new scales for typists were agreed. But the problem of telephonists and telegraphists proved more difficult to settle. Because women in these grades were not under an obligation to undertake night work while their male colleagues were, the Official Side argued that they should not receive equal pay, but did offer 98 per cent of the male scale. The Union of Post Office Workers held out however for equal pay without any change in conditions of work. After prolonged discussions the Official Side offered an alternative – equal pay for all new entrants and for those women who opted for equal conditions of service, unequal pay for those who opted for unequal conditions.

On 18 February 1955, the National Staff Side held a special meeting to discuss the draft equal pay agreement. It lasted for nearly four hours and the discussion was mainly of the Post Office case. The debate was crucial since the scheme had to be accepted by a two-thirds majority and the Post Office group held ten seats out of the twenty-six. In a long debate in which the Union of Post Office Workers claimed that there were numerous other examples in the agreement of equal pay being given for unequal work, Sir Albert Day made the issue one of confidence in himself and in the total agreement. 'If the Staff Side adopted the Union of Post Office Workers motion they must, in the light of the facts now recited, show him (the Chairman) how he could handle the brief, in the face of the Official Side's reiterated refusal to give way on the main issue. If the Union of Post Office Workers persisted with their present attitude they would knowingly be putting the whole settlement in the melting pot; probably delaying the operative date and certainly delaying the payment of arrears. They would moreover be deeply mortifying the Chancellor and damaging the prestige of the National Whitley Council in his esteem, for what reason? – not because the Staff Side or the Union of Post Office Workers had any quarrel with the scheme – its mechanism, its duration, its operative date and the absence of provision for older women – but simply and solely because the Post

Office telephonists and telegraphists were not in it on the Union of Post Office Workers terms.'[1] One of the uncommitted votes was that of the late C. L. Leese. He represented a group of small Post Office associations, and since all his constituents were male, was interested, if anything, in keeping the women down. Nevertheless, he could see the harmful consequences of a setback at this stage. 'Though I had no instructions from my sub-group, I . . . was not going to support the Union of Post Office Workers on that! . . . I looked round the seats and totted up how the votes would go. . . . This would require a two-thirds majority under Standing Orders as an issue of policy, and I realized that . . . even if I abstained', there would still be enough opposition to block the report. So he voted in its favour and against the majority of the Post Office delegates.

The agreed report provided for annual increases for all women civil servants, in addition to their increments, over a period of six years, 1955 to 1961, until they reached the appropriate point on the men's scale. As L. C. White wrote in *Red Tape* in March 1955: 'The equal pay agreement which now comes into operation is not the agreement we would have accepted had the situation been more favourable. I am convinced that we have got from these negotiations everything of benefit that it was possible to get.'[2]

A POLITICAL VICTORY

The campaign for equal pay illustrates the limits of Whitleyism. It could not be achieved by negotiation, because it required a change of government policy. Equal pay could not be justified on the ground of comparability with other occupations, and government does not normally act as a model employer, setting an example to others. The eventual granting of equal pay, therefore, marked a departure from its customary role. 'In this respect, at any rate, the government, for public employment, has gone miles ahead of what private employment does.' This contradicts the habitual policy of the state towards its servants' pay, admitted one member of the Official Side. 'One might say, on that argument, that equal pay is anomalous. I don't personally hold that.' But many people did, and resistance to the measure was (as shown above) tenacious and protracted.

In the end equal pay was achieved by political means. 'We'd been fighting [for] equal pay for . . . years and ultimately the decision had to be made by parliament. The Treasury were not in a position to grant equal pay without the decision of parliament, so that a political campaign was absolutely essential.' Sir Albert Day agreed. 'Equal pay was an

[1] NSS Minutes, Vol. xiv, 18 February 1955.
[2] *Red Tape*, Vol. xliv, 1955, p. 174.

issue that the government said lay outside the sphere of Whitleyism. All right. It's not within the sphere of Whitleyism and my principle of keeping it in the family doesn't apply. Go to parliament if you want to.'

Official Side members saw things in very similar terms. 'The point about equal pay was that it was a wholly political victory, and not (as . . . salary or wage negotiations normally are) primarily an economic victory. In other words, . . . you know that the market rate compels you to pay somebody, or a grade of people, or a class of people, so much, or you won't get them. In relation to women, you knew it was not necessary to pay them more to get the quality you wanted. But the service is finally political. You are politically mastered, and so . . . the thing had to be conceded. I think this is very much why equal pay has made, on the whole, still rather little progress outside the politically dominated organizations, like central and local government, and teachers, and so forth; because it's the strength of the vote that has achieved equal pay, not the economic strength of the women.'

CHAPTER 8

DEPARTMENTAL WHITLEYISM

The Whitley Report provided for Joint Industrial Councils at national, district and works levels. When the Report came to be adopted for the civil service, there was to be a National Whitley Council, Departmental Councils in each of the ministries and local committees in each of the local offices or branches of a ministry. No study of Whitleyism would be complete without some account of how they operate.

There were in 1969 about seventy Departmental Whitley Councils, one in each department and ministry, except the Post Office, which had two (one for Engineering, Factories and Supplies, and the other for the rest of the staff). The first Councils were set up in the period 1919–20 on the basis of the model constitution drawn up by the National Council. The model followed very closely that of the National Council itself. As new departments have been set up, or old ones merged, the structure of Departmental Councils has changed too. The constitutions of new Departmental Councils have to be approved by the National Council.

The original intention was that Departmental Councils should meet quarterly. But annual meetings, as in the Department of Health and Social Security or Inland Revenue, or meetings twice a year, as in the Ministry of Defence or the Post Office, had by 1969 become more common. If Whitleyism were judged from these meetings alone, it would appear far more formal than at the national level. The Permanent Secretary normally took the chair. In the Department of Health and Social Security, for example, it was the practice for the Chairman to distribute in advance a long report on the work of the Department during the preceding year, and then to enlarge on it orally. At Post Office Council meetings, reports were 'given on such topics as the current financial position of the Post Office, the trend of demand for Post Office services and the capacity for meeting that demand, the building programme, and the progress and problems of mechanization, as well as general staffing matters'.[1] It was quite normal for the leaders of the two sides to dominate the discussion, even to the exclusion of all other members. In the Post Office, a member of the Official Side

[1] *P.O. evidence to the Royal Commission on Trade Unions and Employers' Associations*, p. 6.

recalled, they did a good bit of the talking, especially if the atmosphere was tricky, but if – as often – it was informative and non-controversial, several others would take part in the reporting of progress and in the commenting from the Staff Side. There have been exceptions. In the Ministry of Agriculture, Fisheries and Food, for instance, much of the time at annual meetings has been taken up with formal ratification of business done during the year. But on a number of occasions discussions of some importance have taken place as well.

However, any judgment based solely on meetings of full Councils would be misleading, because much of the business was done elsewhere and by other means. Most departments have a joint general purposes committee. In Agriculture, this consisted of representatives of the Establishments Division on the Official Side, and on the Staff Side of representatives from the four Council meetings to discuss the agenda: this gave management a chance to put right any problems raised before Council met. In other departments, the General Purposes Committee met as required: in the case of Health and Social Security, it had not done so for two or three years. There were an enormous number of other joint committees and sub-committees. In Health and Social Security, there were, in addition to the General Purposes Committee, six other standing committees dealing with particular topics. The Ministry of Defence had a general purposes committee, which met four or more times a year, with a number of sub-committees. The Post Office had an elaborate system of committees, some of which linked the two Departmental Councils. Committee business tended to be done much less formally than that of the Councils. In the words of a Post Office Official Side respondent, 'you can openly think aloud at many of these meetings without advantage being taken of the fact'. Much of the negotiation, moreover, was undertaken informally between officers in Establishments Divisions in the ministries, on the one hand, and Staff Side officers and association representatives. One of the interviews on which this study is largely based was punctuated by a telephone conversation in which a staff association officer approved an arrangement provisionally agreed to by a Departmental Staff Side secretary.

Although Departmental Councils have continued to meet formally, there has been a significant change in the attitudes of the two Sides towards one another, paralleling that which has taken place at national level. It seems to have begun in the thirties, when a staff association official 'noticed a very considerable change, a certain mellowing'. 'In big departments like the Post Office, for instance, up to a certain time, round about [1935] they seemed to echo the Treasury's tendency to say "no" in one of the fifty-seven ways they used to say it.' Then came 'the real beginning of . . . what I regard as the humane and sensible approach of establishment officers'.

As might be expected, the trend expressed itself in different ways and at different times in the various ministries. Ministry of Health Whitley in the twenties, for instance, 'was a very stiff and starchy affair'. So little impact did it make that a respondent who served in the Ministry before the war 'was quite unconscious of the existence of Whitleyism, excepting when I was private secretary to the Permanent Secretary, . . . and then, because the Permanent Secretary was the chairman of the departmental Whitley, I used to be dimly aware . . . of this departmental Whitley . . . [he regarded it as] one of those chores you had to go through. . . . He was absolutely hopeless in relation to staff . . . and Whitley to him was just a thing you had to go through.' Things rapidly changed, however, and a post-war Permanent Secretary reported that 'the Whitley affairs of the Ministry of Health . . . were in very smooth waters and I very seldom had to intervene at all. . . . Business was always done informally with the establishment officer and the departmental people. . . . As you would expect [of] someone brought up as I had [been], I did make it my business when first I became a Permanent Secretary – I always said I would do this if I ever reached that rank . . . on my very first day, . . . to send for the chairman of the Staff Side of my new department and have an informal talk over a cup of tea with him. . . . And from time to time, the Staff Side came and sent deputations to me. . . . But relations were always very friendly. We had no serious arguments and troubles.' One of Health's successor departments, Housing and Local Government, inherited a similar tradition. It 'developed very good staff relations. . . . Certainly in my time . . . the reason why you wouldn't need to study our Whitley is "happy is the country that had no history". We had very good staff relations and a relatively uncomplicated staff structure, and a relatively small department, and we were really on very good terms, and all of our discussions were informal, whether with the junior people in the Establishments Division, the Establishments Officer, or if they were very het up, they would [go to the chairman] and [have] a good knock-about.'

Another Council retained the old ways until the late fifties. A new Permanent Secretary who took over at that period 'found . . . that it was still a bit stiff and formal. This wasn't my idea of Whitleyism at all. . . . Before I was here, the Official Side used to put in a document reviewing a whole series of issues that were of Whitley interest – training, welfare, accommodation, . . . and so on. Of course, it's open to either side to put in any documents that they like, but in practice the Staff Side [didn't] put anything in. So . . . the Official Side . . . must take the initiative. Well, we used to put in these great documents and . . . they used to be read through formally, having been circulated in advance, and this I suppose took half an hour, and then there would be a fairly scrappy discussion, and that was it.' Only at that stage, when Whitleyism was about to

L

enter its fourth decade, did things begin to open up. 'I said, "Well, I don't think this is how to do things. . . . Let's try and make it a bit more of a reality. We'll go on putting in these papers, [but], after all, the chaps on the Staff Side can read just as well as we can! Let's take all this as read. I assume before we sit down that we've all *read* this. Now let's go through it and discuss it." And this we do, which . . . has made the meetings of the Departmental Whitley Council rather less stiff, and a good deal more effective, and *shorter*, than they used to be.' But the Council was still meeting, in 1968, four times a year, with the Permanent Secretary in the chair.

Formal behaviour at the top has not prevented an extensive infrastructure of informal relations developing lower down. The Admiralty provided an example. Even as late as 1960 'departmental Whitley was always a bit formal. . . . It was formal in the sense that the meetings of the administrative[1] Whitley Council were meetings that ran to a formal programme. They were set on a regular day of a certain month. We had four a year, and they were always on the second or third Tuesday of [the] month. They were formal in the sense that, on the Official Side, the chairman was almost the only spokesman, unless he invited one of his colleagues to help – which wasn't to say a colleague couldn't butt in and clarify a situation, he did – but for practical purposes the argument took place [through] the Chairman, who was the Official Side spokesman, saying his piece. The majority of the argument on the Staff Side came from the Staff Side Chairman, but not nearly so religiously. Other members of the Staff Side spoke, particularly if the matter concerned very much one grade, and not the other grades. I would have said that, whereas the Official Side spokesman was 95 per cent the Chairman, in other words, the Permanent Secretary of the department, on the Staff Side, the Staff Side Chairman was about an 80 per cent speaker but other members of the Staff Side took part. But there was an air of formality about it.'

Behind the scenes, a different atmosphere prevailed, as described by a pre-war Official Side Secretary. 'A lot of the discussions took place in *ad hoc* meetings organized by the two Whitley secretaries between a group of chaps on the Official Side and a group of chaps on the Staff Side who were experts in their particular fields. Now those meetings were very much more open meetings. They weren't nearly so formal as meetings of the main Whitley Council. Those meetings would argue the toss about something, and out of it would come a report . . . and that document would come to the main Whitley Council. Coming to the main Whitley Council, it would then get into the formal machine. In other words, departmental Whitley was pretty formal in its top level

---

[1] As distinct from the parallel body which dealt with the Admiralty's industrial civil servants.

discussions, but pretty well informal in it medium or lower level discussions.' Very much the same pattern prevailed in the War Office as in the Admiralty up to the time when both departments were absorbed into the Ministry of Defence in 1964.

Why have Departmental Councils not withered away, as the National Council has ? An ex-Permanent Secretary recalled that 'once or twice . . . the Staff Side would say, "We really *ought* to have a Whitley Council . . . just to keep the machine going." But there was . . . never any real need for it, because everything really did get sorted out as far as we were going to be able to sort it out in a much more informal way.' There is no doubt that many Staff Side members, particularly those who are serving civil servants, place a value on such meetings. They see the Departmental Council as a necessary means of involving the Permanent Secretary directly and personally and as a means of 'educating' heads of divisions and others who are not normally involved in staff negotiations. Serving officials on the Staff Side may, moreover, find it easier to meet their hierarchial superiors in a formal setting, rather than informally.

VARIATIONS BETWEEN DEPARTMENTS

What factors explain the differences between departments ? Personality seems to have been of prime importance. Take, for example, a couple of departments whose permanent secretaries had very different attitudes towards Whitleyism in its early days. 'You can't really separate what happened from the attitude of the then secretary of the Post Office, Sir Evelyn Murray, who was very . . . starchy, and, I think, regarded Whitley Councils as nonsense. . . . There was a man who came from Stornoway or somewhere, . . . a representative of some Post Office union, who used to come down to the Whitley Council, spending a day and a half getting down and a day and a half getting back. And Evelyn Murray used to arrange that the Whitley Council never lasted more than thirty-five minutes. And there's a wicked story that he came out of the meeting which he had . . . bull-dozed through . . . and he turned to his secretary and said, "Was the man from Stornoway there this morning?" – which, I think, shows a rather cynical view!' In marked contrast, was the Admiralty, where a style 'of free and frank discussion between the two Whitley secretaries, and to a slightly more limited extent, between two or three people on each side very closely associated with their respective side, . . . was set by a man named William Shorto, who was the first Official Side secretary in the Admiralty, and Oswyn Murray, who was . . . Chairman of our first Council. Murray was sold on Whitley, he believed in Whitley, [and] he tried to make it work. Shorto was a man of great depth and understanding and feeling. I don't think I'd really say he was sold on Whitley in the same way that Oswyn

Murray was. Nevertheless, because Oswyn Murray set the pattern, his Official Side Secretary followed the pattern, and followed it willingly. . . . He wasn't driven into it. He was . . . that way inclined, though he may not have gone as far as Oswyn Murray did if he had not had the encouragement. But those two men between them set the pattern of Admiralty Whitley.'[1]

The personal attitude of staff leaders was important too, of course, And where two or three people on each side were able to provide the drive over a period of years, the most favourable conditions existed for a rapid growth of Whitleyism. Such was the case, for example, in the Inland Revenue. 'Pat Hoey remained Staff Side secretary or member throughout most of the first thirty years (missing only one meeting of the Council between 1921 and 1950); while Douglas Houghton as member and Vice-Chairman spanned the period from 1924 to 1944. For most of the same period there were only three Directors of Establishments, F. A. Barrett and W. V. Bradford (who were founder members of the Council) and Edward Ritson. This long association of leading personalities on either side probably had a great deal to do with establishing a mutual understanding in the long run.'[2] Looking back to the period in question, a member of the Staff Side could not 'recall a single instance where we felt strongly on a subject and said, "We must see the Board!", that we failed to get [a hearing] either at an official Whitley meeting or by means of a deputation. And on things like . . . accommodation . . . – at that time there was considerable disquiet about the accommodation provided for tax officers – . . . we were able to bully the Board and do it quite effectively too!'

The pattern of labour organization within a department has also been influential. The Post Office, with parallel Councils on the postal and engineering sides, provided a good example. The separate engineering Council was set up in deference to the wishes of the telephone staff, which had been brought into the Post Office only in 1911, when the telephone service was nationalized. They wished to retain a degree of independence by having a Whitley Council of their own. The pattern at local level also differed and for the same reason. Non-engineering unionism in the Post Office has been based on local management units, and the Whitley structure took the same form. On the engineering side, by contrast, local Whitleyism has been regionally based, reflecting union structure and tradition.

Geography may count too. For example, most of the staff of the wartime Ministry of Pensions were in Blackpool. The Chairman of the

[1] Cf. L. D. White, *Whitley Councils in the British Civil Service: a study in conciliation, and arbitration*, Chicago, 1933, p. 96.
[2] J. D. Thomas, *Fifty Years of Whitleyism in the Inland Revenue, 1920–1970*, 1970, p. 16.

departmental Whitley Council, on the other hand, was in London. It was a natural development for most Whitley business to be handled informally by the Assistant Secretary in charge of the Blackpool office and the chairman and secretary of the Staff Side. Similarly, the war-time evacuation of most Inland Revenue staff to Llandudno had important consequences. Meeting of the Council had to be suspended, but 'collective relations between management and staff under very hard war-time conditions of work became much more intimate, especially in the Branch Whitley Committees.'[1]

THE OFFICIAL SIDES

Departmental Official Sides consist usually of the Permanent Secretary, heads of specific divisions (for example, the Fisheries Secretary in Agriculture, and the head of the Newcastle-upon-Tyne Office in Health and Social Security) and the Principal Establishment Officer. Provision was made in the past for a Treasury representative to sit on the Departmental Official Side if necessary, in order to ensure that all agreements reached were in line with Treasury policy. It does not appear to have been used for many years. The Permanent Secretary's personal interest in Whitleyism is clearly important to a department in setting the tone of staff relations. An Official Side generally meets together before going in to join the Staff Side. Attendance of Official Side members tends to be lower than that of their opposite numbers. But in the light of the business the Staff Side means to raise, care is taken to ensure the attendance of the appropriate Official Side people. This is especially important in a department like Health and Social Security where members of the Official Side may have to be brought from all over the country.

In a department with an active Council, a good deal of thought often went into the composition of the Official Side. In the Admiralty, for instance, 'about one half of its membership [came] from the establishment field . . . running from the Deputy Secretary down to the establishment branches, and the other fifty per cent came from heads of departments spread over the Admiralty. . . . Quite definitely, it was not a *packed* establishments branch mechanism. We had three, four or five heads of departments, like Director of Dockyards, Director of Victualling, Director of Stores, that kind of thing, on the Council. And they weren't by any means figureheads. . . . They came on and they argued in the Official Side meetings the validity of the departmental line. They didn't often speak at Council meetings, but they had taken part in the formation of the Official Side line. In other words, we did try to make sure that our Official Side was a representative one. There were two reasons behind that: one, because it is utterly essential that in any

[1] Ibid. p. 27.

mechanism you have an opportunity to hear the views of the employers – the Director of Victualling or the Director of Stores, or the Director of Naval Construction, are the chaps who employ the work-people to a far greater extent than the establishment branch do – on what they thought was fair treatment. They could tell you what the men did, they could tell you the complications that arose in their work, to a much better extent than the establishment people could, so you've got to have the representatives of the employers in the broad sense on your Council. And the other reason for it was, of course, that if you went to a Whitley Council which was in effect a packed establishment branch mechanism, the Staff Side would riddle you. They would tell you that in the Director of Naval Construction's department, a third grade clerk is doing this, that, and the other and there would be, as like as not, no one present to contradict. Similar arrangements were made in the War Office for the proper representation of heads of employing services on the Departmental Administrative Whitley Council.

In departmental Whitleyism, it has been by no means rare for individuals to sit on both sides. A young man may early in his career speak for the Staff Side: later, on promotion, he may be nominated to the Official Side. A particularly interesting case was that of Sir John Simpson, who was National Staff Side Secretary, and later became Chairman of a departmental Council. 'Of course, one had a different part to play, but one's approach to it was very much the same. It was always largely a question of reconciling what people wanted with what was possible. I was never very sure whether the Staff Side in the Stationery Office didn't regard me with a certain amount of suspicion. I knew too much! And there were occasions, of course, when – unwittingly perhaps – I revealed a knowledge of the way things were done on their side and [was] able to use arguments which perhaps someone who'd not had my experience couldn't have used. But I hope, and indeed I believe, that it meant that I brought a sympathetic approach to their problems. But as the Chairman of the Official Side, I also had to deal with the Treasury, and I also on occasion had to balance the claims of one part of the Staff Side against the interests of another. I think my Staff Side experience was helpful. Indeed, I think I would have been less efficient as a Chairman of the Official Side if I hadn't served on the Staff Side.'

Such a case was, of course, exceptional. But if the full vertical range of the Whitley system were taken into account, it would not be hard to find a number of cases where service on the Staff Side of a local committee has preceded nomination to the Official Side. Such experience is of course valuable as training. Moreover; it can and does happen that someone sits on the Official Side of a local committee, whilst at the same time representing the staff at some higher level.

THE STAFF SIDES

The make-up of departmental Staff Sides also has features of interest. Clearly there must be enough seats to allow various sections of staff to be represented. For this reason, the Staff Side was sometimes larger than the Official Side, as in the Ministry of Defence for example. This may seem odd, since it might be thought to put the staff in a position where they could out-vote management. But, of course, in departmental Councils, as in the National Council, decisions are not made by voting. So there is no reason for the Official Side to maintain parity, and the extra seats help to solve the problem of representing the diverse groups of staff within many departments.

Even so, the distribution of departmental Staff Side seats poses difficult questions. It is often impossible to give associations seats in proportion to their numbers. To let every distinct group have its individual spokesman might not only make a Council inconveniently large. It could also lead to a situation in which minority interests were able to block policies desired by a majority of those serving in the department. On the other hand, to give large groups places in proportion to their membership might enable them to swamp the smaller interests.

The Inland Revenue is a department which has had its full share of these problems. The first Staff Side consisted of thirteen men and women representing twenty associations. In 1924 the two largest associations almost seceded from the Staff Side because of a dispute about the proportion of seats they should have.[1] In 1944, the Inland Revenue Staff Federation, which had by that come to dominate the Staff side, did secede for several months over an issue closely linked with representation.[2] The imbalance continued. In 1953, for instance, the Staff Side covered 44,194 people of whom 36,500 were members of the Federation. That single union could, therefore, have made out a plausible claim to twelve of the fourteen seats. In fact, it held only four. The remainder were distributed among seven other associations. Thus, a combination of Staff Side members representing only a fraction of the staff could have outvoted the Federation.

Douglas Houghton explained how the system worked in practice. The Federation 'was bigger than all the rest of the department put together. . . . This . . . raised a serious question of representation. If you have a Whitley Council, and you want to give representation to the various staff elements on it you can't give representation . . . solely in relation to . . . number. You have to have regard to different classifications and grades and interests. So that, . . . if you had, say, sixteen members of the Staff Side, how many of those positions should be taken up by the Inland Revenue Staff Federation, that had enough members to swallow

[1] Thomas, p. 19.   [2] Ibid. pp. 26–7.

up everybody else? If we were going to have more members on the Staff Side than all the rest of the Staff Side put together, it would make it unwieldy in size, if you were going to give representation to the others. It would also mean that there was this intimidating sight of the block of the Inland Revenue Staff [Federation] who were there to vote down anybody else if they wished. . . . Well, we had to come to terms with this situation and we were content with a distinct minority of seats on the Staff Side, but we did ask that we should be given the right to veto. This was something unique. We should be given the right to veto decisions of the Staff Side which we thought were inimical to our own interests. In fact, the veto was never used. . . . With the acknowledgement of the position of the [Federation] and mutual understanding, to this day, that veto has never been used.' Another former official of the Federation, James Callaghan, confirms Houghton's analysis. 'The essence of Whitley discussions', he writes, 'is that a Staff Side rarely acts on any major issue save with the consent of all the important elements on it.'[1] Hence, the use of the veto would have been, not so much a way of preventing a collapse of Staff Side consensus, as a sign that that consensus had already ceased to exist.

The Staff Side representatives are elected by the Section Committees of the various associations within the department. Local branches of an association send a delegate to the Section Conference which elects the Section Committee. Usually one of the Staff Side representatives of the larger associations is a full-time officer. These officers are consulted frequently, in some departments daily, by Staff Side Chairmen. Departmental Staff Sides normally meet once a quarter and as a rule the meetings are long ones. The Section Committees may meet the day before to brief their representatives. Much of the business is, however, done through committees and the Staff Side meets to direct and ratify their work.

Officers of departmental Staff Sides are usually serving civil servants who are allowed by their departments to have a light official job which leaves them time to undertake Staff Side duties. Occasionally the Chairman may be a full-time association official, as in the Ministry of Defence. In the Ministry of Defence also, the Staff Side secretary and assistant secretary were paid by the Ministry and provided with a clerk and typist. In this way, a large part of the cost of Whitleyism was borne by the department. This is reasonable, for the considerations which applied in the case of the Inland Revenue were of general application. 'On the Official Side [Whitley] work is part of the official's job; but many Staff Side members have had to do much of this work in their own time, and very demanding it can be. It took ten years before the Official Side

[1] James Callaghan, *Whitleyism: a study of joint consultation in the civil service*, Fabian Society, London, 1953, p. 15.

gave adequate recognition to the contribution by the Staff Side by providing for [its] business to be conducted during official hours, and by ensuring that as far as possible official duties should be arranged so as to enable Staff Side representatives to devote sufficient time to Whitley work.'[1]

Nevertheless, the officers are servants of the associations. Some chairmen regard their job as simply to carry out the instructions they are given, but others appear to take a greater initiative. The associations retain the right to negotiate directly with the department on such questions as promotion, seniority, and individual grievances: but a Staff Side officer may attend the negotiations to demonstrate support for the claim and to safeguard the interests of the other associations. Staff Side officers have a delicate role. In the course of discussions with senior members of their department, to whom they have wide access, they often acquire information which is not generally known to the staff. The department may tell them things they would not tell a staff association as such. Again, a Staff Side Chairman may, as in Agriculture, Fisheries and Food, have the opportunity to comment on departmental policy affecting staff. His comments in such a case would give weight to the efficiency of the department as well as the welfare of the staff. Anyone placed in this position needs to be trusted by both sides, yet is in per-petual danger of losing the confidence of staff, or management, or both.

Most members of Departmental Staff Sides, unlike their counterparts at national level, are serving officials. There are few full-time association officers. 'This makes life . . . for both sides very much easier. . . . Where you are able to have your discussions with people who are serving civil servants, you have a realization on the Staff Side of the problems of the Official Side and of the limits beyond which . . . the Official Side cannot go. . . . You are talking more of a common language when you are both . . . working in the same organization than when you are having to talk with people whose professional job is to represent the staff interests. When I was . . . Chairman of Departmental Whitley, one of the subjects which was often a matter for discussion between us, and rightly, was the appalling accommodation which much of the staff had to occupy. You know how abominable accommodation is – really dis-graceful, something I think Whitley should have taken more seriously a long time ago. But our civil servants, although they were representing staff who were really aggrieved and fed up, . . . did realize that . . . there was *nothing* we could do. . . . By and large, . . . we were as angry as they were, and trying as hard as they could wish us to, to batter at the Ministry of Works . . . to try and improve things. . . . Maybe this meant that the working of Whitley was muted because in the end both sides shrugged their shoulders and said, "We know exactly how hard your

[1] Thomas, p. 19.

problems are. We know how hard you're trying." But of course it meant at the same time a very easy relationship.'

But one man's ease is another's unease. Whitley negotiations often brought together individuals whose places in the departmental hierarchy were widely separated. Civil servants of lower rank could feel the consequent strain. 'It was always a little difficult when one was dealing with one's own superior officer to tackle him freely and without fear.' In the Inland Revenue, according to Douglas Houghton, senior staff assisted the rank and file to overcome their nervousness. 'The readiness of the higher grade organizations, like the Valuers and the Tax Inspectors, to provide the initial Staff Side leadership was of great help. They were less in awe of the Board of Inland Revenue than those of us who had never seen them before.'[1] For a similar reason, as James Callaghan has pointed out, the role of salaried association officers in departmental Whitley is essential although they are relatively few in comparison with serving civil servants. 'Full-time officials have the advantage of providing the expert knowledge that comes from continuous study, and can meet the Official Sides on equal terms. Moreover, as they are not civil servants, they have a greater feeling of independence than can be expected of a junior official meeting his departmental superior even in the atmosphere of a Whitley Council. I do not intend to imply that civil servants serving on departmental Staff Sides do not freely express their views or differences with the Official Side and I have heard much plain speaking where important issues have been at stake. But in the last resort, where relations between Official Side and Staff Side become strained, as they do from time to time, there are no sanctions that can be applied to the full-time trade union official if he speaks over-plainly, and his independent position constitutes a reservoir of strength, even if it does not have to be tapped.'[2]

The first full-time officers to join departmental Staff Sides were not always welcomed even by their colleagues. One of them recalled his debut in 1925. 'When I went on the departmental Whitley Council, . . . I was the first full-time officer ever dreamed of in the Ministry of Labour, and the Staff Side barred me, never mind about anyone else! The Staff Side would not go on with their discussions because I was there. My union had to move that I come in as a member . . . and there was a hell of a row before I got in . . . I went in, and then it was quite clear that the managers . . . and the senior officers on the Staff Side went and saw the Official Side, because the Official Side came in and took the reports – "Agreed, agreed, agreed" – and it was all over in about eight minutes, which absolutely staggered everybody.' The deadlock was broken by a

[1] In his foreword to J. D. Thomas, *Fifty Years of Whitleyism in the Inland Revenue*, 1970.
[2] Callaghan, p. 14.

member of the Official Side, T. W. Phillips, who 'slowed his steps as the Official Side went out, put his arm through mine, and said "I'd like to talk to you, my boy!" . . . I went in, and he said "Don't take things to heart! You'll settle down. Come and see me in a day or two and talk to me." And Tommy Phillips then lived in Wallington. I lived in Carshalton, one station back, and again and again, when he wanted to talk to me, he would tell me to buy a transfer ticket from 3rd class to 1st [and] to travel with him in his carriage and talk to him, just privately, off the record. . . . It helped Ministry of Labour Whitley tremendously!'

RELATIONSHIP WITH THE
NATIONAL COUNCIL

Given the existence of a National Council, together with a number of Departmental Councils, it is obvious that problems of demarcation and co-ordination must arise. Uncertainty as to the level at which a given matter should be dealt with might cause delay, or might be exploited by either side with the object of causing delay. A department might be hampered in its efforts to carry through some change with national implications because of the necessity to carry other departments along. Departments might render national agreements dead letters by failing to implement them. But to postulate things that could happen is not to demonstrate that they have happened. Which of those theoretical possibilities – if any – has left traces on the historical record?

Difficulties in implementing national agreements at departmental level were among the most acute of Whitleyism's teething troubles.[1] The Staff Side felt that the Treasury, by determining departmental action in this matter, was exercising a concealed veto on the agreement which had been reached. When the Staff Side complained to the Treasury, they were told it was a departmental matter, and when the complaints were transferred to the departments, they were referred back to the Treasury. The issue was raised several times by the Staff Side on the National Council, particularly with reference to the implementation of the Reorganization Report. Eventually, they met the Chancellor of the Exchequer to discuss the question. But the Official Side was determined that the National Council should not become a court of appeal from the Departmental Councils. In the end, the National Council's constitution was amended – the only amendment that has ever been made – to allow a committee to be set up to investigate allegations of difficulty in implementing a national agreement in a department. The provision has rarely been used, and never since 1946.

The distinction between national and departmental levels has, however, continued to pose problems. 'There was a continuing problem

[1] Cf. White, p. 31.

of demarcation', an old Treasury hand recalled. 'In other words, was a particular topic a general topic and, as such, proper to be discussed by the National Council, or was it essentially a departmental topic which should be discussed by a Departmental Council? I think . . . it's fair to say . . . that the staff sometimes felt that there were matters which could have been settled departmentally, but which were argued to be a national issue and therefore [had] to go to the National Council, and vice versa.' Neither side was 'entirely guiltless of the tactical argument that "No, no, this ought to be there rather than here and vice versa". And whilst I wouldn't claim that the Official Side were entirely guiltless, I would not accept that the Staff Side were little angels in this respect either!'

As to the implementation of national agreements, the same respondent admitted that 'certain national decisions were reached with greater enthusiasm by certain heads of departments than by others. . . . At times . . . certain heads of departments thought perhaps that one was making too many concessions to the Staff Side.' Such an attitude might cause delay. But a Staff Side leader did not think it could absolutely block a reform. At the departmental level, 'we often made them do things they didn't want to do on the basis of a National Whitley decision. But I can never conceive the possibility that the Departmental Council would be able without gross neglect on the part of the Staff Side' to frustrate a National Whitley Council decision.

An ex-departmental Council Chairman explained how national considerations impinged on the business of the body over which he presided. 'We quite often said . . . "We're bound to be governed or affected in our study of this problem by the conclusion of the National Council. . . . Our problem is to determine how far we can apply the arguments, the reasons, the solutions, to our departmental problem." . . . We very seldom referred back to the National Whitley Council matters that arose from us. . . . I can recall examples in which I have said, "I am sorry we can't get any further with this departmental problem, because the National Council, in respect of a National Council grade, had laid down this, that, and the other. The Official Side here can only apply that decision to the departmental field, and if the Staff Side are not prepared to accept that solution, there's nothing I can do about it" – which meant, in effect, that they must apply for arbitration, if that's what they wanted to do. The reverse problem could happen, and I would have said, did happen, though I can't for the moment recall an example. In other words, a departmental problem arises which the Official Side sense has a wider implication than a department, and therefore [feel] "The most we can do is to report to the National Whitley Council that here is a problem. We can't find an answer to it without the help of the National Council." ' A former member of the Admiralty Official Side supplied a hypothetical example. 'The Admiralty had a grade called overseers. Their job was to oversee the contract building of warships. We put these people into a shipyard to see the job was properly done. Now these people were detached from dockyard homes, they were working in industrial neighbourhoods like Newcastle or Glasgow, they were there for two years, three years or four years but not for life, they were doing a job which, although it demanded a knowledge of dockyard procedures, was separate from their dockyard work. . . . They might well have said that, subsistence-wise and lodging-allowance-wise, they ought to have rather special conditions. If they raised this question, the Official Side of Admiralty Whitley would have had to say, "All right, we can understand this, but we're not sure we can provide the answer, because whatever we might think was right, we should have to make sure that we weren't in fact imperilling some agreement which exists already in a parallel field, or conversely, that the parallel field hasn't already provided the answer which we ought to [follow], but we don't know." '

CO-ORDINATION ON THE OFFICIAL SIDE

In such a situation, a Departmental Official Side could have asked their colleagues on the National Council to put the matter before that body. Alternatively, they could have raised it directly with the Treasury. It was the latter pattern which prevailed. 'In practice . . . it very seldom got to National Whitley, and the national aspect of it was discussed between Official Side Admiralty Whitley and the Treasury. The Treasury came back and said yes, or not, or three bags full, and Official Side Admiralty Whitley then talked to Departmental Whitley and said what we could do.'

In dealing with problems of this kind, it was not always the Treasury that said no. Other departments might be even more difficult. A former Departmental Council Chairman recalled that 'the greatest problem I ever had . . . was to get other departments to agree that we could pay our professional staff adequately. . . . I felt terribly strongly about . . . the contribution made by the professionals and the appallingly bad way in which the civil servants had treated its professionals before the war. . . . I found the real difficulty . . . was to carry the departments that were, so to speak, linked with us, . . . that had . . . corresponding posts, some of whom still cherished this appalling theory that a professional was in some way inferior to an administrator – a theory that I think now has very nearly wholly disappeared.'

CO-ORDINATION ON THE STAFF SIDE

In the early years of Whitleyism, the National Staff Side used to convene regular meetings of Departmental Staff Side secretaries and other representatives to discuss matters of policy and common interest. This was the province of the Co-ordinating Officer, W. E. Llewellyn, but the post was abolished for reasons of economy in 1925. Meetings continued into the thirties, although the attendance at times fell below twenty. During the same period, and with a similar aim, the *Whitley Bulletin* was publishing the minutes of selected Departmental Councils alongside those of the National Council. These devices were useful, but in more recent times, new mechanisms have come into being which have rendered them no longer necessary.

There is now remarkably little direct contact between National Staff Side officers and their departmental opposite numbers. The channels of communication run through the associations. In some cases, association officers are members of Councils at both levels. Whether this is the case or not, a full-time officer of each major association normally sits on the Council of each department in which it had any considerable number of members. In many instances, such officers belong to more than one Departmental Staff Side. Furthermore, when a departmental Staff Side officer wishes to consult an association, he normally approaches a full-time officer, who is in this way closely involved in all discussions. It is up to these officers to take departmental problems to the executives of their associations, and for the representatives at the national level to bring them to the notice of the National Staff Side. With so many informal contacts, there is little need of formal machinery to co-ordinate the work of the Staff Sides on the various Councils.

THE SCOPE OF DEPARTMENTAL WHITLEY

Departmental Councils were set up to deal with matters peculiar to a single department, while the National Council was to deal with questions affecting two or more departments. The trend has been towards centralization. Following the Joint Reorganization Reports of 1920 and 1921, a large proportion of civil servants were assimilated into Treasury classes for whose conditions of service the National Council was responsible. Over the years, the conditions of departmental classes have been brought more and more into line with those of the Treasury classes, so that such questions as annual leave and standards of accommodation have come to be settled by national agreements which are applied, with some variations, by the Departmental Councils. Certain training and promotion procedures have also been brought within the ambit of national Whitley, leaving only the detailed application to be worked out at departmental level. Many variations remain, of course, and where, as in the case of substitution in the Post Office, the rules were more liberal than those in the national agreement, the Staff Side was staunch to defend them.

There remains a great deal for departmental Whitley to do, subject always to the operation of the Whitley proverbs: 'Whitley superseded nothing' and 'Whitley is an umbrella'. Lord Geddes explained how the first worked. 'The Departmental Whitley, properly used, was absolutely first-class. . . . The Post Office Whitley . . . always had been a very, very, important part of the negotiating machine subject to the fact, certainly in my day, that it was only used when you wanted it to be used and you only took to it the things you wanted to take to it – and those things where you had to get a unified policy. Now clearly there are some things on which you had to get a unified policy . . . which was essential before [going] to the Official Side.'

But Lord Geddes was speaking of a union which was great and powerful, both absolutely, and in relation to the department in which its members served. To others, the umbrella had more appeal. 'Large and strong unions frequently make independent representations to departments where the interests of their members alone are involved. but numerically small unions tend to seek the help of the Staff Side in order to get a proper consideration of their claims.'[1] Even large associations, however, could find the umbrella useful. Sir John Simpson recalled the skill with which Douglas Houghton manipulated it. 'Houghton was a first-class example of a man who could use the umbrella. He had innumerable discussions with . . . people on the Official Side . . . under the umbrella of Whitleyism, but you wouldn't find [the business] covered in the constitution. For instance, if the Department wanted to transfer Brown from Pontypridd tax district to Tavistock, and this chap had family ties, or some domestic trouble, which meant that it would be a very unfortunate move, Houghton was able to go to the people who were responsible for transfers and say, "Look, don't do this, it is going to be a great hardship." Now this was done under the umbrella of Whitleyism, but it wasn't contained in the constitution, and it was never reported . . . back to a sub-committee.'

In most departmental Councils, issues such as grading, promotion procedures, dispersal, and general questions relating to the organization of a department and its work kept Whitley very much alive. Each department has problems peculiar to itself; the perennial topic of civilianization in the defence field, for instance.

The mere range of topics dealt with in the Post Office (to take just one example) was impressive, The list covered, among other matters, the following: computers; engineering stores distribution; field trials of new tools and techniques; Giro; health; industrial safety; post codes; STD; training; two-tier post; and welfare. Suggestions, awards, and produc-

[1] Callaghan, p. 21.

tivity were dealt with apart from Whitley, but clearly in the same spirit. Lord Geddes recalled the establishment of one of these special purpose bodies. 'We were the only people in the whole of the service . . . that set up a Productivity Council. And it was set up on the basis that the proceeds of the productivity should be shared, and they were shared, and in fact we got about £200,000 out of the Treasury. . . . This was under Sir . . . Alexander Little. And he was a first-class man, absolutely first-class. . . . And we used to sit there, and we used to discuss ways and means. . . . [I remember] the first meeting of the Productivity Council. . . . In the normal way . . . the Staff Side were always in their place first, and then the Official Side filed in, in order to show their superiority. In this case, we were all in, and Little said . . . "Come over here, Geddes, you sit next to me. There's no both sides of the table here. Take your seats!" And the Official Side just went to the nearest seat they could and sat beside a member of the Staff Side.'

In the Chief Inspector's Branch of the Inland Revenue, as early as the thirties, Whitleyism reached the point where no instruction was issued to the staff without the Staff Side being consulted. Sir John Simpson recalled, as an example, a purely procedural circular being drafted. 'It had no direct effect on the staff in terms of pay or conditions – none whatever! It was just a new system being introduced, and we were given a copy of this circular and asked to comment on it, and our comments had nothing to do with Staff Side interests in the narrower sense. Our aim was to try and help the Official Side to produce the system in [such] a way that it would work! . . . We found their proposals wholly unacceptable. We were convinced, since we knew what it was going to mean at the working level, that it was badly conceived, and had a lot of things in it which just wouldn't work! . . . I went along, together with a colleague, to see the Chief Inspector, who was then Sir Edward Harrison, and I ticked off one by one the faults in his memorandum, and well remember his putting his hands above his head and saying, "Simpson, Simpson, as you are strong, be merciful!" And they took the draft circular back and it was completely recast. . . . This I regarded as a great achievement because it meant . . . that without going as far as the staff participating in management, we were getting as near to it as you could really hope to get. We were being consulted on the way the department was being managed, and given the opportunity of making representations, which didn't only come from me. I had a number of correspondents all over the country, and I was able to either bring them together or do it by correspondence, and say, "What do you think of this draft circular?" I was thus able to give the Official Side advice, or criticism, or sometimes commendation, from people who'd got to work the [system]. . . . And I felt that we'd really reached the furthest that Whitley could be pushed when you'd got the [Official Side] bringing you their draft instructions on purely procedural matters to get your views before they were put into effect.'

Dispersal is another example of a topic that came within the orbit of departmental Whitley. 'It's not a thing that's likely to be wildly popular with anybody.' But discussion can go a good way towards sweetening the pill. 'It isn't so much that . . . a Departmental Staff Side automatically tries to fight it. But every Departmental Staff Side, when the prospect of a major dispersal of staff arises, obviously gets on its hind legs and pipes up because it has a number of very legitimate interests which it must safeguard – questions of domestic hardship, questions of . . . promotion . . . going awry, questions of redundancy and people who don't want to leave . . . and the departments are now well accustomed to handling these things in collaboration with their Staff Sides in a way which brings as much satisfaction, or as little dissatisfaction, as the circumstances render possible.' Inland Revenue provides an example. Between 1948 and 1950, a number of units were dispersed to Cardiff, Edinburgh, Hinchley Wood, Liverpool and Worthing. 'The moves did not all go smoothly but a functioning Whitley system of consultation certainly eased management's task and secured humane conditions for the staff. Valuable experience was gained by both sides, not only in clearing away internal obstacles but in negotiating with outside bodies over housing, social amenities and so forth in the dispersal areas.'[1]

Paradoxically, concentration of staff raises much the same problems as dispersal. A notable recent occasion has been the automation of PAYE work. This involves the setting up of nine new regional centres, and it is estimated that ultimately some 20,000 Inland Revenue personnel will have to move. East Kilbride was chosen as the site for the first centre, covering Scotland, and in 1964 the East Kilbride Liaison Committee was brought into being. It has concerned itself with the impact on the staff of the technical and organizational planning, and with the gamut of human problems which the creation of a computer centre with 1300 staff must entail. These have included accommodation and amenities in the neighbourhood of the new centre, local recruitment, transfers from other offices, travelling and removal allowances, transport, and facilities for education, sport and recreation. It would be idle to pretend that so great an upheaval could be carried through without causing hardship to anyone. But it can be kept to a minimum by full use of consultation procedures.

PROMOTION

Promotion is a matter of prime concern in all departments. 'The Staff Side of Departmental Whitley Councils keep a sharp eye on methods of promotion and also on the types of individual selected to fill vacancies.'[2]

[1] Thomas, p. 34.   [2] Callaghan, p. 16.

Since qualified officers are normally more numerous than vacancies, competition is keen. Both sides share an interest in maintaining a system which the staff in general regards as fair. Widespread resentment among those who do not secure promotion is a serious source of friction within an organization. But though the interests of the two sides may converge at one level, at another they may be far apart. To the typical member of the rank and file, the fairest claim to promotion usually appears to be that which rests on seniority. There is no blow to self-esteem in admitting that another man is older, or that he has served longer. It is a rare individual, on the other hand, who is prepared to admit that another person has more merit than himself. Yet those responsible for management ignore merit at their peril when making promotions. And the higher the post, the louder are the claims of merit over those of seniority.

In some departments, methods have been worked out which involve the Staff Side in promotion procedures. This was notably the case in the Post Office manipulative grades, where the Staff Side was invited to submit a nomination for each vacancy as it came along. The great majority of Post Office branches took advantage of these opportunities, often putting forward the name of the most senior claimant. Promotions to grades below the rank of Assistant Postmaster were made locally, not from a national list. But, of course, staff nominees were sometimes passed over, charges of favouritism became frequent, and the staff lost faith in the system. The Union of Post Office Workers, through the Departmental Staff Side, pressed for a new procedure. In 1950, agreement was reached on a new method, to be tried in selected offices. After putting forward names according to the previous practice, the Staff Side was now invited to send not more than three representatives to discuss the merits of candidates with the Promotion Board. Discussion was frank, and the Boards explained in confidence their reason for passing over certain officers in favour of others. The Staff Side had the chance to express views about the suitability of candidates, drawing on knowledge of the individuals concerned which could well differ from what was in the hands of the Board.

In the clerical and executive branches of the Post Office also, the Staff Sides could make representations before promotions were announced, but the opportunity was rarely taken except where special considerations applied, as for example in the case of welfare officers. In this respect, their attitude was more typical of the civil service as a whole. The typical Departmental Staff Side holds 'that it is the responsibility of the Official Side to select individuals but that of the Staff Side to see that the ring is fairly held.'[1] To go further involves representatives of staff associations in discriminating amongst their constituents. For example, one aspirant may have the better claim on seniority,

[1] Callaghan, p. 17.

another on ability. If the Staff Side supports the former, it is likely to annoy the younger and more ambitious who hope to advance more rapidly than by waiting for dead men's shoes. If, on the other hand, the Staff Side supports the candidate who appears to be more able, it will alienate those – normally the majority – whose chances of promotion are greater where seniority prevails.

A typical procedure is to give the Staff Side the chance to make representations after a promotion list has been drawn up but before it is published. The opportunity is sometimes taken. It is quite common, however, for a Staff Side to take the view that, so long as no candidate within the agreed range had been overlooked, the whole responsibility for selection should rest with management. When several promotions are to be made simultaneously, it is normal to keep back a few vacancies so that they can be awarded on appeal if it seems desirable. The Staff Side watch the process closely to ensure that it is operating fairly and in particular, that aggrieved officers who have been passed over have adequate opportunity to appeal. At this stage, the Staff Side is often willing to help the individual in preparing his appeal; for example, by reading his written statement in draft, or by advising him to lay more stress on certain points whilst playing down others. If it is the practice of the department to call applicants before an interview board, the Staff Side may give advice about the sort of questions likely to be asked, so as to help the officer feel at ease. In some departments an appellant may even invite a union official to accompany him before the board. However, where such representation is allowed, and the official is willing to comply, he may still advise the appellant to go in alone. A man who lacks confidence to do so is hardly likely to convince a board that he deserves promotion to a post of greater responsibility.

REGIONAL AND LOCAL COMMITTEES

Provision was made in the Ramsay–Bunning Report for committees at local levels to deal with such matters as leave arrangements, accommodation, and the application of national and departmental agreements. An extensive and complex network of such committees has developed during the first fifty years of Whitleyism. The Council in a department has to approve the constitutions of Whitley Committees, but is not in any sense a court of appeal from the lower levels. The channel of communication runs mainly through associations and can be very effective. They carry news from the Council down to local branches with the result – to quote an Official Side member – that 'we are always getting complaints from local management that their union representatives know things before they [i.e. management] do'. Discontent expressed at a local Committee is not brought to the attention of the Departmental

Council by the Committee itself. It must be raised by one or more associations through their spokesmen at departmental level. The associations are very jealous of this prerogative.

Departmental Councils are, as a rule, keen to encourage local Whitleyism. As one example among many, when the Department of Health and Social Security was set up, its Council approved a circular to be sent to heads of local offices and brought to the attention of all members of staff. It began: 'in the local office, as in other spheres, it is important that there should be a close relationship between the management and representatives of the staff associations concerned. . . . The Department cannot of course, limit its freedom of action in the exercise of managerial authority, but staff consultation must be genuine and full, and not be merely a convenient means of conveying decisions to the staff through their accredited representatives.' This is a good expression of the spirit in which Whitleyism is carried on at the local level.

An illuminating tribute was paid by Lord Geddes, looking back to the start of his own career. 'I used to use my local Whitley a very, very, great deal, because it was the only way in which I could get a dialogue. It was the only way in which you could force . . . the Official Side to talk to you. In the very early days, there was a time-honoured phrase used by the Official Side. You could talk for an hour, and they'd sit there silent, without an expression on their face, without a change in their eyes, and when you finished, they'd say, "We have taken down what has been said, we will give it our most careful consideration and let you know." And that was the end . . . Whitley stopped that, because they had eventually to accept the fact that Whitley was [a forum for] discussion – not consultation only – but discussion on things. . . . In those early days, the top people were very high up the divine ladder. . . . They weren't quite gods but they were demi-[gods]. . . . And the only way . . . was to get them round a table, [for] which Whitley gave you the opportunity.'

Of course, the business of a local Whitley Committee is necessarily limited in scope. Men and women working in a Post Office (for example) might formulate a demand for a shorter working week. But major changes of this kind clearly have to be made at a higher level – the department or even beyond. 'It was no use a local Whitley saying, "Well, we want the forty hour week." If you wanted the forty hour week, you'd got to pursue it at the National Whitley level.' But once the reduction had been agreed, it was precisely at the local level that it had to be realized in the form of more days off. In some cases, this could be done simply by closing the offices on Saturday. But in the Post Office – to retain the example – that would obviously have been unacceptable to the public. So systems had to be devised in which offices stayed open six days, while individual employees worked only five. It is in tasks of this kind that local Whitley Committees excel.

To deal adequately with local Whitley Committees would require another volume at least the size of the present. A brief sketch of those in the Inland Revenue must stand in the place of the full account which will no doubt one day be written. The local offices of the Board are, of course, very numerous and the scope for local Whitleyism proportionately great. Some committees had developed spontaneously prior to 1946, and were doing effective work in regard to such matters as hours of attendance, accommodation and arrangement of work. The Inland Revenue Staff Federation then called for official encouragement of office committees. After about a year of such encouragement, local Whitley bodies were functioning in more than 70 per cent of the tax districts, in more than 50 per cent of collection offices, but only in 16 per cent of the valuation offices where the numbers were usually small. In the middle fifties, a further review of local Whitley activities found that 97 per cent of tax districts, nearly 70 per cent of collection offices and 78 per cent of valuation offices had local committees. The historian of Inland Revenue Whitley concludes that all this activity, though useful, still has great scope for development. 'The subjects discussed were indeed for the most part of the local "comfort and convenience" variety, and valuable enough since these are essentially the matters that could either clog the Branch or Departmental machine, or, if neglected, be spreading roots of discontent. Hygiene of this kind is not to be held in too little regard because it merely avoids ill health in the organization: but it is much more desirable of course to see local Whitley make a positive contribution to efficiency as both sides would have it do. . . . A mere list of subjects on the agenda of the local Whitley meeting is no true indication of the total contribution made to the Whitley idea, for local Whitley is a training ground, and provides the grass roots for Branch and Departmental Whitley where the main issues are worked out. But it still seems probable that after fifty years of Departmental Whitley and twenty-five years of local office Whitley the full potential of the latter has not been realized.'[1]

[1] Thomas, p. 38.

CHAPTER 9

WHITLEYISM AND THE INDUSTRIAL CIVIL SERVICE

The government accepted the Whitley principle so far as industrial civil servants were concerned in July 1918 – a year before it was adopted for their administrative brethren. In 1969, there were 213,400 industrial civil servants. The vast majority were in the three defence departments (70 per cent), and in the Ministries of Technology and Public Building and Works (25 per cent between them). But a number of other departments also employed industrials; for instance the Home Office (3200) H.M. Stationery Office (3803), the Royal Mint (965) and the Department of Employment and Productivity.

The Whitley machinery for the industrial civil service is separate and different from that for the non-industrial service. There is a Joint Co-ordinating Committee for Government Industrial Establishments. This Committee was set up originally to deal with general conditions of service, allowances and other matters not related to pay. Since 1966, however, following Report No. 18 of the National Board for Prices and Incomes, it has by agreement taken over responsibility also for central pay negotiations. The Committee is under the chairmanship of the Civil Service Department and consists, on the Official Side, of representatives of the main employing departments, i.e. the Ministry of Defence and the Department of the Environment, and of the Department of Employment in its capacity as the department responsible for industrial relations. The Trade Union Side consists of twelve members, three from Trade Union Sides of each of four Trades Joint Councils who sit as representatives of the Councils and not of their individual unions. The Committee normally meets every three months but more frequently when necessary.

There are four Trades Joint Councils, for Engineering, Ship-building, Works Services and Miscellaneous. They meet every two or three months and deal with pay matters, other than central pay negotiations, relating to the industrial civil servants in their respective spheres of interest. They do not, however, deal with the pay of the small minority of industrials whose pay is linked more specifically with that in a particular outside industry, e.g. printing. The Engineering, Ship-building and Miscellanous Trades Joint Councils are under the chairmanship of senior officials from the Ministry of Defence; the Works Services Trades Joint Council is under the chairmanship of a senior official from the Department of the Environment. In each case, the Official Sides consist of representatives from the main employing departments together with a representative of the Civil Service Department and of the Department of Employment. The Trade Union Sides consists of representatives of the relevant unions. On both the Official and Trade Union Sides, often the same person represents his department or trade union on each of the Councils.

There are five Departmental Joint Industrial Councils, one in the Department of the Environment and the other four in the Navy, Army and Air Force and Procurement Departments of the Ministry of Defence, and a Joint Negotiating and Consultative Committee in the Science Research Council. The Official Sides consist of representatives of the department plus one member of the Department of Employment and Productivity. The Chairman of the Councils in each of the three service departments of the Ministry of Defence are the Parliamentary Under-Secretaries of State, the only examples in the whole of civil service Whitleyism of a minister being directly involved. The Trade Union Side is again composed of representatives of the unions concerned, one or two of the members holding a seat shared by those unions not large enough to secure separate representation. The departmental Councils meet every two or three months and deal with matters domestic to the department other than pay. The Committee in the Science Research Council meets when necessary and deals with both pay and conditions of service.

Finally, most establishments have local Whitley consultative committees at works level where matters such as local working conditions and the local application of national agreements are discussed between management and employees representing their various trade unions. In the Royal Dockyards, for example, there are three main levels of local committee; the Yard, the Division (Department) and the Shop. The Yard Industrial Whitley Committee is usually chaired by the Senior Naval Officer in the area who, among his other responsibilities, is the Admiral Superintendent of the Dockyard. The subordinate committees are chaired by line managers who may be either naval or civilian. Linked to the Yard Committees, there are also Joint Production Committees which deal with all matters affecting efficiency and production. Recently, Joint Productivity Consultative Committees have also been established to provide a forum for discussion of factors affecting the individual Yards' productivity agreements. All these committees involve a considerable number of employees who sit on them as representatives of the various trade unions. In other establishments, on the other hand, there may be only one local Whitley committee which deals with all these aspects of joint consultation. In the Royal Ordnance Factories, however, there is a 'dual' system under which matters relating to the improvement of production are dealt with on Joint Production Committees and other Whitley matters on Joint Factory Committees. An interesting feature of this arrangement is that every factory employee, including non-union members, is entitled to vote for his representative to sit on the Joint Productivity Committee who, though they themselves have to be members of a trade union, do not sit on the Committee as trade union representatives. There is also a Central Production Committee, under the chairmanship of the Controller of Royal Ordnance Factories and consisting of representatives of Ministry of Defence Headquarters and national trade union officials, which meets quarterly to hear reports on production at individual factories, and to co-ordinate the activities of the Joint Productivity Committees at individual factories.

THE TRADE UNION SIDES

Twenty-six unions have a stake in civil service Whitleyism on the industrial side. They are all national unions, and none of them restricts membership to civil servants alone. Some of the largest unions in the country are involved, including the General and Municipal Workers, the Transport and General Workers, the Amalgamated Union of Engineering Workers and the Electrical Electronic and Telecommunications Union. The Trade Union Side members at national level are full-time officials, except for two seats on the Navy Department Joint Industrial Council where two unions are represented by one executive lay-member each. There is a great deal of interlocking membership on all the Councils. Nine unions are represented on each of the nine Councils. In 1969, Mr. J. Cousins, of Transport and General, and Mr W. John, of the Amalgamated Union of Engineering and Foundry Workers, each served on all the Councils, while Mr J. P. Bishop, of the General and Municipal, served on seven. Only about fifty persons all told were involved in representing the trade unions on all the Councils. The Councils tend to be officered by the larger unions, which supply the Vice-Chairmen and Trade Union Side Secretaries. The smaller unions accept this, because the officials concerned are paid by their unions for their Whitley Council work and this makes it possible for the Trade Union Sides to operate on extremely low budgets. The affiliation fees were in consequence merely nominal, in some cases as little as £5 per seat per year.

PRINCIPLES OF PAY

The underlying principle on which the rates of pay of all industrial civil servants is based derives from the Fair Wages Resolution of the House of Commons. The Resolution itself refers only to government contractors and requires them to pay rates of wages and observe hours and conditions of work not less favourable than those observed by the appropriate trade or industry in the district in which the work is carried out or, alternatively, than those generally observed by employers in similar circumstances. The original Resolution dates from 1891. In 1910 the government of the day undertook to apply the terms of the Resolution to its own employees; this undertaking was re-confirmed by the then Chancellor of the Exchequer in the House of Commons in January 1948, in relation to the current version of the Resolution which was passed on 14 October 1946. By 1950, however, national agreements on minimum wages and on some other conditions of service had become common in other branches of public employment and in several outside industries. From this time onwards, therefore, in negotiations on the appropriate Trades Joint Councils, the Fair Wages Resolution was increasingly interpreted in terms of nationally-agreed rather than locally-agreed minimum time rates; though the industrial civil service retained separate rates of pay for Coventry and Northern Ireland until very recently and there is still a separate rate for London.

Industrial employees received the basic skilled or unskilled rate of pay, as appropriate, plus a lead rate appropriate to the nature of their occupation and the degree of responsibility. The lead rate was determined by reference to differentials for analogous work in comparable outside industry. Basic rates were reviewed at six-monthly intervals; but lead rates rarely changed. The pay of a small minority of industrial civil servants, e.g. printers and electricians in the works services area, were not covered by these arrangements but followed the trade rates agreed between unions and employers in the relevant outside industry.

When this system of fixing the pay of industrial civil servants was investigated by the National Board for Prices and Incomes in 1965-6, the Board reported that the take-home pay of some industrials was seriously out of line with that outside because of the practice of having one general rate with supplements. A more serious criticism was that the system deviated from the policy of the White Paper on Prices and Incomes in four respects; it simply followed on from outside rates, it failed to recognize the variety of conditions existing both inside and outside the service, it based its averaging formula on wage rates rather than actual earning, and it ignored the essential relationship between incomes and the effective use of man-power. For all these reasons, there should be a new set of pay structures which would recognize the different industries existing within the civil service. These would be based initially on the pay of time-workers with a forty-hour week in similar occupations, taking into account fringe benefits. Negotiations should in future take place in a Trade Joint Council for each industrial group. 'The negotiations would be concerned not, as now, with a statistical comparison with outside movements in basic rates which may or may not have been determined in accordance with the White Paper, but with the needs of each industrial group assessed in the light of the consideration set out in the White Paper – in the light, that is, of any national standard for pay increases laid down by the government and of criteria for exceptions from the standard on the ground, for example, that a major change in working practices had taken place.'[1] In order to use manpower more effectively, the government should consider giving local management more responsibility to decide the numbers and grades of workers to be employed.

Both the Official and the Trade Union Sides had some doubts whether the concept of separate industrial pay groups envisaged by the National Board would work out satisfactorily in practice. Nevertheless, the industrial civil service was divided into ten pay groups in 1967 following the Board's recommendations. Separate Trades Joint Councils for each industrial group were not set up. Six of the new pay groups, which reflected predominantly engineering functions, became the province of the Engineering Trades Joint Council; two became the province of the Miscellaneous Trades Joint Council; the pay group for the Royal Dockyards remained the province of the Shipbuilding Trades Joint Council and one new Trades Joint Council was established for the Works Services pay group.

Experience showed, however, that the doubts about the practicability of having ten separate industrial pay groups were well founded. Apart from the management difficulties of deciding the yardsticks by which to assess the pay needs of each separate industrial group, the main criticism from the industrial employees concerned was that the different bases of pay determination for the new industrial groups meant that a man doing a job in an establishment in one group received quite a different rate of pay from another man doing a precisely similar job in a neighbouring unit in another group. Common pay increases averaging $3\frac{1}{2}$ per cent were given to all pay groups in 1968. In 1969, in the face of mounting dissatisfaction with the ten group pay structure, agreement was reached on an interim revision reducing the number of pay groups from ten to four, corresponding with the four existing Trades Joint Councils, and the pay of government industrial civil servants was referred once more to the National Board for Prices and Incomes. Their report, published in April 1970,[2] recommended that a single system of basic rates should

[1] National Board for Prices and Incomes, Report 18, *Pay of Industrial Civil Servants*, Cmd. 3034, para. 39.
[2] National Board for Prices and Incomes, Report 146, *Pay and Conditions of Industrial Civil Servants*, Cmd. 4351.

be introduced related to two key grades (basic grade craftsman and unskilled worker) whose rates should be determined with the aid of comparisons with the basic pay for comparable outside work as shown in the Department of Employment and Productivity New Earnings Survey. These basic rates would exclude any payment for productivity which the Board recognized would, in the circumstances of the industrial civil service, have to be negotiated separately by line management organizations. Up to the time that the Board reported, productivity schemes had been implemented for only a few establishments; but many were in the planning and negotiation stages and, during the rest of 1970, agreements were implemented covering about half of the industrial civil service.

The industrial civil service is predominantly a masculine concern, with women forming only 17 per cent of the total. The Equal Pay Agreement of 1954 did not apply to industrial civil servants, on the grounds that to do so would mean a change in government policy towards industry generally. Until 1970, women continued to be paid 85 per cent of the men's rate if they were employed on work which could be done equally by men or women. Following the Equal Pay Act, 1970, which applied to the Crown and required the introduction of full equal pay by 1975, a first step was taken in the 1970 pay settlement towards this objective by reorganizing industrial civil service women's rates and increasing the standard percentage relationship with men's rates to $87\frac{1}{2}$ per cent. Women industrials do not appear ever to have come under the marriage bar. The Royal Commission of 1929–31 noted that unestablished women industrials (almost none were established) were not required to resign on marriage but were stood off or asked to leave a certain time before a child was expected.

The basic working week for industrial civil servants is generally forty hours net, as for outside industry; and overtime pay arrangements similarly follow outside practice for the most part. Other conditions of service such as leave, sick leave, travelling and subsistence allowances etc. are determined with an eye both to outside practice and to non-industrial civil service arrangements. The National Board for Prices and Incomes recommended in both of its reports on industrial Civil Service pay, etc, that the government should make it its aim, over a period of time, to build on what is common to the industrial and non-industrial civil services with the ultimate objective of according all workers equality of status.[1] Much has been done to bring other conditions into line; but on conditions which have a relationship with pay and hours, e.g. payments for overtime and shift working, the broad fair comparisons principle on which pay is determined means that practice in outside

[1] National Board for Prices and Incomes, Report 18, *Pay of Industrial Civil Servants*, Cmd. 3034, para. 55.

industry is the more significant consideration, and therefore some differences between industrial and non-industrial conditions may well remain.

In superannuation, all civil servants enjoy the same conditions. In 1948, the Trade Union Side of the Joint Co-ordinating Committee made a claim for the establishment of all industrials after three years' service. It was acknowledged in discussion, however, that this would mean that more people would be established than the departments could expect to employ in future. An element of selection was, therefore, incorporated into the scheme. Minimum service before establishment was to be three years, establishment was to depend nine-tenths on seniority and one-tenth on selection, and establishment was to carry liability to transfer. The Committee also agreed the total numbers of staff to be established in each department, but the distribution of these totals among each grade and complement was left to the departments. Departments also determined the rules of selection other than seniority. Only 40 per cent of industrial civil servants are established, as compared with 75 per cent of non-industrials. This results partly from the policy of maintaining a smaller core of permanent staff in the industrial field. But in addition there is a much higher turnover of staff. The conditions for the two groups are the same, however, and for the purpose of the review of superannuation which was proceeding in 1969, the Chairman and Secretary of the Joint Co-ordinating Committee sit with the Staff Side of the National Whitley Council on the Joint Review Committee.

It was characteristic that the joint review of superannuation should have been entrusted to an *ad hoc* body. Indeed the lack of systematic machinery for co-ordinating the industrial and non-industrial aspects has always been a curious feature of civil service Whitleyism. The need is recognized when conditions common to both come under review. But generally speaking, the two systems operate in separate worlds. Sir John Lang explained how it worked in the Admiralty. 'There was no cross-linkage between the two Councils. . . . The Chairman of the administrative Whitley Council was not the Chairman of the industrial Whitley Council. The linkage came at quite a low level. . . . The establishment branch . . . serviced the [administrative] Whitley Council. . . . The branch which serviced the Admiralty industrial Council was not civil establishments, but labour branch. . . . Labour branch and establishments branch were friendly enough. They got together . . . when a joint problem came up which both of them could see. But they were awfully inclined to gang their own gait unless they could see the other fellow's concern. And the point of contact there, the man who in a sense had got a foot in both camps was . . . the Principal Assistant Secretary(C) – C meaning civil. You had a head of civil establishments, you had a head of labour branch: those two assistant Secretaries reported to a Principal Assistant Secretary . . . and it was his responsibility to co-ordinate industrial and administrative conditions. The two Councils themselves were quite separate.'

In retrospect, Sir John felt that the arrangement had not been satisfactory. 'In a department like the Admiralty, where something affecting the industrial workers either directly affects the non-industrials, or can lead to repercussions on the non-industrials, . . . there ought to be a real positive linkage between the two. Such a linkage never was invented in the Admiralty. We reckoned that the absence of a positive link never got us into trouble. . . . The Official Side linkage was good enough to avoid it.' Part of the reason why the system worked was the small amount of business common to both Councils. 'There wasn't a great deal of overlap, though there could be. . . . You could get a trade union problem affecting what the Admiralty called "mechanics", in other words, the fitters, the shipwrights, and other tradesmen. What happened to them could very easily affect the inspectors of shipwrights, the inspectors of fitters and turners, who were in an administrative grade as contrasted with the industrial grade they supervised.'

Sir John agreed that it was quite possible to imagine a situation in which the two Councils could be acting at cross-purposes, though he could not recall one. 'But that's really a testimony to the efficacy of the Official Side mechanism, because the Official Side was the only field of Whitley in which those two things linked.'

CHAPTER 10

CONCLUSION

'It is one of the ironies of history', Sir William Armstrong has pointed out, 'that [Whitleyism] was not originally intended for the civil service at all, but as a solution to . . . the problems of industrial relations generally.'[1] Why has it proved so much more successful in the civil service than in the private sector? The first factor is the absence of fundamental differences of interest between the two sides of the kind which so often bedevil staff relations in profit-making industry. It is true that W. J. Brown, one of the ablest of staff side leaders, thought otherwise. 'Behind all the amenities and cordialities of Whitleyism,' he wrote, 'there is a real and permanent antagonism of interest between the two sides.'[2] But the antagonism is not between the sides: it is between the staff and an abstraction which may be variously labelled the state, the public, the taxpayer, or society at large. The distinction may not be so clear at departmental level as it is at national level. And it may be less clear in a department with large numbers of low-paid staff whose conditions of work approximate to those of the private sector than it is in a department where a high proportion of the work is related to policy processes. Nevertheless, the distinction does exist, and helps to exclude from the great majority of Whitley negotiations the bitterness which is all too common a feature of collective bargaining in the private sector. It is possible for society, like any other employer, to exploit those who work for it. But this does not mean that there is a divergence of interest between the two sides – two groups of human beings meeting to transact business. A member of the Official Side is not an employer; he is an employee of the state. Hence, although the Official Side plays the role of employer, its members can also, as individuals, sympathize with the staff point of view. It would not be easy for a Staff Side representative to persuade himself that anyone – and certainly not those on the other side of the table – is making exorbitant profits out of those for whom he speaks. Awareness that ultimately the employer is society at large goes some way towards mitigating the disappointment staff representatives feel when their claims are rejected or cut down. 'Civil servants, whether they are for the moment behaving like Staff Side people or Official Side

[1] *Whitley Bulletin*, Vol. xlix, 1969, p. 155.
[2] *Whitleyism on its Trial*, (n.d.) p. 18.

people, do all have a perfectly genuine feeling of togetherness and of common purpose and service to the community.'

It follows that the two teams of negotiators understand one another much better than is normally the case in the private sector. Although convention favours the expression of a united Official Side view, and a united Staff Side view, the thoughts of those involved in the discussions are a good deal more complex. As a member of the Staff Side put it, 'you may find yourself, some of you, . . . in agreement with the Official Side. And the Official Side may be split. . . . But eventually you arrive at a common view, not necessarily a Staff Side view, as originally you started, but a joint view.' The war atmosphere was, of course, especially favourable to this way of looking at things. 'You got to the stage . . . where men no longer were discussing things from that and this side of the table. They were really a body co-operating together to try and find a solution to so many of the wartime problems.' But, Lord Geddes went on, the new understanding reached in wartime was the 'commencement of a dialogue . . . between the Official and the Staff Sides and it has ended with the two sides ceasing to be two sides in that sense and becoming a corporate body which is acting on behalf of the whole of the civil service'. This was very close to the basic belief of Sir Albert Day. 'My philosophy about the Staff Side and Whitleyism rests on the thought that a Whitley Council is an entity. It's not two entities brought together, it's a single entity, consisting of members who, like a jury, are charged to agree if they can. And if they can't agree, that's not because one or other of them is being cantankerous, but because [of] some point of principle'.

Secondly, once the Staff Side had overcome their early suspicions of the Official Side, they came to place a high value on the decision-making power of Whitley. The requirement that all decisions must be adopted *nem. con.* might seem a prescription for impotence. Must not the Official Side always be unwilling to grant all that the Staff Side demand? Must not the Staff Side always ask more than the Official Side will give? Will not the Staff Side always go to arbitration rather than accept the Official Side's offer – to say nothing of industrial and political action? Yet the system does not break down because neither side wants to break down. 'When we could make a decision, it was effective, really effective', said one member of the Staff Side. Douglas Houghton spelled out the same point more fully. 'When you're negotiating with the Official Side, you're negotiating with people who already know the room for manoeuvre they have. They've already cleared their position with ministers. So when you reach agreement . . . it is definitive. Nobody turns it down, because what they would not agree to anyway, you could not get in negotiations. So that you were really negotiating with those who were in a position to give you the final answer. And sometimes, if the Staff Side said, "Well, if you could go a little further, then we might reach agreement, if we could do this, if we could do that, can't you give some easement here, can't you do this and that there", and so forth, if the Official Side knew it was outside their room for manoeuvre, in cost or range of concession or whatever, then they would say, "Well, we'll adjourn and we'll refer back to ministers." But when they came back, whatever they came back to say, you knew that you could do business.' If the price of having a decision-making body was that decisions could be reached only by consensus, the Staff Side accepted that it was a price worth paying.

The third factor making for the success of Whitleyism was the realization by the Official Side that the system helps in securing the co-operation of the staff. This realization was slow to dawn. 'In the early days there was great resistance on the part of the Official Side to consult or to recognize that the Staff Side could make a contribution on many of the questions with which they were concerned. . . . It was a great fight . . . to obtain recognition that the Staff Side could make a really substantial contribution to the administration of the departments.' One of the first departments to appreciate the value of the Staff Side was the Inland Revenue. 'Since the Staff Side were . . . made aware of what was projected . . . they were able to . . . demonstrate that they had been consulted. In other words, they participated, and they were able, therefore, to give the staff some confidence that what was being done was not being done in an authoritarian way. It was being done after consultation with people who represented their interests – even in cases where they disagreed with what was being done!' That was in the thirties, as recalled by a member of the Staff Side. Since the Second World War, a like awareness has spread throughout the service, with the result that the Official Side has become fully convinced of the value of Whitleyism when confronted with a practical problem such as implementing the recommendations of the Fulton Committee. It has made possible agreements 'which had the acceptance of the accredited representatives of the staff, which had been hammered out with them, and to which, when it came into effect, they were committed'.

From some members of staff associations has come the charge that their leaders have committed them too deeply. A militant union leader has called Whitleyism the 'clever dialectic of enlightened management and co-operative union officials'.[1] Sir Albert Day was aware of the danger. When he retired, the system 'was coming to be regarded almost as a part of the administration'. Whitleyism had reached the limit of consultation. 'Go a step further, and you get directly into the field of management and I would be opposed to that. I don't think it would be a good thing . . . to have participation in actual management.' Cyril Plant,

[1] J. D. Thomas, *Fifty Years of Whitleyism in the Inland Revenue, 1920–1970*, 1970, p. 41.

the General Secretary of the Inland Revenue Staff Federation, has said much the same thing. 'When there was less understanding by the Official Side of Staff Side aspirations the association conferences vented their anger and concern at the Official Side. Today, because there is close co-operation, some members regard the Staff Side as a part of the administration and this may be a reason for the gulf between some members and the leadership. Conference agendas today criticize Executive Committees; no voice seems to be raised against the Official Side. Looking at my agenda my members seem to think I am the Permanent Secretary.'[1]

Is there a serious threat that militancy may endanger the continued operation of the Whitley system? The National Staff Side has noted that 'within the last two or three years . . . several organizations have adopted a strike policy. The annual conferences of other organizations have declared their intention to take militant action if exceptionally they find it impossible to reach satisfactory settlements through the normal negotiating machinery.'[2] One of the organizations referred to has published a well-considered statement of the problem, which has important implications for staff associations generally. It recognizes the value of Whitley. 'The system was introduced to avoid conflict and will continue to have that important function. . . . But the reality of collective bargaining the service is . . . that when there is a disagreement between employer . . . and trade unions, there can be no resolution of the conflict apart from arbitration. . . . A great deal can be done by argument, persuasion and compromise, but in the last resort – subject to certain issues regarded as suitable for arbitration – the will of the government prevails. The government can force through a decision by what is variously described as "administrative action" or "executive action". The reality of service negotiations is that at the end of any bargaining process the employer can refuse to accept arguments or interpretations other than his own – the employer can exercise the ultimate sanction.' As things stood, staff associations could not exercise their ultimate sanction, if only because they had no strike funds. The conclusion was that a strike policy was 'necessary because collective action is an essential part of the collective bargaining process'.[3]

A full discussion of the factors making for increasing militancy in contemporary society would extend far beyond the scope of this book. The historian of Inland Revenue Whitley refers to some of them. 'Along with unification of structure and a new outlook on efficient management is developing a feeling among public servants that their restrained col-

[1] Ibid. p. 40.
[2] Civil Service National Whitley Council (Staff Side), *Explanatory Note on the Civil Service Staff Movement*, mimeo, July 1970.
[3] Civil Service Clerical Association, *CSCA Strike Policy*, 1969, pp. 10 and 18.

lective methods are out of date. The stresses and strains of contemporary life are bad enough. There are signs in our society of disenchantment with security, rejection of authority, and increasing material expectations. Over much of the department lies the apparent endlessness of the prospects of under-staffing, of always having arrears and never being able to feel at the end of a week that the job has been well done. It is scarcely surprising that a new mood of militancy is growing up.'[1] But there are factors specific to Whitleyism that must be looked at in some detail.

Civil Service Whitleyism, and the system of arbitration with which it is linked, has come to rest on three principles. The first of these is that it is practicable to separate the state in relation to its employees, from the state in its capacity as state. This distinction was inherent in the original wording of the constitution of the National Whitley Council, which spoke of 'the state in its capacity as employer', implying that there remained other functions of the state outside the Council's scope. Similarly with arbitration. Clearly no sovereign state can submit itself in its totality to the ruling of a tribunal set up within its territory. If it submits at all, it does so in respect of a defined aspect of its function; in this case, as an employer of labour.

The second principle is that of fair comparison as a means of determining pay. As shown above, the doctrine had been in the air for a long period before it was given operational form by the Priestley Report of 1965.[2] The principle has been accepted by both sides, and there is little doubt that it provides the best basis for negotiations that anyone has yet been able to devise. But it has the drawback that pay in the public sector tends always to lag behind that in the private sector. Had a Pay Research Unit been set up simultaneously with the Council itself, this feature would sometimes have worked in favour of the staff. When pay in the private sector was falling, pay in the civil service would fall less fast. In fact, it came into being in a period of continuous inflation. By the time the Pay Research Unit began work, a pattern of periodic wage settlements was already established. Every settlement was in an upward direction. Since fair comparisons take time to work out, the principle has meant in practice comparison with the private sector at an earlier point in time; that is, at a lower point on the inflationary spiral.

The third principle has been that of an incomes policy; that is to say, that a contemporary government, having a responsibility for the management of the economy, must regulate not only the pay of its own employees, but the incomes of the community as a whole. The light thrown by this principle on staff relations has, admittedly, been rather like that of the moon on a landscape. At best, it has done little to assist those who are trying to find their way about. Often it has shone fitfully

---

[1] Thomas, p. 41.   [2] See p. 59.

through gaps in clouds. Sometimes it has been altogether obscured from view. But even in eclipse, everyone realizes it is still there, and will presently emerge once more.

If any government can succeed in finding a way to make an incomes policy work, all may very probably be well. Until then, the three principles will continue to conflict with one another. Private sector wages will tend to rise faster than governments, on incomes policy grounds, desire. On the basis of fair comparison, civil service pay should follow. Naturally, governments will be reluctant to let this happen, for the reasons stated by one of the major staff associations. 'As the government develops an incomes policy which is supposed to apply to the country as a whole and implements policy criteria rigidly, for exemplary reasons, in respect of its own employees . . . would be fiercely resisted. No government can afford to be observed retreating from fundamental policies because of strike action by its own employees.'[1] It is hard enough to persuade others to listen anyway. If the government as employer appears to be ignoring the government, as author of an incomes policy, it would be unreasonable to expect anyone else – employer or worker – to take any notice of it. But in so far as the government enforces an incomes policy on those who work for it, the distinction between the state, as state, and the state, as employer, tends to break down. Clearly something will have to give.

As shown above, Whitleyism is criticized by some association activists on the grounds that it restricts the full operation of trade unionism in the civil service. The Fulton Committee criticized the Whitley system for the diametrically opposite reason that it reduces the flexibility of management.[2] 'In some respects', they wrote, 'we consider that management, constrained by the existing structure of the service, has allowed the Whitley system to operate in ways that hamper effective management.'

The criticisms were expressed in very general terms and it is not too easy to see exactly what the Committee was getting at. Six points appear to merit consideration here:

1. 'The first [defect] is the structural framework of the service within which Whitleyism has had to operate. . . . It is because staff associations represent groups whose careers are largely limited to a single class that they are so sensitive on such matters as promotion within it, late entry into it and the number of jobs allocated to it.' The truth or falsehood of these judgments can be relegated to the category of historical questions. Since the Committee recommended a complete remodelling of the structural framework, and since major changes in the former

[1] Civil Service Clerical Association, *CSCA Strike Policy*, 1969, p. 12.

[2] Cmd. 3638, paras. 269–74 inclusive, from which the quotations in this and the next nine paragraphs are taken.

class structure are in process of implementation, the important question now is, how will the new structure affect Whitleyism?

Changes in the service structure can hardly fail to have repercussions on the staff associations themselves. The Committee recognized this. 'Our recommendations . . . are bound to have a profound effect upon the pattern of joint consultation. The introduction of a common grading structure; manning the work by job evaluation rather than by reference to membership of a class; training arrangements that lead to fast promotion routes; career management that will open up new and wider prospects of promotion; an increase in late entry and short-term appointments – all of these will call for co-operation and goodwill between departments and the Staff Side centrally, departmentally and locally. The changes will surely also lead to structural changes among the association themselves.'

But would a changed structure make staff associations less sensitive on such points as those mentioned? For example, in response to the Fulton reforms, and the absorption of the administrative and executive classes in the new administration group, the First Division Association may merge with the Society of Civil Servants. It would be the function of such an amalgamation, as it is of any trade union, to protect, not merely its members as a whole, but the various categories of its members. There are bound to be differences of interest between the various categories. The interests of the young will not coincide with those of the old, nor those of the lower-paid with those of the higher-paid. How does this apply, for example, to one of the points mentioned above – 'training arrangements that lead to fast promotion routes'? An innovation designed to turn this aspiration into a reality is the creation of the new grade of Administration Trainee, most members of which are likely to be members of such an amalgamation. The major milestone in the career of every member of the new grade will come when he is selected, or passed over, for rapid promotion. Since a minority of the grade will be non-graduates, it is to be expected that the association to which they belong will closely scrutinize the qualifications of those selected. If it appears that they are largely Oxbridge graduates with good degrees in arts subjects, the suspicion will be fostered that they are merely old-style assistant principals in a new guise. The training given to the grade will be scrutinized to see whether everything possible has been done to achieve parity between graduate and non-graduate Administration Trainees. Surely it would be perfectly legitimate for their association to raise such questions through Whitley channels – even at the risk of being castigated by some future committee of enquiry for undue sensitivity? Whatever the structure, staff associations are bound to do the best they can in the interests of their members. The Fulton Committee seems here to be attributing to a particular civil service structure characteristics of staff relations which are in fact inherent in the very existence of labour organizations.

2. 'The second [defect] is that management is sometimes less active and determined than it should be; arguments are allowed to go on too long, and rigid procedures are accepted where flexibility should be insisted upon.' One word calling for emphasis here is 'sometimes.' The Committee has already paid a striking tribute to the way in which Whitley has been used to promote change. 'Co-operative responses to the wide-ranging changes brought about, for example, by the introduction of computers; the acceptance of domestic disturbances involved in the policy of dispersal of office staffs from London; and the smoothness with which pay settlements are generally reached and accepted, are attributable in no small measure to the activity of the staff associations in reaching agreements with management and subsequently defending them to their members.' If the call for more active and determined management is a variation on the major Fulton theme that senior civil servants should behave more like industrial executives, there may or may not be something in it. But the logical consequence is that staff associations may come to behave more like industrial unions. It is significant that the withdrawal of the Post Office from the National Whitley Council, in consequence of its re-constitution as a public corporation, was followed not much more than a year later by an official strike of the Union of Post Office Workers. The Civil Service Clerical Association faced the implications in the context of its strike policy. 'The civil service is no longer unique in its conditions of service. The most distinctive features of civil service employment are now frequently matched and often improved upon in large, private firms. The concept that a person in the civil service had a "job for life" with slow but steady progress up long scales neither meets the needs of new recruits nor does it, in fact, meet the demands of those who want to make the civil service more efficient. As new management techniques have been adopted in the civil service so employment in it has come closer to the experience of those employed on similar work in private industry. The future, if the most significant Fulton Committee recommendations are implemented, will produce a civil service almost indistinguishable in its attitude to staff and its conditions of employment from large private organizations. . . . To the extent that these conditions change and the civil service becomes less of a "protected industry" so will forms of trade union action change. If there is a desire, as there appears to be to create a civil service on modern business lines then it can be expected that civil service trade unionism will change to meet the new aggressive competitiveness inherent in such changes.'[1] The changes recommended, like all changes in human life, will have to be

[1] Civil Service Clerical Association, *CSCA Strike Policy*, 1969, pp. 8–9.

evaluated in net terms. The very effort to improve sets off other changes, some of which may not be improvements. If active and determined management leads to working to rule, go-slows, and strikes, the last state might very well be worse than the first.

3. 'Management has entered into agreements that have produced rigid arrangements in the promotion system in which seniority plays an excessive part.' What does 'excessive' mean in this context? Many areas of civil service work consists in the detailed application of general rules to particular cases. In work of this kind, seniority may in fact be a good guide to promotion even though not invariably decisive. Then again, seniority has the merit of being objective. There are cases, of course, where one candidate is older while another has been longer in the service. But as a rule, seniority is a fact admitting of little dispute. Merit, on the other hand, leads to endless controversy. What looks like merit to one may appear to another more like favouritism. Moreover, nature doles out seniority with an even hand: it comes to everyone in time. The distribution of natural merit is, however, notoriously inequitable. Those who lack it often resent its possession by others. One mark of a successful promotion is that it should be acceptable to those over whom the new man is set. It is easier to accept seniority than merit. In short, it is by no means simple to strike a due balance, or to say when the recognition given to seniority becomes excessive. In any case, are Whitley agreements the cause? The argument about seniority versus merit is much older. It was already venerable when Northcote and Trevelyan wrote about it. 'The theory of the public service is that . . . promotion from class to class is the reward of merit. . . . This salutary principle is, however, in practice often overlooked, and promotion from class to class . . . is more commonly regulated by seniority than by merit. The evil consequences of this are too obvious to require lengthened comment; it is, perhaps, more important to point out some of the difficulties which lie in the way of amendment. If the opinions of the gentlemen engaged in the civil service could be taken on the subject of promotion, it would probably be found that a very large majority of them would object strongly to what is called promotion by merit. The reason they would assign would be that promotion by (so called) merit would usually become promotion by favouritism. . . . Constituted as our official system now is, men feel, and not unreasonably, that the recognition of their merits, even within their own departments, is extremely uncertain, and that there is no appeal to any public tribunal if injustice is done them there. . . . In an office, if a clerk fails to please his immediate superior, he is probably condemned to obscurity for his whole life.'[1] And if the promotion problem is older than Whitley, it also

[1] The Fulton Committee, Cmd. 3638, p. 116. It is, of course, unlikely that

occurs in areas where Whitley's writ does not run. At the present time, the absence of a Whitley agreement covering promotions in the higher civil service does not safeguard it from the suspicion that there, too, seniority counts for more than it should. With or without a Whitley system, many promotions would be influenced by seniority in any organization of the size and complexity of the British civil service. The Fulton Committee did well to draw attention once more to the phenomenon. But the explanation offered is an over-simplification of a very complex problem.

4. 'Resistance to changes in organization tends to become formal and institutional; this has inhibited management from experimenting in the use of grades and classes.' Resistance to change is, of course, normal in organizations of every type. It was widespread in the British civil service long before Whitley, and would continue if Whitley were wound up next week. What merits a closer look is the implication that informal and uninstitutionalized resistance to change is preferable to what exists now. Would it in fact enable management to experiment in the use of grades and classes? Shipyard managers try such experiments from time to time by giving, for example, work to fitters which is claimed by boilermakers as their prerogative. The unpredictable nature of the disputes that ensue, and the difficulties that often stand in the way of a settlement, are largely due to the lack of formal and institutional machinery for consultation. The fact is that there is ample room for improvement in every kind of enterprise in Britain. Management generally has been slow to experiment, and workers have shown suspicion towards proposals for change. In the civil service, the Whitley system provides at least a forum where changes can be proposed and discussed. By recommending that Whitley channels should be used in implementing its own proposals, the Fulton Committee itself recognized their potential for promoting reform.

5. 'Managers of "operating" divisions are reluctant to become involved in questions of organization and staffing, which are often the subject of complex and delicately balanced agreements with staff associations. These agreements are the responsibility of the personnel and organization division of the department, and questions of organization and staffing come to be regarded as their exclusive province. As a result, the manager is apt to see himself as less than fully responsible for the effectiveness of his branch.' This is one aspect of a problem common to all large organizations: centralized versus decentralized management. Each has merits, but it is impossible to enjoy all the advantages of both systems simultaneously. The National Whitley Council is admittedly a centralizing force in the British civil service, though not

'gentlemen engaged in the civil service at the present day' would respond in the same way.

199

the only one. The Civil Service Department (in succession to the Treasury) and the Civil Service Commission are others. It is possible to imagine all the complex and delicately balanced agreements swept away, and much greater freedom in questions of organization and staffing delegated to managers of operating divisions. There would undoubtedly be advantages in such an arrangement, but not necessarily net gains. Improvements in some directions would be counter-balanced by losses in others. For example, staffing standards would become less uniform than they now are – perfect uniformity in such matters being unattainable even with the most highly centralized management. If they did not, the whole exercise would be pointless. Staff in divisions with favourable ratios would defend their privileged position. Staff elsewhere would develop a sense of grievance with consequent harm to morale. Managers of operating divisions, having been made fully responsible for the effectiveness of their units, would have to cope with the ensuing problems. Some would succeed brilliantly, some would fail hopelessly, and most would muddle along somehow as most human beings do under most circumstances. Supposing such a transformation possible – a large assumption, in the light of such things as ministerial responsibility, parliamentary questions, the Public Accounts Committee, etc. – it is conceivable that the new system might prove on balance better than the old. But the benefits would not come unalloyed, as the Fulton Committee seems to imply.

6. 'Success in reaching agreement with the Staff Side comes to be treated as an end in itself, and failure to reach agreement as a failure by management; this means that negotiations are sometimes too long drawn out.' Again, the criticism is couched in terms so vague that it is not easy to answer. How often is 'sometimes'? 'How long is too long'? Numerous examples have been given throughout this book where, disagreement having registered, management has dealt with a problem by executive action. Examples have also been given of important changes being introduced through the Whitley machinery. The implementation of the Priestley recommendations are a striking example. It is hard to imagine that it could have been done faster without Whitley; indeed, it would probably have taken longer. Again, the category of business has to be considered. If the alleged procrastination involves large numbers of people and/or large sums of money, it is clearly a more serious charge than it would be if affects only minor and marginal issues. As shown above, the agreement on pay and arbitration contains something analogous to a penalty clause to safeguard against the risk of negotiations being excessivly protracted. And pay is likely always to be the most sensitive topic dealt with in Whitley. Is there anything wrong in management taking failure to reach agreement seriously? A wise manager always considers the

alternative. If the alternative is a political campaign, or some form of industrial action, agreement is very well worth striving for, even if it takes time. Civil servants are not meek and docile creatures who will simply do as they are bid when they feel their reasonable proposals have been overriden. But perhaps the best evidence that this criticism need not be given too much weight is provided by the Committee itself, since it suggests that the Whitley machinery should be used to implement its own recommendations. 'We have been much impressed by the thoughtful and constructive evidence that staff associations have sent us, and by the interviews we have had with their representatives. They can assuredly play a vital part in promoting and smoothing the way for the major reforms we recommend. We feel confident that they are willing, and indeed eager, to do so.'

The Fulton criticisms are vague and unsubstantiated, amounting to little more than a statement that the civil service is not exempt from problems common to large organizations in general, and that Whitley-ism – like all human institutions – is not perfect. Little positive guidance is given as to what changes are desirable.

It is not possible to make a detailed forecast of the character of civil service Whitleyism even ten years from now. For example, the recent Industrial Relations Act is likely to bring big changes. But what they will be no one can yet say. It is however possible to make a shrewd guess at some likely developments. On the Staff Side, the departure of the Post Office unions when that department became a public corporation in 1969 has already had important consequences. The opportunity was taken to reduce the number of seats by two. The remaining seats have been amicably redistributed among other associations. Throughout this book, stress has been laid on the distinctive role of the postal unions in the work of the National Staff Side. The departure will leave it an even more homogeneous body. On the Official Side, it is reasonable to assume that the Head of the Civil Service will continue to give the strong, positive, leadership that Sir William Armstrong has given so far. His attitude was clearly indicated in his Whitley memorial lecture. 'It has been said that one leading member of the Official Side crystallized all [his Whitley] experience into the maxim "when in doubt, consult". I myself would go further than that and add: "even when in no doubt, still consult." It seems to me that on the occasions when the Official Side is absolutely certain of the rightness and reasonableness of its position, that is the time when it would do well to consult. That remark, incidentally, is based on my own personal experience which, though short, has been, shall I say, salutary.'[1] The post-Fulton reversion to a pattern in which a higher proportion of such consultation is done through joint

[1] *Whitley Bulletin*, Vol. xlix, 1969, p. 154.

committees may be expected to persist; though there should be a fall in the absolute amount of work once the Fulton recommendations have been fully implemented. The emergence of giant departments in central government should mean that the principal employers can participate more fully in National Whitley discussions than was usually the case in the past. The creation of the Civil Service Department should provide more effective intelligence and research support than the Official Side has had in the past, for instance in regard to the consequences of new management techniques for the staff.

Having examined its criticisms in some detail, it is fair to close by quoting what the Fulton Committee says by way of praise. 'Whitleyism in the civil service . . . has made an invaluable contribution to good staff relations. The high morale of the staff, and the fact that industrial disputes are rare in the civil service, owe a great deal to the universal acceptance of the principle of joint consultation. . . . It is very much in the public interest that this atmosphere of agreement and of co-operation should be preserved. . . [The defects we have noted] are in no way inherent in the Whitley system itself. Its principles are fully compatible both with a different structure and with more flexible methods of consultation. . . . We are convinced that its principles are of immense value to the service and will continue to be so.'

INDEX